FORESTERS, BORDERS, AND BARK BEETLES

FORESTERS, BORDERS, AND BARK BEETLES

The Future of Europe's Last Primeval Forest

Eunice Blavascunas

INDIANA UNIVERSITY PRESS

This book is a publication of

Indiana University Press
Office of Scholarly Publishing
Herman B Wells Library 350
1320 East 10th Street
Bloomington, Indiana 47405 USA

iupress.indiana.edu

Manufactured in the United States of America

Cataloging information is available from the Library of Congress.

ISBN 978-0-253-04958-2 (hardback)
ISBN 978-0-253-04960-5 (paperback)
ISBN 978-0-253-04959-9 (ebook)

1 2 3 4 5   25 24 23 22 21 20

To the forest

CONTENTS

ACKNOWLEDGMENTS

THE FOREST, NAMED AS YOU ARE, BIAŁOWIEŻA, OF tree, moss, mushroom, animal, human—for twenty-four years, you have been the humus from which this book emerged. I know you because of the time I have spent under your canopy and at your edges. I know you because of the stories people have told me about you and because I have read about you. I know you from multifold actions and conversations that flow around you. Through history and lived experience, I acknowledge you.

Writing this ethnography after decades of research raises the fundamental question of what belongs to whom. As much as I secluded myself to write this book and painstakingly crafted its sentences, paragraphs, and chapters, I do not believe that I am an atomized, individuated subject who has solely produced the story. Like the forest, this writing has existed in relation. It is here that I acknowledge how others contributed, whether they fed me a steady diet of encouragement or served up platters of critique. A book is produced through a series of negotiations and tensions that the author learns to navigate. I thank the people and institutions named here for their medicine, mud, recipes, suggestions, edits, personal stories, assistance, political positions, and science.

This book traveled far from my doctoral thesis, yet I would like to acknowledge my teachers and mentors at the University of California Santa Cruz. The contours of their knowledge projects shaped who I am as a thinker and writer. Ravi Rajan, my doctoral advisor and friend, you invite difference and treat it hospitably. Your pioneering work on the history of forestry and colonial sciences influenced this book's *longue durée* coverage of the sciences. I hope that I have followed your sage advice and just "told a good story."

Melissa Caldwell contributed rigor and compassion, continually working to strengthen my ideas by pushing me to always reach just beyond my intellectual limits. Donald Brenneis helped me defend the value of a now rare long-term ethnographic engagement. Carolyn Martin Shaw and Dan Linger taught me how to successfully write applications for the many grants that funded this project. Anna Tsing taught me the art of noticing and how to ethnographically explore entanglements between humans and nonhumans. Donna Haraway deserves credit for helping me use different intellectual senses than I was used to. To all my graduate student colleagues, with whom I grew, you opened oysters full of wisdom: Conal Ho, Riet Delsing, Jessica O'Reilly, Kristine Baker, Bettina Stoetzer, Alisa Puga Kessey, Kristen Cheney, Scout Calvert, Harlan Weaver, Eben Kirksey, Jeremy Campbell, Noah Tamarkin, Meghan Moodie, Jake Metcalf, and Heath Cabot. While exploring the forest through the lens of geography at the University of Texas at Austin, Robin Doughty, along with Bill Doolittle and Karl Butzer, encouraged me to trust my intellectual creativity and always remember small acts of kindness.

The writing of this book began in earnest through a generous fellowship at the Rachel Carson Center in Munich, Germany. Thank you Christof Mauch and Helmuth Trischler for crafting a creative space for scholars. My colleagues at the center read and commented on multiple early chapters; my thanks to Nicole Seymour, Ruth Oldenzieil, Seth Peabody, Donald Worster, Jenny Price, Celia Lowe, Ursula Muenster, and Shen Hou. Thank you also to Markus Krzoska, Thomas Bohn, and Aliaksandr Dalhouski at the University of Giessen for your own book on Białowieża and for including me in your formative historical workshops on your coverage of the topic.

I finished writing this book at the Leibniz Institute for East European History and Culture. Dietlind Hückter facilitated this opportunity and pushed me to think in new ways about Poland and materiality. Frank Hadler enabled me to make global linkages I would not have otherwise made. Christine Goelz deserves a special mention for background support. In Leipzig, Tracey Wilson shared ideas about Polish scholarship on the environment. Marc Allen Herbst animated thinking about antifascist organizing when it comes to all things "environmentally related."

Indiana University Press series editor Jennika Baines deserves credit for her judicious and gracious go-betweens. Two anonymous reviewers also made careful efforts to help me see the holes in the manuscript and fill them with substance.

I would not have reached this forest had it not been for the US Forest Service, its Pacific Northwest Research Station, and Dr. Steve Berwick. He was kind enough to share his contacts and library with me before my first visit in 1995, and this proved indispensable in terms of who I would have access to and how. Simona Kossak generously introduced me to Białowieża. She and Polish State Forests' Forest Research Institute ensured that I was housed and hosted. They endured my evolving questions and fulfilled some

of my basic needs, as did Ella Kudlewska; her mother and father, Wiesława and Stanisław; her daughter Karolina, who assisted me with translations; her sister Gosia Kudlewska, who often cut my hair; and her brother Adam, who let me accompany him and Dr. Elżbieta Mahlzahn to distant forest hamlets. Thank you to Małgosia Buszko, Lars Briggs, Lars Christian, and Olimpia Pabian for including me in your 1995 amphibian workshops, which brought laughter, meetings with farmers, and knowledge of what it means to sleep with the mosquitoes. Thank you, Monika Kurzawa, for traveling by my side in after that workshop and teaching me about Polish history. Krzystof and Joanna Zamojski kindly opened their house, making holidays more bearable. Jadwiga and Staszek Sawrycki fed me many pierogi stuffed with garden cabbage and forest mushrooms and shared their love of bees on many a cold winter night. Andrzej Bobiec took my project and young ideas very seriously. I am deeply indebted for the amount of time and energy he gave me. Andrzej Antczak facilitated many introductions and always ensured that I would hear multiple types of stories in the forest region. Kazi Borowski provided tech support when the internet was pretty new in Białowieża. Thank you to Joanna Kossak for needed translations and teaching me that difficult circumstances can lead to joy.

The scientists and staff at the Polish Academy of Science's Mammal Research Institute were extremely gracious. They let me follow them on radiotelemetry outings; talk with them while they collected bat, bison, and weasel data; and generally spend time with them in their lunchroom and homes. Thank you to Jan Wojcik, Rafal Kowalczyk, Ireneusz Ruczyński, Krzysztof Schmidt, Karol Zub, Krzysztof Niedziałkowski, Paulina Szafranska, Bogumiła Jędrzejewska, and Tomasz Borowik for maps and conversation and to Tomasz Samojlik, who explained Białowieża's history in his *Pompik* comics just as thoroughly and professionally as he does in his scholarly writings. Joanna Łapińska assisted with fact checking.

I remain wiser and with eyes wider for knowing the Society for Landscape Protection and Janusz Korbel, whose footprints I can still see in the snow—my dear friend who encouraged dissent, whose life was the forest, and who showed me what it means to be single-minded. Leszek Szumarski, the Black Stork, your arthritic wings carried Adam Wajrak and Nuria Selva and me in all our conversations and excursions. Grażyna Kowalczyk, your friendship and grace in the face of adversity, I do not forget.

For forest walks and talks and for opening of hamlet homes, thank you to Kasia Wappa; Lech Wilczek; Beata Hyży-Chłopińska; Zenon and

Dorota Kruczyński; Kasia Bielawska; Łukasz Ławrysz; Arek, Mateusz, and Lucyna Szymura; Romuald, Marysia, and Romek Wołkowycki; Sławomir Dron; Ewa Moroz Keczyńska; Andrzej Keczyński; Bogdan from the bike rental; and Basia, Mateusz, and Pani Bańka. In Teremiski, thank you to Pani Nina, Pani Sylwestruk, Pani Ciesia, Pani Falinska, and Pani Luda for your songs, sweaters, and stories. Thank you to Ella Poleszuk for tours of the sawmill. Thank you to Adam Bohdan for sharing updates on the campaign for the forest. Thanks to Dorota Gryka, Karol Gryka, and Władysław Gryka of Suszczy Borek, whose lives intersected with mine in ways that still move me. Borys Russko saw poetry in every tree and narrated his boyhood memories of World War II.

Uniwersytet Powszechny (UP) and the Jacek Kuroń Foundation gave me countless opportunities to become intimate with what it means to be Polish and to live in Poland at a historical juncture. Danusza Kuroń showed such exceptional kindness, which was always tied to thinking of the greater good and how to transform society. Had you not shown such kindness only a few weeks after Jacek's death, I would have never had the opportunity to meet so many important figures in Polish history. Kasia and Pawel Winiarski offered many meals and conversation in addition to historical and sociological materials. I thank you for seeing me through growth and changes. Thank you to all the students at UP who broke bread with me for sharing meals and sentiments and to Agata Konczal for helping me better understand the politics of Polish forestry. Thank you to Jodie Baltazar, chronicler-artist of urban plants and compost who made the film *Black Stork White Stork* with me, and my thanks to Emma Sieverson and Borys Labeda for camera work.

As the country supported the urban, in a reversal, the city often supported me. Thank you, Ben Cope, for making intellectual work center around play. Thank you to all current and former residents and participants in the Ząbkowska apartment and the vegetable orchestra Paprykalabra, including Diana Barańska, Irka Jazukiewicz, Eliza Czech, Krzystof Polek, and Siarhie Liubimau. Jakub Grygar always had good ideas for research directions in the borderlands. Myroslava Keryk enabled many professional opportunities in Poland.

My supportive colleagues at Whitman College provided encouragement or lifelines in many ways during the writing of this book, including Suzanne Morrissey, Chas McKahn, Kirsten Rudestam, Lisa Uddin, Ewa Hoffman, Elyse Semerdjian, Timothy-Kaufman Osborne, Stan Thayne,

Susanne Alterman, Rachel George, Jakobina Arch, and Phillip Brick. Thank you to Jamie Warren for tinkering with words and seeing the forest through the trees and to Chris Leise for coaching. Thank you especially to Jason Pribilsky for reading a whole draft and making substantive comments.

The Switzer Foundation, the National Council for East European and Eurasian Research, the Fulbright Foundation, the Ford Foundation, the National Security Education Program, the Kosciuszko Foundation, and Whitman College provided research or language funds.

At the University of Washington, Gene Anderson encouraged the production of this book and the advancement of my career by carefully reading and reviewing early drafts. I also thank Julia Parish at Program on the Environment, for keeping me at the interdisciplinary table, and Sara Breslau, whose efforts to cross-pollinate artistic projects with social science projects provided a model for my film.

Thank you to the Foundation of Civic Space and Public Policy in Poland for the invitation to workshop my manuscript at Recovering Forgotten History: The Image of East-Central Europe in English-Language Academic and Text Books, where Michał Buchowski, Tomasz Zarycki, Rigels Halili, and Maciej Janowski performed close reading and prevented me from making historical errors. I assume full responsibility for any remaining inaccuracies.

To my parents, Norma and Robert Blanchard, you taught me that the basis is love. To my mother-in-law, Yvonne Otterness, whose dedication to the land inspires me. Thanks to Greg Lalish, who, like Janusz, demonstrated his care for land and people and was a maker of forest trails, memorial and secret.

Anders Otterness, my life partner, the morning porridge, the staple meal, and the sweet and savory dessert—your labor and your thoughts undergird this book. Every idea in this book has first been fleshed out with you. To Milena Blavascunas-Otterness, may there be ancient forests for you.

TIME LINE

Fifteenth Century

1409   Władysław Jagiełło (Lithuania): First Polish Lithuanian Union. Crown Kingdom of Poland joins with the Lithuanian Commonwealth and first confers royal protection for Białowieża.

Sixteenth Century

1569   Union of Lublin makes one state out of two, forming the Polish-Lithuanian Commonwealth.

Seventeenth Century

1632–48   Władysław IV Vasa (Lithuania): The "Białowieża Royal Forest Decree" is established, freeing peasants and dividing the forest into twelve distinct areas.

1648–68   John II Casimir Vasa (Lithuania): Iron ore deposit and tar production interests brought populations to establish small villages around the forest.

Eighteenth Century

1765   King Augustus Poniatowski surveys royal lands in Białowieża, anticipating the "wise and rational use" of the forest for future timber production.

1772–95   Partitions of Poland: Kingdom of Prussia, Habsburg Austria, and Russia divide commonwealth lands, giving themselves various pieces of Polish territory.

1772   First partition treaty ratified by signatories.

1790   Second partition: Polish-Prussian Pact signed, bringing Poland into alliance with Prussia to save some lands.

1795   Third partition: Lands further divided. Poland loses rest of territorial land base; Białowieża falls under Russian control.

All royal guards turned into serfs and land distributed among Russian aristocrats.

Nineteenth Century

1830–31   First Polish uprising against Russian occupation.

1855–81   Czar Alexander II: In 1860, the czar reestablished protection of bison after a visit to the forest. Consequently, all predators of the bison—including wolves, bears, and lynx—were killed.

1863–64   January Insurrection against Russia.

1888–1917 Russian czars decree Białowieża to be a royal hunting reserve.

Twentieth Century

1915   German occupation: industrial forestry begins with production center developing in Hajnówka.

1918   Last wild bison becomes extinct.

1918   Poland regains independence as the Second Polish Republic.

1921   First forest reserve established in Second Polish Republic to protect remnants of ancient forest.

1924–29   English firm Century European Timber Corporation heavily logs forest.

1928   Lasy Państwowe (Polish State Forests) established and assumes management of Białowieża in 1929.

1929   Two breeding pairs of bison brought from zoos to Białowieża—breeding program is underway.

1932   Białowieża National Park established under control of Polish State Forests.

1939   Soviet occupation of Białowieża.

1941   Nazi occupation of Białowieża.

1945   Poland "liberated" by the Soviets. World War II ends.

1947–1990 Polish People's Republic (Polska Rzeczpospolita Ludowa).

1980   Solidarity Trade Union formed.

1989   First semifree elections in Poland. Round Table negotiations. Third Republic of Poland.

1999   Poland joins NATO (North Atlantic Treaty Organization).

Twenty-First Century

2001   Law on the Protection of Nature established, meaning national parks cannot be expanded except with consent from local municipalities.

2004   Poland joins the European Union.

2011   Annex to State Forests management plan reduces the amount of timber that can be logged from the commercial forest for ten years.

2017   Annex to State Forests management plan triples the amount of logging in the Białowieża commercial forest.

2018   EU Court of Justice requires Poland to stop logging or pay fines for breaking Polish law and EU law.

FORESTERS, BORDERS, AND BARK BEETLES

1

PUSZCZA

Of Forests and Time

PROTECTED ANCIENT FORESTS ARE RARE IN EUROPE. MOST European forests have histories of intensive logging and management. The only protected lowland primeval forest lies on the border between Poland and Belarus. In Poland it is called Białowieża (pronounced "Biaow-oh-veah-zha") and in Belarus, Belovezhskaya. In both places the forest is referred to simply as *puszcza* or *pushsha*, meaning "ancient forest." In media, the most commonly represented trait of this forest is its primeval character. Oak, ash, and linden trees, hundreds of years old, tower over a dense understory. Moss-covered logs slowly sink into the layered ground cover. The preeminent symbol of the forest, European bison, are featured in their temperate woodland habitat, grazing in the mist of riverine meadows. Such images remind the world that modern and civilized Europe was once fully forested from the Ural Mountains to the Atlantic coast and rich with wildlife such as wolves, pygmy owls, and moose. The forest is evidence of a European past, a relict that did not survive in the rest of Europe.

The majestic oaks standing today were never turned into ships for the global grain trade of the sixteenth and seventeenth centuries or into wine casks or furniture in the twentieth century. The trees are not all single species growing in straight rows for the economic logic of modern forestry, nor did the forest spring back after farmers abandoned the land. Białowieża has been evolving as forest since the end of the last ice age, twelve thousand years ago, a geologic event that marks the start of the Holocene. Given this deep time, how does a primeval forest shape multiscalar historical projects, some intensely local and all ideological?

Today in Poland, the Białowieża Forest is split between national park lands (Białowieski Park Narodowy)—projected as primeval and untouched—and highly utilized State Forests (Lasy Państwowe) lands, forming a complicated blend of highly protected zones and commercially logged areas. Those who advocate for the conservation of this outpost of lowland mixed-deciduous forest defend its pristine nature and focus on the forest's primeval character. In the conservationist narrative, the forest is evidence of a European past that survived only there. In this vision, the forest and its unique nonhuman inhabitants urgently need protection against logging. But to those who log and manage the Białowieża Forest (through Polish State Forests), the forest is a testament to a tradition of intensive human management and the economy and culture supported by such management. Forestry and hunting align in their ethos. The forester plants and cuts the trees and keeps them safe from deer through regulated hunting, and the village residents respect the forester. In this view, the forest would not exist without the forester's care.

Since the fall of communism in eastern Europe following the revolutions of 1989–91, the Białowieża Forest has garnered its share of international attention, first for being rediscovered as the last remaining primeval forest in Europe and then through outrage at the Polish government for logging the ancient woods. Polish nature conservationists, including biologists, activists, artists, and journalists, assumed that the introduction of democracy in the postsocialist period would benefit their cause. For them, democracy meant that merit-based science and meritorious managers could decide the fate of the forest. Over the past three decades, conservationists submitted proposals to the Polish Environmental Ministry to enlarge the small national park and curb logging in critically sensitive habitat. At the same time, Białowieża's foresters (employees of Polish State Forests) mobilized powerful social discontent against the inequalities of the new era to solidify their political base, even as State Forests downsized more than 75 percent of its workforce following the end of full employment under state socialism.

Białowieża Forest is both logged and protected in part. It sits on the border of the European Union in a formerly communist region and is Europe's last primeval forest. Contests rage among locals, biologists, conservationists, and foresters, who struggle to determine what the forest has meant and what it will become. The forest is both purifying and in need of purification. Purification takes on many meanings—not just whether the forest will be logged or protected but also which ethnohistories of the region should define the woodland, how the border of the European Union will influence the forest, and how communism will be remembered as an

Fig. 1.1. Białowieża National Park, strict reserve. Photo by Janusz Korbel. Used with permission.

artifact of institutions and social practices. Loss and desire are part of the experience of being there. Histories of inequality and ethnic violence have been suppressed. Many local people long for an era of full forestry employment. The forester promises modernity through what is extracted from the forest, a vision in which people forever plant and manage the woodland. There is also grief over logging the ancient woodland. Moreover, the deep past of primeval nature is invoked through conservationists' visions of a modern future facilitated by tourism.

No place is without a human narrative about its past. Is Białowieża's conservation conflict unique in terms of its troublesome pasts, which involve communism, the struggle for national identity, world wars, and insurrections? Białowieża's and Poland's pasts have not been put to rest—they remain open to reinterpretation and repurposing. In communist Europe, the past as a category in and of itself was used as a tool of control. For Poland as the People's Republic of Poland (Polska Rzeczpospolita Ludowa) in 1952–89, socialist ideology controlled interpretations of the past from the center. Following World War II, Poland came under Soviet control, and the first egregious attempt to control history came with the ideology that Soviets liberated Poland from fascism, and any other attempts to narrate

Poland's victimhood during and after the war at the hands of the Soviets was summarily forbidden. Following Marx's theories, communism would unfold as a historical inevitability. Despite this supposed inevitability, or perhaps to ensure it, eastern European socialist states felt the need to control interpretations of the past.

Intense social and political debates have ensued since 1989 in all eastern European formerly communist countries to reevaluate how the communist period reshaped history and collective memory and to reclaim the pasts that were erased, in an official sense, by communist rule. The past and future roles of the primeval forest are significant parts of this potent mix of questions about what "truthfully" happened in the past and deeply tied to the fundamental restructuring of people's relationships to that past and to the forest.

Nature Conservation and Postsocialism

Communism was well known for its ineffective environmental protection, resulting in forests destroyed by acid rain, the Chernobyl nuclear accident, soils contaminated by heavy metals, and industries belching dioxides into the sky (Pavlinek and Pickles 2000; Dawson 1996; Petryna 2002; Snajdr 2008; Manser 1993). The failures of communist modernity—perceived as failure in the sense that communist states never "properly" modernized and that they caused health and environmental catastrophes—also had unintended benefits for landscapes valued as natural and pristine. Socialist industry and development left many wide tracts of land open and virtually free of industry's direct manipulation and pollution (Schwartz 2006; Franklin 2002). Conservation occurred not necessarily because Communist Party ideologues pressed for protection but rather because inefficiencies in the system heavily industrialized some areas and neglected development in others. In other cases, nature conservation within the Soviet system was the biologist's "little corner of freedom," as Douglas Weiner (2002) has argued in his book of that title.

In the mid-1990s, Polish and western European nature conservationists promoted ecology as a new modernity in Poland. Through nature conservation, they argued, the past could be neutralized and the remains of the primeval forest made timeless. At that time, however, both the long-term residents of Białowieża—mainly those who worked on their farms and as forestry employees (the official designation was "peasant/worker")—and a small intelligentsia felt the stigma of being "backward" because of Communist underdevelopment in this region. Communism was a political system, and peasants or smallholders formed systems of production and sociality outside the logic of modernity. As these locals, biologists, foresters, and others reported to me, Białowieża had not sufficiently modernized.

Communist authorities redistributed large estates to small farmers after World War II and then attempted to collectivize them, but the drives ended in 1956 because of peasant protests, leaving a legacy of farms under ten acres. From a development perspective, there were too many small farms and dilapidated wooden houses, not enough cars, and the wrong kind of "elites." Five decades of communist rule undermined the chances for a "proper" Polish elite (with manners and a taste for literature, music, and the arts). Many upper-class Poles were exterminated by Soviets and Nazis during World War II, and others escaped Poland during Communist Party rule. The one-party state promoted villagers and the labor class to administrative positions and sustained apparatchiks that used favoritism and bribes. This history caused embarrassment in different ways for different people and gave rise to intertwined concerns about the past. Residents who lived in dilapidated houses challenged me, asking, "Are you going to write about our 'mud'?"—meaning poverty. A forester or scientist might redirect questions about who was a Communist Party member. Young people revived painful histories of Polish and Belarusian violence during and after World War II. Everyone I met over twenty years of research visits (1995–2018) invested hope in a time of change during the early years of postsocialism.

For nature conservationists, the way to bring about change seemed obvious. One mark of a developed nation, they argued, is that it can successfully preserve nature. Rather than wait for conservation in Poland to come in the wake of western European salaries and a car for every family, they asked, why not conserve nature to prove to the rest of the world that Poland was developed? Why not define modernity as the successful protection of a national park or nature preserve? Białowieża had flourished during an era of royal protection and again during an interwar logging boom. By the mid-1990s, it had become one of the poorest regions in Poland, even by Communist Party standards. Given the dire economic situation, ecological projects seemed both necessary and frivolous. Would worker peasants be left behind economically if conservation were prioritized over forestry? In the process of modernization, which pasts would be forgotten, resurrected, or celebrated?

The Importance of the Past for Forest Management

Białowieża has a preeminent position among globally designated cultural sites in Europe. The United Nations Educational, Scientific, and Cultural Organization (UNESCO) recognized a section of the Polish side of the forest as a World Heritage Site in 1979, and the whole forest in Poland and Belarus became a UNESCO World Heritage Site in 2014. Polish State Forests had to apply for this designation, and UNESCO threatened to remove it in response to egregious logging in 2017. The forest is divided not just by the EU border between Poland and Belarus (Poland has joined the European Union but Belarus has not) but also by its logged areas and protected reserves. In Belarus, the entire forest area (900 square kilometers) became a national park in 1991 (Belovezhskaya National Park). One might assume the result would be preservation; however, clear-cuts routinely appear along the national park tourist trails and deadwood is removed. Other areas, especially those running the length of the border with Poland and the European Union, receive strict protection, but I and others have seen logging within these reserves, and endangered animals such as wolves and bison are hunted. In Poland, more than 80 percent of the area (600 square kilometers) is a commercial forest belonging to Polish State Forests with a series of protected reserves (122 square kilometers within the 600-square-kilometer area). Forest-wide protective measures have prevented cutting stands more than one hundred years old. Another 18 percent (101.7 square kilometers) is managed as a national park. Of that, about 9 percent (57.3 square kilometers) is a highly protected strict reserve, where no management is carried out and entry is forbidden except with a trained guide. The other half of the national park includes active management to better preserve biological habitat (e.g., mowing riverine meadows and selectively logging some trees). This dizzying abstraction of management and numbers is often reduced to simple portraits. It is either all pristine *or* all planted and managed. In fact, the story is more complex.

The strict reserve in Poland (part of Białowieża National Park) often gets cast over the whole forest in strategically essentializing conservation discourses about "Europe's last primeval forest." Foresters and their supporters enlist a five-hundred-year history of use to contest such descriptions. In their narrative, administrators (later foresters) long maintained the forest for the hunt and later to serve economic needs through potash and furniture production. Foresters want to show that the forest needs the

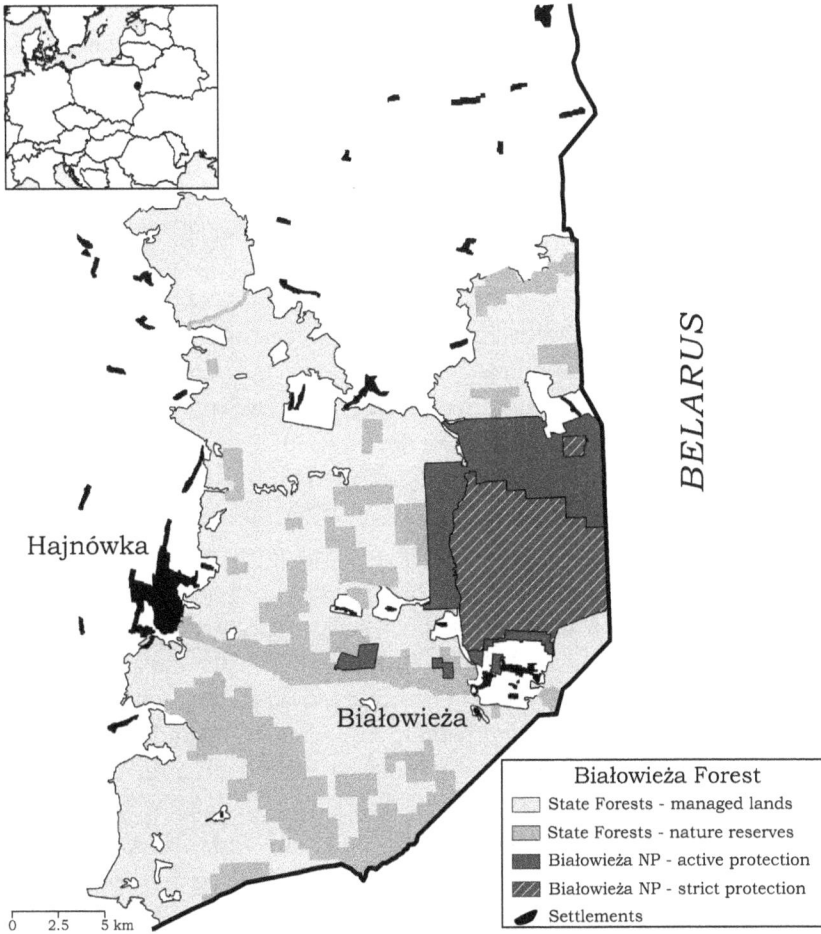

Fig. 1.2. Map of forest ownership. Produced by Tomasz Borownik. Used with permission.

forester, that nature and biodiversity are actually better with logging. Much has changed since Poland joined the European Union. The village hamlets hemmed in by the forest have seen rapid increases in wealth and sustainable development projects spurred by both the forestry sector and by funds for nature conservation.

Defining the Forest

What is Białowieża Forest? This question is about more than just management designations or defining the correct baseline of plant and animal species.

How to define the *puszcza* is entangled in the past and the future, in the identities of contemporary Poland and Europe, in the legacy of communism, and in the country's understanding of the "peasantry" in a decidedly postpeasant populist moment. What we consider to be the forest existed before human history, but there is no way to tell its story outside of nature's entanglement with culture. The past does not precede the forest any more than the forest precedes the past; nature and culture produce each other.

To depict a narrative of the forest during the course of human time, biologists and archaeologists have interpreted questions such as how open the canopy was in the Middle Ages (Vera 1999; Birks 2005; Latałowa et al. 2015) or whether Slavic grave mounds date to the ninth or sixteenth century. The pasts I am interested in are more recent. They center on Poland's peasantry and the birth of Polish State Forests in the twentieth century, the founding of the Białowieża National Park in the interwar period, the communist period in Poland (1945–89), and the postsocialist period (1989 to present). The twentieth century and start of the twenty-first cannot be understood without also referring to earlier periods, which I will explain below. As people fight over forest management, they use various pasts to link arguments for their projects—to Europe, as a representation of an idealized moral framework for solving problems; to Poland, as a misunderstood nation; or to Belarus, which can be understood both as a relic of the communist era and as an orderly nation where a dictator "gets things done." Entanglements between Poland and Belarus, and their relationships to Russia, arise in the course of celebrating or eschewing different pasts. I will highlight vital dimensions of Poland vis-à-vis Belarus and how these political bodies and ethnic groups relate to the ecology of the Białowieża Forest.

Above all, the forest mediates nostalgia and othering. It eludes those who try to define it. The forest remains unknown even as competing groups argue for different forest management and define its known qualities through science (forestry science and biology). Białowieża is both the last primeval forest of Europe and a commercially logged woodland. In other words, it is both pristine and imperiled, "already ruined" and the best hope for knowing a "wild" European forest. Its ambiguity increases when tourists and landscape aficionados discuss the forest as Belarusian, Russian, or Polish.

"Domes of Darkness" and Socialist Modernity

Returning to the primeval past, consider Europe at the end of the ice age, when wandering bands of humans survived by hunting. Glaciers retreated, the European continent warmed, and forests encroached. Humans moved around the globe, crossing into North America. In Europe, agriculture spread north from the Fertile Crescent. Many centuries later, settlements and then cities arose. Robert Pogue Harrison (1992) reminds us that forests would have shadowed European civilization. These "domes of darkness" (61), indifferent to time, began encroaching on humans accustomed to treeless expanses of ice. Europeans created their civilization not under the canopy trees but in its clearings: "One could not remain human in the forest: one could only rise above or sink below the human level" (ibid.). In other words, as the idea of European civilization developed, so did the ideas of cities and towns, agriculture, and eventually writing. The forest is antithetical to civilization. During the Roman Empire, for example, barbarians lived in the forests to the north. In this pan-European *longue durée*, the west cleared or exploited Europe's vast forests (Oosthoek and Hoelzl 2018). By the nineteenth century, most European forests had succumbed to the logic of German scientific forestry, which transformed forests into even-aged tree stands growing in straight rows. Few European forests survived unlogged or uncleared with continuous forest cover since their initial evolution after the ice age. Especially in continental Europe, to be left in the forest, poor and undeveloped, and without logging to rationalize it (Scott 1998), was the mark of backwardness. In Poland's postsocialist era, with its anticipation of a renewed attempt at modernity, whoever would win political power over the forest would have to define the markers of modernity in relation to this past.

The west's refusal to see the east as fully human, as fully civilized, has long divided the nations of eastern and western Europe. The category of "eastern Europe," according to Larry Wolff (1994), was invented only in the Renaissance as "western" European philosophers traveled and encountered "eastern" Europeans. Educated travelers deemed eastern Europe uncivilized. Reformers in Russia, such as Peter the Great, pursued a series of projects to "catch up" to western Europe. No project to modernize the entire region of eastern Europe had such a central organizing principle as communism under the ideological direction of the Soviet Union.

One Past, One Future

Throughout the 1990s and well into the twenty-first century, Poles and other citizens of formerly communist countries reckoned not only with state control over the economy but with temporality, defined here as the way one experiences time. Is time cyclical, future oriented and messianic, dragged out, sped up? Because of state socialism's efforts to suppress information and knowledge, state-sponsored historical narratives did not lend context and meaning to personal experience, and thus memory and unofficial stories became a way to overcome the disjuncture between individual recollections and official historical accounts (Wanner 1998; Gal 1991). Communism seized people's perceptions of time and projected an inevitable, glorious future that never came (Verdery 1996; Kaneff 2004). The past in official accounts did not consider suffering to be the suffering of national and ethnic groups in World War II. They turned relations between peasants and gentry into unified narratives about class, although many differences existed within those categories. They also turned great feats of Polish history into narratives of voracious empire.

During the communist period, the state promised its citizens that there would be one future, a future of communist utopia when the workers owned everything. By the time the communist future brought harmonious industrial development and goods and services similar to those in western Europe, classes and the state would supposedly no longer exist. Eastern European state socialism, or rather the command economy with its hierarchy of apparatchiks, was intended to advance the communist project. However, disillusionment with this vision, given the violence needed to maintain it—including shooting down protesters, beating and jailing dissidents, and fostering a network of secret police—brought the system to a moral breaking point.

With the end of that system, followed by Poland joining the North Atlantic Treaty Organization (NATO) in 1999 and then the European Union in 2004, people on the former eastern side of the Berlin Wall were led to believe that they might be able to obtain a kind of western European "normalcy" (Berdahl 1999; Kaneff 2011). For some, that normalcy meant the advancement of a legitimate intelligentsia. For others, it meant the ability to afford more consumer goods. The certainty of a European normalcy was surely doubted by many people on both sides of the former Iron Curtain. Nonetheless, the possibility still looms, and people in Białowieża fight over how to advance—how to turn this formerly poor peasant region into a model of modernity. The Białowieża Forest has the potential to drive and represent progress; however, the definition of progress depends on determination of the forest as primeval or dependent on human stewardship and forestry. These conversations and fights ensued in a country that had positive economic growth since 1989 and an economy that was growing beyond expectations but where the average annual salary was still equivalent to US$15,000 by 2017 and many manual workers made less than US$500 a month.

For conservationists, normalcy would consist of establishing a large protected area with minimal to no logging and placing the highest priority on protecting ecological processes that create the conditions for old growth, including allowing dead trees to remain standing and fallen trees to rot on the forest floor. Downed and standing dead woody debris provides critical bird habitat, creates more trophic (energy-exchanging) interactions, and constitutes half of the biomass in the strict reserve—the core part of the Białowieża National Park. Moreover, parks would be administered by scientists and foresters trained in the new era, in western European countries or by "western" standards of higher education. For foresters and the local lobby that supported them, normalcy would look quite different. It would mean removing dead wood on the forest floor, using all available resources to employ people, and relying on established social networks to provide a secure and bountiful future.

The narrative of a transition to normalcy, whether referring to the forest or to Polish society as a whole, has enforced the perception that modernity is spreading east over time. Maria Todorova (2004) wrote about this time lag as a condition of modernity for all regions that are not included in "the west." Visions of the future in such places depend on this belated time of arrival. Countries wanting to achieve European normalcy had to open themselves to free market reforms. Eastern Europe entered its postsocialist phase of modernization during the global era of neoliberalism, characterized by David Harvey (2005, 2) as a theory "that proposes that human well-being can best be advanced by liberating individual entrepreneurial freedoms and skills within an institutional framework characterized by strong private property rights, free markets, and free trade. The role of the state is to create and preserve an institutional framework appropriate to such practices."

This idea was certainly different from the welfare state that characterized and modernized much of western Europe during the postwar era. Western Europe rebuilt itself on generous social benefits and protections and in Germany on the US-funded Marshall Plan. Poland and other Soviet-sphere countries used the paltry resources of the Soviet Union and Warsaw Pact countries to rebuild cities, factories, and infrastructure that experienced more World War II destruction than other parts of Europe. After 1989, Poland embraced the challenges of transition. Poles followed Western consultants' advice. They privatized banks and sold off apartment buildings, factories, and shipyards. As with the Communist regime in its early postwar years in Poland, change was supposed to be accomplished quickly. In 1989, the Third Polish Republic implemented Finance Minister Leszek Balcerowicz's "shock therapy." In response to Poland's efforts in the first decade of postsocialism, money flowed copiously from the United States and Europe (US Agency for International Development, PHARE [Poland and Hungary Assistance for the Restructuring of the Economy] Program, World Bank/ International Monetary Fund) in the forms of both loans and grants; however, this approach backfired by seeding corruption and stunting democratic development (Wedel 1998). The change from state to private ownership often benefited the former class of apparatchiks. In the first decade after communism, ordinary citizens—often those who had fought and demonstrated against the Communist regime—lost their jobs and pensions and descended into a new kind of poverty. They had more material goods but less security about the future, a precarity also increasingly common in the west.

I came to know the Białowieża Forest during these economic, political, and cultural ruptures. Politics would appropriate history in ways that were different from the communist era but no less impactful. The conflict over the forest is not just a conflict about control of land and resources: it is about whose pasts will be recognized or ignored and how recognition can ensure that those living in the Białowieża Forest region are not left behind. People in Białowieża drew my attention to difficult, proud, embarrassing, and celebrated pasts. Although the people I knew disagreed about what should happen in the forest, they were passionate about the past, particularly the communist era and a past that supported a large group of smallholder farmers. The people who live in the forest clearings of Białowieża helped me understand that the forest itself, as opposed to politicians or governments, could bring about modernity, westernization, and civilization.

Fieldwork/Forestwork

The revolutionary wave of the late 1980s and early 1990s had tremendous power for me. The end of the Cold War influenced my generation and infused me with a sense of optimism and possibility. Growing up in the United States in that era taught me that the Cold War meant the fear of nuclear war. The largely peaceful revolutions added to the allure of traveling to this region and participating in the spirit of openness between people on both sides of the Iron Curtain. In 1989, I recall sitting in my college seminar on evolution when a fellow student rushed in ten minutes late commanding us to turn on the television—the Berlin Wall was opening and millions of people were climbing both sides. I had the distinct feeling that I wanted to join the masses of people as they assembled new worlds. While these images today might seem like the clichés of media reports, they drew me to Poland and Białowieża in subsequent years and would ricochet through my expectations over two decades of research stays.

After graduating with a bachelor's degree in environmental studies in 1994, I worked for a year at the US Forest Service to save money for my travels to eastern Europe. I was part of a team conducting research on the endangered spotted owl and its habitat loss in old growth forests in Washington State. This Pacific Northwest context pitted loggers against environmentalists. The radical ecology group Earth First spiked logs and "monkey-wrenched" harvesting equipment. In that year, a contingent of Polish foresters visited our laboratory as part of a US State Department exchange and told us about a similar conflict over old growth forest in Białowieża, Poland. It was my first awareness of nature as part of the postcommunist world, which I had imagined only in cities such as Berlin and Prague and in the Gdańsk shipyards. I arrived in Poland in June 1995 seeking out contacts provided by the visiting foresters.

Researchers from the Białowieża Forest Research Institute (Instytut Badawczy Leśnictwa) immediately found volunteer projects for me. I joined an international group of students collecting data about the presence of the rare fire-bellied toad (*Bombina bombina*) on farmland adjacent to the forest. I stayed in foresters' cabins and met foresters, biologists, farmers, and others. This era was a time of promise both for me and for Poland in terms of what was possible. People were eager to talk with me because of my interest in their future. The visit led to promises of collaboration for a master's thesis project. The scientists I met, including those working for State Forests, spoke to me proudly about their activities in the Solidarity movement—the trade union, which was instrumental in bringing communism to an end. In the 1980s, the ten-million-member organization (more than a third of the adult working population) constituted a civil rights movement. I met farm families piling hay, flax, and rye onto drying racks in what looked like timeless traditions of smallholder agriculture. Western European tourists were everywhere, studying forest biology or writing articles for major news outlets and telling me how the villages of Białowieża and the forest itself reminded them of their not so distant European rural pasts.

In 1998–99, I lived in the village of Białowieża for one year doing master's thesis research in cultural geography. I kept an office at the Polish Forest Research Institute connected with State Forests, and I spent this year learning how to speak Polish, neither my native tongue nor a heritage language. Inspired by humanistic geographers such as Yi Fu Tuan, Edward Relph, and Anne Buttimer in their writing about sense of place, I wanted to tell a presentist tale about the arrangement of space between village and forest—about how villagers shared responsibilities for herding cows and went to the forest to look for mushrooms and what colors they painted their wooden cottages. In the tradition of humanistic geography, I described the Orthodox and Catholic wooden crosses on the road as a way of thinking about ethnicity. The world conformed with my expectations based on that literature not just because I was blind to other kinds of stories but because people graciously endured and entertained my questions about goshawks stealing their chickens and how the rowan and raspberry shrubs grow out of the upturned spruce root plates. The forest had a kind of magical realism for me, and when I entered as a young woman, not asking burdensome questions about the past but curious about the arrangements of their daily lives, I developed strong and trusting relationships that enabled me to pursue research on more difficult topics later. This type of questioning also coincided with the eastern European tradition of ethnology in which the anthropologist is expected to lovingly record customs, which will eventually be used to build the nation.

Białowieża has a story of tradition paired with primeval nature. Although I found material to match my interests over two decades of research visits, I would be pulled, time and again, into obsessions with unresolved and painful pasts. I now realize that the way I experienced and interpreted meaning, time, and history at the start of my research was part and parcel of the West's need to see Poland and eastern Europe on its terms. As James Mark (2010) observed in *The Unfinished Revolution*, Western media, funders, and institutions asserted a triumphalism at the end of the Cold War and the inevitability of liberal democracy's sweep over eastern Europe. The West saw people on the other side of the former Iron Curtain borne along in the desire to be free from communism. But as a formative scholar coming out of ahistorical disciplines (environmental studies and humanistic geography), I wanted to believe in and present a world that was not overdetermined by history and modernity. And in many ways, the subconscious appeal still pulls me, as if I could rescue the forest and its inhabitants from ideological mobilizations and show the more mundane struggles of village life.

This book is laden with self-reflection on the ways in which the West has tried to peripheralize and orientalize eastern European societies and their historical experiences. But I also want to get to the urgent matter of forest ecology at a time of decreased and diminished old growth forests around the world and in a moment when right-wing nationalism tries to run off with the narratives of multicultural places.

Because of my own internal tensions regarding my position as a western chronicler of place and the unavoidable traces of other types of stories, I turned to a cultural anthropology program for my doctorate. Cultural anthropology asked ethical questions about fieldwork and culture in a different way than geography (Clifford and Marcus 1986). It encouraged sensitivity to the unspoken and close participant observation. During another seventeen-month stay in Białowieża (2005–6), a period of years heightened by the politics of memory in Poland, I learned that I had to catch myself in my historically conditioned modes of thought. In those years I held an office at the Polish Academy of Science's Mammal Research Institute, the premier center for conservation biology in Białowieża. I also lived with an experimental live-in college for teenagers from former state farms who moved there from other parts of Poland. This school, Uniwersytet Powszechny, was connected with the legendary Solidarity agitator, the "godfather" of anticommunist organizing, Jacek Kuroń and brought in scholars and intellectuals from Warsaw, who would expose me to why and how the past mattered in the region and in Polish politics at that time. My involvement also led me to many people I would never have had contact with otherwise, such as performance artists connected with the legendary director Jerzy Grotowski, architects of the Solidarity movement, and officials in the Polish government. My research visits to Białowieża continued until the completion of this book in 2019.

My formative romantic images of anticommunist organizing, small-scale independent peasant farmers, and an enchanted old-growth forest all came undone over the course of these years. The fight for the forest polarized inhabitants and the institutions with which I was affiliated—a situation that put me in the difficult position of taking sides, with allegiances that will emerge in the chapters of this book. Above all, a self-conscious attempt to reflect on my ethnographic authority gets to the heart of the politics at the center of this story. The West has misunderstood Poland and eastern Europe more broadly, which is why a primeval forest cannot simply rest in its primeval status and commercial logging cannot promise undifferentiated sustainable modernized development for all inhabitants of the forest. But as this book will explore, is the answer to let my ethnography become a tool for strident nationalists and to write this forest as a history of Poland in the time of climate change, an era that begs for internationalist action on the environment?

The two main trends in European anthropology, meaning here studies that take place in the amorphous area understood as Europe, have been ethnology for the purposes of "national awakenings," as developing bourgeoisie found their souls in peasant customs (Gellner 1998; Buchowski 2004), and anthropology for empire (Hirsch 2005; A. Zimmerman 2001), as imperial powers tried to describe the peoples they sought to control. Precisely because of the disappointments of both the communist and now the postsocialist eras, heightened attention has been paid to the way ethnographers of Europe position themselves (Hann 2017). An ethnographic emphasis on the past requires careful attention to the concept of "propriety" in management of the forest and the idea of a "proper" nation. Propriety is the way one behaves; what is proper is the conduct that ensures belonging (Rose 1994). A proper nation, such as what Poland was striving to become in the eyes of the West or by its own nationalist turn in recent years, must project itself as a nation that is powerful and self-determined, that will not be taken over by a foreign power, and that is respected by other countries. I take it as my ethnographic responsibility to guide you through this tension in my book.

Two ideas are interrelated: How does the forest, logged or preserved, further notions of Poland as a modern nation with a historical predisposition between eastern and western Europe? And which national people, if any, belong to the soil and forests of Białowieża within these narrations about modernity, morality, and belonging as the forest is logged and protected? Nations often cling to their relationship to nature to define their rightful place as a nation among nations. Nationalism has both an inward gaze ("this is ours") and an outward gaze ("not ours"; Gellner 1983; Anderson 1983; Hroch 2000). Białowieża has always been a multicultural region, and its future as a preserved forest without logging increasingly rests on the forest as world heritage, beyond borders. As logging intensifies (covered toward the end of the book), foresters stand convinced that conservationists are "ecoterrorists," meaning illegitimate oppositionists out to sabotage the nation, and that a vision of self-made nature—nature without human intervention—is the vision of foreign saboteurs. For Polish nature conservationists, only an EU-oriented politics or an outward internationalist focus will save the pristine treasure within Polish political boundaries from the nationalists.

Like the trees, plants, animals, soils, and management boundaries, the forest's pasts are places where expectations are defied. Those who might be accustomed to reading the social sciences literature on nature conservation will note that this is not a "top down to bottom up" ethnography—that is, this ethnography is not about global conservation agendas or nongovernmental organizations (NGOs) imposing conservation and how the local people resist those impositions. In environmental anthropology, the model that reflects this relationship best is political ecology (Robbins 2012) in which a great variety of relationships deal with economic centers and resource peripheries. Although my book draws on some insights from political ecology, as in how neoliberalism drives conservation, it also diverges from much political ecology. I am not looking at how the neoliberal turn subordinates all relationships to its theory of power, borrowing from Foucault's theory of governmentality. My book is an ethnography about the way different pasts trouble nature conservation, which here also involves the globalized and globalizing project of scientific forestry. My role is to interpret through the outsider's lens of anthropology, triangulating a narrative that can be recognized as familiar by those in the location of the forest but also providing a perspective that people in the forest do not see as obvious. I pay close attention to individual people in this book and often those who are outliers in their world, a focus on identity that Paul Rabinow (1977) reflected on in his classic book about fieldwork in Morocco. It is the misfit, the person who often does not fit in his or her own group, who can lead the anthropologist to the most meaningful understandings of another society. And yet I also use archetypal figures, especially the figure of the forester, to understand the roles that people play across historical terrain.

Like Erica Lehrer (2013) in her book about Jewish tourism to Poland, I see ethnography as a process of reengagement with uncomfortable and awkward pasts. Lehrer's work illustrates that ethnography can have the purpose of catalyzing change, that we can be committed to creating "ameliorative narratives and healing spaces" (20) in ethnography. Albeit an attempt to ameliorate more than heal, my work leaves room for changing one's position, just as politics, social configurations, and forests change. At the center of this story, though, is the biophysical entity that humans refer to as "forest," which includes a myriad of nonhuman and human-dependent relationships. All of those relationships are products of evolution, of history, and of different administrative regimes the forest has endured. I would betray my readers and myself if I pretended to be indifferent to the outcomes of both logging and preservation regarding the biological integrity of the forest and the social and economic welfare of the diverse inhabitants of this region. I am a nature conservationist, a person from a lower-middle-class background who has socially advanced through the study of science, a former US Forest Service employee, and someone who has wanted life to be "improved" and "normalized" for people who live in this region.

Engaged ethnography is neither "activist research" nor purely "cultural critique" (Hale 2006). I am not narrowly supporting a group that seeks to gain political legitimacy, nor simply serving to unveil what my informants cannot see for themselves (or what I missed the first time around). Like Anna Tsing (2015), I want to use the ruins of the present moment—ruins of capitalism and communism displayed through climate change and the disappointments of postsocialism—to show how a moment of uncertainty can also be one of wildly creative possibility, but this can be painful. There is often a deep sense of betrayal when people change positions, when those left holding up an obsolete or critiqued way of doing something are shamed for their role. This will become apparent repeatedly in the following chapters. My aim is not to expose and leave vulnerable but rather to uncover human foibles and frailties while looking at the ways people sustain relationships. This book is centered on characters and people that I knew over long periods of time who have been in those positions. I show how they changed and were changed and hold open the possibility that an anthropologist's work is toward becoming rather than a closed account of what was (Biehl and Locke 2017). This is especially important in an era of climate change.

Route Finding: Six Hundred Years of Administration

To get to the village of Białowieża, you head east from Warsaw for 220 kilometers to the industrial mill town of Hajnówka (population twenty-one thousand), the center of a large Belarusian (some would increasingly identify as Ukrainian, a newly discovered category of ethnicity for the forest region) and Orthodox (religion) minority in Poland. In an otherwise majority Roman Catholic, Polish-speaking country where the political boundaries align with ethnic boundaries, Białowieża's ethnic difference is a significant social fact.[1] From Hajnówka, you drive twenty kilometers along the Szafer Nature Reserve, a protected area within State Forests holdings. When you reach a clearing in the forest, you have arrived in the Białowieża village. Billboards advertise forest attractions, such as an adventure train ride, a spa experience, and the local supermarket. In this "village," which hosts three churches (Orthodox, Roman Catholic, and Baptist), two large hotels, several dozen smaller pensions, three scientific research institutes, and State Forests offices, there are approximately twelve hundred year-round residents. There are villages on other outside rims of the forest, but Białowieża village is the mainstay for tourism and the administrative headquarters of the Białowieża National Park with its museum and tour guides. The cultural, class, and occupational diversity here is rare for a Polish village of this size.

For those completely without knowledge of Poland, this brief historical overview will situate Białowieża within the regional history. Białowieża has been a quintessential borderland for centuries, which explains much of the diversity, and a site for understanding the historical union between Poland and Lithuania, where "Old Belarusian" served as the language of administration (Woolhiser 2003) and many people were called "Ruthenians," a term that no one identifies with today. As far back as 1409, when King Władysław Jagiełło set off on an eight-day hunt in Białowieża to supply his men at the Battle of Grunwald (against the Teutonic Knights in 1410) with bison meat and other game, Białowieża has been a site of governing intervention. Royalty and then the state have chosen this site as deeply symbolic for retaining and demonstrating power.

Although the date is uncertain, Jagiełło was born in Lithuania roughly around 1352. Foregoing his pagan upbringing, he converted to Catholicism through a royal wedding to the twelve-year-old Polish Queen Jadwiga. As the king of Poland, he established a centuries-long dynasty that ruled a territorial expanse known as a biconfederation: The Crown Kingdom of Poland and the Grand Duchy of Lithuania. This biconfederation created a space for cultures to coexist. It lasted until 1572 and was the largest Christian state in Europe at that time, reaching from the Black Sea to the Baltic.

Jagiełło built a lodge on a tourist site now known as Stara Białowieża, and most historians think this was the beginning of formal forest protection. Archives report an official administrator of Białowieża, Bohusz Bohowitynowicz (1510), and a delegation of more than one hundred guards, game managers, beaters (those who drove game toward horse-mounted dignitaries), and others who trapped animals for fur or took care of the lodge. The story of Jagiełło's dynasty is understood as marking the Christianization of the last outposts of pagan Europe. Pagan Lithuanians had worshipped earth goddesses under sacred groves of ancient oaks.

In the nature conservationist's rendering, Białowieża was spared the ax and plough during these times only because of royal hunts. In that view, kings and grand dukes like Jagiełło mark a turn away from a more idyllic pagan past of worshipping and belonging to the forest. Foresters, in contrast, recognize echoes of Jagiełło's hunting practices in their own present-day administrative structures. Also due to royal influence originating in Jagiełło's hunts, Białowieża continues to have a mix of people who descended from aristocrats and managers as well as from peasants and lowly functionaries. In any case, wrapped up in the legend of Jagiełło is an articulation of borderlands (the Polish-Lithuanian border), the importance of the hunt, and the symbolism of the bison for national identity. It is the origin story of this forest and has a special place in the way competing interests call upon the past.

With the Union of Lublin in 1569, Poland and Lithuania became a joint commonwealth. The Polish-Lithuanian Commonwealth was a multiethnic, multireligious empire for much of the late Middle Ages and the Renaissance. In the relatively liberal democracy of nobility, diverse linguistic groups coexisted, including Poles, Lithuanians, Ruthenians, Germans, Dutch, Tartars, Jews, and Armenians. Catholics, Mennonites, Orthodox, radical Anabaptists, Jews, and Muslims were only some of the religious confessions of this period. From the mid-seventeenth to mid-eighteenth centuries, the commonwealth was one of the first experiments in European democracy, meaning rule by the elite but not necessarily the king. Poland elected its kings between 1572 and 1791, and several were foreign born. Ten percent of the population counted as nobility, and each of the men had the same parliamentary power. This parliamentary device, known as liberum veto, often led to stalemates and chaos that made the commonwealth look weak in the eyes of its imperial neighbors. Austrian Habsburg, the Russian

Fig. 1.3. Hunting party of Czar Nicholas II, 1903. From Białowieża National Park archives.

Empire, and the Kingdom of Prussia partitioned Polish lands among themselves beginning in 1772 and lasting until 1795. These more despotic rulers prompted a strong Polish resistance and claim to Polish moral superiority. The resistance grew into a Polish ethnic and nationalist identity without a land base and state of its own.

The partitions mark the "martyrdom" of Poland, the idea that Poland built democratic structures long before the rest of Europe and would be punished by other European countries for doing so. The division of Polish territory planted the desire for a formidable and unified national project that could build support for an independent Poland abroad. During the partitions, Białowieża belonged to Czarist Russia, which used it as a private hunting ground.

After 120 years of fighting for independence, Poland regained its independence in 1918 after World War I, a period in which the forest was industrially logged by German occupying powers. Białowieża also became one of the first Polish national parks in the interwar period (1931). After World War II, the geopolitical configurations of the Yalta agreement (1945) had a cascading effect on the region. Churchill, Stalin, and Roosevelt divided Europe into spheres of influence, and Poland became Stalin's first agenda item. At the time, the Soviet Union already occupied Polish territory, and Churchill and Roosevelt sought to keep the peace between the two formerly warring nations. To that end, the leaders divided Białowieża between Poland and the Soviet Union. The Soviet Union kept its side of the forest as a private hunting reserve for premiers, rather than logging it. Soviet engineers drained the forest bogs to create two lakes stocked with fish. Polish State Forests set up felling and planting schedules.

Poland created a chaotic yet peaceful transition to multiparty democracy and free markets. Former Communist Party members were permitted to run for political positions, which was not the case in many formerly communist countries. Poles elected Solidarity leader Lech Wałęsa as the first president of the Third Republic of Poland in 1990 in what seemed like a huge victory for the movement.[2] But while Wałesa's original trade union goals demanded better conditions for workers in the Lenin Shipyard in Gdańsk, his government largely gave way to the creed that Poland would open to Western loans and investment, showing its gratitude and loyalty through quick and painful reforms that hurt the working class and the large rural population. On May 4, 2004, Poland, along with seven other formerly communist countries, joined the European Union. Membership brought benefits in the form of subsidies to farmers, direct monies for infrastructure, and representation in Brussels. It also brought many expectations that went unfulfilled, with the result that Polish politics swung from pro-EU candidates and parties toward anti-EU positions over the next decade. The political parties that had either majority support or parliamentary positions included center-left parties, such as the Democratic Left Alliance (Sojusz Lewicy Demokratycznej), which thought ousting communists had too high a social cost and rejected religion in schools; Solidarity Electoral Action (Akcja Wyborcza Solidarność), a coalition of more than thirty parties that grew out of the momentum of the Solidarity Union; the centrist Civic Platform (Platforma Obywatelska), largely pro-EU and socially conservative; populist agrarian parties, such as Self Defense (Samoobrona), which never reached parliamentary majority but symbolized discontent with the new European Union membership; and the right-wing, anticommunist, and EU skeptics in power today, Law and Justice (Prawo i Sprawiedliwość [PiS]).

This greatly abbreviated sketch of history and postsocialist politics is intended as a preliminary chronology for reading the rest of this book. Although Polish readers and historians would surely have much to add or clarify, I direct them to the chapters that follow. Each chapter covers different facets of history in greater depth, interweaving historical background with people and forest ecology. However, the following points are essential for understanding how the past informs conservation politics in Białowieża today. First, although nature conservation is seen by some as a modern-day Western imposition, it has been part of the region in various forms since Jagiełło and since the International Union for Conservation of Nature and Natural Resources (IUCN) cofounder Władysław Szafer initiated designs for the Białowieża National Park following World War I. Second, Białowieża has long been a borderland, which means its ethnic populations are mixed while nationalist political movements try to override plural interpretations of history. Third, the area's past use as a hunting ground can be conveyed to different ends. At times, this use has spared it from logging. However, at other times, logging and hunting were inseparable and both seen as critical to the economic well-being of the area. Fourth, there is a longstanding antipathy between Poles and Russians, stemming from the time of the partitions and represented in Communist Party rule. Poles participated in communism, but it is seen within many political factions as a Russian-directed project. However, the dramas that will play out in this book all center around the question of who is secretly collaborating and openly on the side of Russia, even as they might outwardly appear anti-Russian or anticommunist. It is also worth noting that Belarusians living in the greater forest region are often stereotypically linked to Russia, which is part of a far larger historical project of Pan Slavism, dividing Slavs into eastern and western Slavic-speaking regions. Little distinction is made in Białowieża between Russians and Soviets. This distinction, although critically important in a historical sense, is often collapsed in Białowieża. Fifth, communism never successfully collectivized Poland's peasants, leaving a huge legacy of small subsistence farms throughout Białowieża in the postsocialist era. This has had an impact on how locals perceived themselves as backward in the 1990s and early 2000s. Sixth, the postsocialist period modernized Poland in some respects but created huge gaps in wealth, leading to a sense of disillusionment. Logging and preserving the Białowieża Forest cannot be interpreted outside of this notion of modernity and progress for the nation.

Fig. 1.4. Polish State Forests, Białowieża District, logged oaks, 2008. Janusz Korbel. Used with permission.

History and Ethnography

As Marshall Sahlins (1985, vii) noted, "History is culturally ordered, differently so in different societies, according to meaningful schemes of things. The converse is also true: cultural schemes are historically ordered." A Pole or Belarusian (and many who are of mixed ethnicity) in Białowieża would identify differently with the significance of certain historical events. They would also become Poles and Belarusians, or conservationists or foresters or peasants, because of events far from their interpretation and control. And to borrow from Sahlins, anthropologists working on historical topics will need to incorporate the notion of rupture to understand the structure of a culture or society at different moments in time. In other words, there are undeniable breaks, such as the discovery of the Americas by Christopher Columbus in 1492, World War II and its postwar divisions of territory, or the anticommunist revolutions of 1989–91, that organize people in different cultural, social, and economic ways. But, as this book struggles to understand, are the ruptures understood as ruptures at the time they occur or in the places they unfold? Scholars of postsocialism have been arguing for the need to see continuities where others see rupture.

During the first twenty years of postsocialism, anthropologists took up the weakening and retreat of the state as a central organizing theme, looking particularly to record the ordinary person's view of history (Creed 1993;

Kaneff 2006; Verdery 1996). Anthropologists today need to pay increasing attention to Poland and other eastern European nations' retreat to nationalism in the wake of both rising prosperity and vast inequality. In other words, there seems to be another historical break, not as covered by the Western media as the anticommunist revolutions but significant in terms of culture ordering history and history ordering culture. That rift is producing adoption of a nationalist understanding the "glorious past," referring to Poland during the Polish-Lithuanian Commonwealth or as resurrected in the interwar period, and Poland as the martyr of Europe as a political raison d'être for the Law and Justice party, especially martyrdom at the hands of Soviets. The glorious past, in which even something like the failed Warsaw uprising during World War II can look like a victory, fails to discern distinctions within these periods and uses selective emotional symbols from these eras to affirm Poland's greatness. There is widespread agreement that the west betrayed the east in the postsocialist period, just as it did in the post–World War II era when Roosevelt and Churchill "gave" Poland to Stalin after Poland had fought alongside the western allies. If the communists spent four decades emphasizing fascism's (i.e., Nazi Germany's) role in former injustice, nationalists now emphasize the greater role of Russia and the Soviet Union. Right-wing politicians with strong electoral victories talk about the glories of the precommunist past, when nations experienced a level of "civilization" that the West had not attained, for example, during Poland's eighteenth-century experiment with democracy. The West does not see and never saw these civilizations (Hann 2015). In turning toward stories of the past, the nation isolates itself, believing that its own superior national culture will provide the antidote to the West's arrogance and globalization. The European Union is now seen by many nationalists in Europe, not just Poles, as a force of globalization and fast capitalism rather than a moral center for European values (Holmes 2000).

The crucial distinction for anthropologists writing about how the past troubles nature conservation now is that postsocialism itself is no longer seen as part of a transition toward a desired, normal modernity. Extensive everyday changes, geopolitical relocations, and reorientations to planned market economies have only caused perpetual uncertainty (Knudsen and Frederiksen 2015). When writing about postsocialism today, scholars refer to the period as one of disillusionment, frustration, and a turn toward nationalism as the antidote to failed reforms. But this is hard to understand given Poland's astronomical economic growth, charted at 4 percent annually by economists, and electoral support and representation for right-wing nationalism in countries like Germany, Britain, Italy, and the Netherlands. But economic conditions still merit consideration in eastern Europe. Frustration stems from the inequalities embedded in Poland's growth. Postsocialism no longer has an end point in sight. Transition is an end in and of itself. And political support for the right-wing PiS party is a vote for a right-wing welfare state as a response.

Experiencing "constant transition," the forest sits in that ambiguity (primeval, managed, EU border, Polish, Belarusian, under constant rewriting of management plans and protective schemes). Yet foresters and scientists are in the forest, measuring and collecting data and inscribing stories about the past through the allegiance they build. And each memory, measurement, and interaction takes place in the loaded field of the past, as it is remembered and interpreted by these individuals.

Ethnography as Entanglement

My ethnographic commitment is to personal and community accounts that acknowledge particularlisms and agency in the face of these large histories that accompany the accounts. Instead of reflecting only on the inequality and miseries wrought by the past thirty years, for there were inequalities and miseries in former periods, I turn to the logic of my informants as a lead-in to discussing theory but without letting this book become constrained by a single theory or argument. My work is a unique "village ethnography," in a village with three scientific institutes and a growing number of tourists. It pulls details from my engagements with individual people and types of social actors into histories that undergird the structure of the book. I source history through archives, secondary sources, popular written local accounts and oral histories, as told in fragmentary ways by my informants. Unlike a classic village ethnography, it is also an ethnography of institutions, with a focus on State Forests and biologists working at different types of state research centers.

I rely on vignettes, but my book does not relate the kind of outdated village ethnography that comes from an ethnographer knowing almost all inhabitants in the village, their kinship ties, and daily rituals. Rather, I investigate the future of the village and forest by looking at usages of the past, especially the communist past. I push against the totalizing narratives of neoliberalism as the future. For example, many ethnographies of contemporary conservation choose neoliberalism and the creation of governable subjects as their main analytical lens (Heatherington 2010; Buscher 2013; Escobar 2008). Sherry Ortner (2016) wrote recently about "dark anthropology," meaning an anthropology in which there is no escape from power. In this type of anthropology, every crevice of life is infected and succumbs to this logic (Ortner 2016).

Working in the circulation of this logic, many scholars of postsocialism intervened in debates about structure and agency. Did cultures—often meaning nations—have their own cultures in which they could act as agents, as parts of cultural groups? Or did state socialism and the Communist Party create a culture that became apparent when the west tried to impose reforms (Dunn 2004)? In multiple postsocialist ethnographies, citizens of the newly independent, noncommunist states and nations succeeded or failed in the capitalist era as a direct result of the cultural and social acumen they developed in the communist era (Ghodsee 2005; Berdahl 1999).

Culture and its relationship to the past is a process of, as Tsing (2015) and Donna Haraway (2016) have called it, "world-making." World-making involves humans and the natural world that extends beyond them in an emergent moment of global change marked by global formations such as migration flows, refugee crises, and climate change. The Białowieża Forest is dynamic and a primeval relic not only because of human activity but also because of assemblages of eras, forests, humans, and modern technologies, which are themselves shaped by communism, postsocialism, and neoliberalism—all projects with great spatial and social reach. In this book, I will resist totalization or any argument that claims to explain all phenomena about all people's relationships with the past in the forest. Instead, I will let each chapter explain patterns by way of anthropological insight. To let the book be guided by a single argument would betray the complexity of people and the forest and my relationships with them. This is not to say that this book is atheoretical, but it comes first and foremost from the place of encounter and leads to a place of becoming through theory.

Anthropologists have long viewed cultural identity as emergent rather than fixed, as dynamic and changing based on the circulation of discourses (Lowe 2006; Brosius 1999) and individual agency as people interact (Hathaway 2013; Tsing 1995; Barad 2003). This allows the understanding that one's sense of identity can shift among the village, local, provincial, national, regional, and global spheres. At other times, identities coalesce not around place but rather displacement. Humans act strategically, informed by their cultures, and so they change their positions over time. In times of historic transformation, the horizon of possibility for choosing what to identify with is opened (Razsa 2015). In Białowieża, the forest is at the center of people's worlds and identities. As we will see at the end of this book, Białowieża's nature and management become synonymous in a fight for the nation. If we think of the postsocialist era as an attempt to modernize Białowieża by pitting a "backward" Belarus and Russia against a "civilized" Europe, we are easily deceived by this stereotype. It backfired. The result of attempts to modernize by looking to Europe has been a spiral into nationalism and populism.

Over the course of my fieldwork in Białowieża, the preoccupation with the distinctions between east and west, with communist and peasant throwbacks and the possibility of western normalcy, was on everyone's mind. I was forced to grapple with how people working at a particular type of institution or holding a "stakeholder" position might choose an unexpected alliance, in spite of those distinctions. What animates this book are portraits of people in complex interaction with each other in ways that defy easy categorization. This approach demonstrates friendships, betrayal, and advancement, as well as degradation, exploitation, and engagement. But most importantly, I show how difficult pasts have come to be negotiated in the forest in the present. The stories I know, through two decades of visiting and living in the forest, show that the positions people take are best understood by linking individuals to one another and to their mutual historical past of royal forest protection; of an intertwined Russian, Polish, and Belarusian history; of the rise of resource institutions such as State Forests and biological research centers; of peasant agriculture under communism; and of Poland's entry into the European Union.

The outcome of the historical constellation of the communist and peasant pasts as they intersect in views of the forest is worth exploring. For all those who care about how to best protect and use the forest, this story offers many lessons and explores the question of why a forest's history is so important.

Organization of This Book

Each chapter that follows shows foresters, conservationists, and local people interacting and relying on different understandings of time and history for their identities. In chapter 2, I open the ethnography with the figure of the forester. Who is the forester, and what is the forester's role in local society? This chapter will largely explain how and why foresters retain power in the postsocialist era. This history of Polish State Forests also has a significant impact on the protection and use debates of the present. Previously, forest-ers advanced peasants, offering them a chance at the coveted position of bureaucratic manager. After socialism ended, there was and continues to be an expectation that State Forests would provide education and job security in otherwise unstable and changing times. Białowieża enables us to con-sider the legacy of a state institution on how people respond to authorities, both old and new, when it comes to interpreting the forest. This chapter is an institutional history in part and an ethnic and class history that explains how an education and career in forestry was a means of social mobility in the twentieth century.

In chapter 3, I take readers into the world of science research in the Białowieża Forest. I discuss the salience of the communist past on scien-tists' field biology careers and how discourses about communism infiltrate institutional identities, "proper" interpretations of the primeval forest, and perspectives on how the forest should be studied. At the center of the chapter is a biologist of aristocratic descent, Simona Kossak, who is at once mystical, anticommunist, and a defender of a peculiar position among scientists—animal rights. Through her story, we see the slippery boundary between what seem like distinct political positions. A scientist and descen-dant of the aristocracy can facilitate cronyism as much as former apparat-chiks. All actors in this chapter profess a desire for transparency at the end of the communist era, but they hide from each other and become exposed in ways they do not predict.

Chapter 4 tells a story of how the peasant past has been both cele-brated by conservationists and reinvented by local people to promote their respective agendas. I feature an aging misfit bachelor, Leszek, and look at his struggle to adapt to the changing social and economic climate of the postsocialist years. This chapter asks how a man of the forest survives and even remakes himself in an economy driven by consumerism and tourism. Leszek turns the ideas of peasant and cosmopolitan, wild and tamed, past and future, capitalist and socialist, upside down. This chapter also explains the fate of the peasant class by looking at Poland's complex pattern of pri-vate agricultural land holdings during the socialist period. I give a brief his-tory of the peasantry in Poland and a distinctive overview of why peasants in Białowieża were never "true peasants," acknowledging the staying power of a term long separated from its feudal origins.

Chapter 5 looks at the attachments of tourists and landscape lovers to the ethno-landscape of the Białowieża Forest at the site of the Belarusian border. Białowieża also allows us to explore why notions of romantic pristine nature persist. Europe's last primeval forest was also the home to Europe's last dictatorship under Belarusian President Alexander Lukashenko. The site creates an opportunity for ethnic Poles to play out their victory over the communist past, and this can be seen in the social practices of tourism. Visitors explore the forest, themed hotels, and restaurants and cross the border on adventure tours of the Belarusian forest, which reinforce what it means to be Polish as Europe enfolded Poland into its union. I will explore the question of what kind of nostalgia is facilitated by experiencing a relic forest and communist-like dictatorship. How is eastern Europe recreated as a category from the past in the politics of ecological activism and ecotourism?

The book then veers into the nationalist turn in chapter 6, prompted in no small way by spruce bark beetle outbreaks. If the forest is narrated peripherally to the Polish nation in the preceding chapters, it become a defining pivot point here, where we are able to reflect on how conflicts over control of land and resources are also conflicts about national distinctiveness and the negotiation of national peripheralism. What can the anthropologist offer that is more than a report of competing ideologies in the age of climate change and European disintegration? Can there be a way to think with the bark beetle outbreak about the past?

In conclusion, I look at how foresters, biologists, tourists, and locals project Białowieża as past and future. Chapter 7 provides a telling account of humans' attempts to use nature to support cultural ideas about themselves and the world around them as both shift and transform.

The approach I have settled on involves naming people by their first and last names if they are dead or famous and providing everyone else with a pseudonym. However, I realize this is problematic as many people I write about are public figures in the regional context, and any details of their lives will break the anonymity I have given them through an alternative name.

Notes

1. Some estimates put the country's ethnic Polish-speaking and Catholic population at 97%, but the 2014 statistical yearbook of Poland puts Catholics at about 86% of the population.

2. General Jaruzelski was the first president, elected in 1989 by the joined Lower and Higher Chambers of the Polish Parliament. In the popular vote of December 1990, Wałęsa became the first publicly elected leader of the Third Republic of Poland.

2

THE FORESTER

YOU CAN DETERMINE A FORESTER'S RANK BY HOW many oak leaves and diamonds appear on the lapel of his uniform. Marek's has two oak leaves and three diamonds, meaning he is a midlevel forester. Like all foresters, he wears his uniform most days, which can include during non-working hours if he is running errands. The uniform includes a white or beige collared shirt under a tawny-green suit coat with a forest-green tie. His crisp pants match the color of the coat. The cap is peaked with a brown leather strap and adorned by a Polish eagle—the national coat of arms.

It is September 2004. I ride with Marek, a forty-year-old forester, in a State Forests Jeep to do a routine survey for timber theft. We stop first at the local shop where he can acquire some bread and sausage. I stand at the entrance, as the small shop is full of people, while there is a warm and jovial exchange between Marek and several others in front of the glass counter with large blocks of cheese and plastic kefir bottles. He shakes hands with several men and jokes with the shop attendant about his recent hunt. Then Marek and I are back in the vehicle, headed to a unit of forest near the hamlet of Teremiski. We travel a narrow stretch of road where one has an expansive view of the border of the Białowieża National Park, striking for its uneven silhouette of trees against the large overgrown meadow filling in with shrubby willows.

When we get to the sites that he patrols, Marek takes me to a spruce and pine stand with an admixture of birch and a few young oaks. He admires how straight and strong the spruce trees are. All of the seedlings for this stand and others come from nurseries within the forest. The tree genetics belong to this forest and no other. The pedunculate oaks grow amid a few stumps. The young trees about my height have protective plastic covers to prevent browsing. If the forester had not created this opening in the canopy, there would be little future for oak, he explains, but boar are also a problem, which is why he hunts them: "Boar can dig up roots when consuming acorns. If we have less boar, we have better oak regeneration."

I raise the topic of timber theft. Who steals timber and how? Marek is a bit unspecific. "People come at night and sometimes just drive away with the logs piled on the side of the road," he says. "Sometimes they cut timber from the forest, which is why we're checking for any suspicious stumps that we did not authorize to be cut." I ask if these are local people or organized industrial operations. He suggests some of both, indicating that local people have been more known to take a smaller fallen birch, and then only those who are really poor and in need of fuelwood for heating. "But people wouldn't need to take from the forest if State Forests and the mills could employ more people," he says. "Not long ago everyone worked for State Forests. There was no unemployment. We found people, took them by the collar if necessary, and put them to work."

To solicit more details, I share anecdotes I heard from the grandmothers who sit on the benches along the road most days. They frequently boasted to me about how many trees they had planted over their lifetimes and how much they missed the time when the forester knocked on the door, asking them to come out for work in the nurseries. "The forester is boss and chief," and "he is the right kind of expert," the women say. "He is like the aurochs [now extinct], because he keeps the canopy open for new growth."

Marek reaffirmed the significance of his profession, forester (*leśnik*), for the village while adding historical context. He too wanted me to understand that the forester created this world of people and forest. "We [foresters] carry a tradition. Forest protection goes back to the fifteenth or sixteenth century, and that's how deep our tradition is. From generations back, if you stayed in the forest, you worked in the forest. It was a question of heritage. If you lived in the forest, you were a forester. We are all one family here." In this sense, Marek and the women I had spoken with earlier wanted me to see the forester as a figure of belonging, a figure who had been here for centuries, who created the forest and sustained culture in the forest.

How does a role become transhistorical in a place that is part of what Timothy Snyder (2010) has called "bloodlands"—the part of Europe where more than 14 million non-combatants died outside of concentration camps between 1933–1945. How does a type of social actor keep his or her status even as borders, administrations, economics, and societies change? It was tempting to take the forester's and the local people's pronouncements about him at face value. Wasn't this part of the optimism of the postcommunist era?

Topographies and Figures

There is a topography to places that becomes wrapped up in roles or figures—a precise description of a place embodied in qualities ascribed to the figure. The forester is such a role or figure in Białowieża. The forester has to be written about in the singular, as in "the forester." First and foremost, the forester represents his organization (State Forests) with a unified approach to the Białowieża Forest—namely, that the forest needs the forester. In this rendering, the forest risks certain peril without him. Bark beetles (*Ips typographus*) would strip valuable spruce of its life force, leaving patches of dead standing timber. Oaks and maples could not mature unless seeded and protected from browsing ungulates. If foresters were not overseeing species composition, tree stands would degrade into nothing more than gnarled unmarketable hornbeam or, worse yet, grassland.

There is a set of relations packaged as the forester; an entire social world, an ecological and aesthetic forest world circulates back to this figure. The forester plants the forest, cares for the forest, and ensures a forested future. This figure is useful in supporting a social order, one in which history is present but collapsed to fit a tidy portrait.

The forester is a masculine figure that promises development under paternalistic care; development out of the primeval forest past, with its pest insects; and development out of the peasant past, with its cramped wooden houses, farm animals, dirt roads, and outhouses. In some cases, it even harkens back to the communist past, a past that was associated not necessarily with the ideology and implementation of Marxism and Leninism but rather, for locals, with an era of unquestioning obedience to the authority of the forester—an era in which the community was optimistic about its future.

With the chronic threat of underdevelopment in the postsocialist era, a gap is left open for the forester to fill, just as the forester fills in canopy openings with juvenile trees. He holds onto hierarchical and patrimonial power, including the customs of that power such as chivalry and hunting. The forester in Białowieża is able to become transhistorical as a result. He collapses different historical periods, ethnic conflicts, and identities as a way of maintaining a hold of social power and forest management after the fall of communism.

I listened to countless people talk about foresters as *the* forester, always in the singular. It was a curious distinction. Scientists, referred to as *naukowcy,* and nature conservationists, referred to as *ekolodzy,* were both always spoken of in the plural, as in "nature conservationists come here with their pseudoscientific ideas" or "scientists are the cause of our poverty." But the forester—"He should decide the fate of the forest," "He is the proper manager," "He sells us wood," "He hired us for work." And "he" was accepted as a local, in the most charged political sense of that word, even if he arrived in Białowieża from elsewhere to be a forester.

Some women work for State Forests at administrative levels in Białowieża, but for the most part, a cadre of male foresters can be found in the field and in higher administrative positions. When people speak of the forester, they refer to the person who sells them wood and decides which trees to cut. Loggers and equipment operators, for instance, are not foresters. They are private contractors. The forester inhabits a house in the forest or village and oversees a forestry operation, but not every village has a forester or a forester's house.

The forester condenses inhabitants' memories of different eras by reminding them of better times, particularly the 1980s, which was a good period for worker-peasants in terms of stability, independence on the farm, and a village full of people who had physical work in the woods. He gave people work. He held opportunities for social advancement in the State Forests administration. There was collective work in the forest, hand planting trees, removing brush, and cutting trees. The state provided its workers with solid houses in the decade before communism ended. Houses were especially hard to acquire in the city or even in many villages, where people had been living in blocks of flats. The villages in the forest, inhabitants repeatedly told me, were brimming with life, multiple generations, and a sense of future, even if the material conditions were difficult in that era.

By placing the forester as central to the local, central to the forest, an oppositional identity developed. Local inhabitants rejected the European Union and international nature conservation and, generally, people from outside. The oddity of this was that the forester in Białowieża could not be removed from his role as a bureaucrat of the central state, and yet locally he fronted opposition to the outside. Countless foresters emphasized their primary commitments to developing and protecting the local society. The forester symbolized times of social cohesion in the village, and no one ever spoke of him as being responsible for the reduction of State Forests staff during the 1991 reforms.

In those reforms, State Forests adopted a corporate model, keeping 80 percent of communist-era holdings (nationalized in 1944) and cutting 75 percent of its workforce. Its total forest holdings added up to more than a third of Polish territory. State Forests privatized state-owned homes, supported the private property relations of local people, and sold off state-owned equipment, such as tractors and harvesters. The institutional model became more corporate, reserving profits for its employees in the form of bonuses and providing little revenue to the central state. State Forests had a monopoly on wood sales, and only since 2014 has the central government reserved a 2 percent share from forest profits for the national budget.

In all of these official obligations, local inhabitants, together with foresters, crafted the forester as a figure of belonging outside privatization and the break with communism. Krzysiek, a private sawmill owner, shared his regrets with me that he had not pursued forestry far enough: "I should have become a forester. Look at them. They have it made." Sourcing oak from the Mazury region of Poland or even Ukraine and Belarus was cumbersome in terms of finances and labor and especially insulting given the trees surrounding his house. He lived more comfortably than his workers, other men in the village who often labored under the table, but he lived a less comfortable life than a forester, many of whom had refurbished interwar residences with roman pillars and solid gates to demarcate their domains. Krzysiek wanted the prestige and quality of a forester's life. Although he attended the Technical Forestry High School (Technikum Leśny) in Białowieża, considered one of the best in the country, he began the 1990s focusing on building up a private business instead of asking for work at State Forests. Some of his peers had risen through the ranks to become foresters, even without a master's degree in forestry.

One friend, Staszek, who lost his son to a suicide with a hunting rifle, recalls how his local forester nurtured him back to mental health, going far beyond what any other villager would do for him under the circumstances: "He stayed with me for months in my grief." Staszek, who tried to make a living taking EU subsidies for ecological sheep grazing and meat production, also regularly hunted with foresters and gifted them with his award-winning cured meats and the honey he produced on the farm.

Arek, one of the young men who labored privately for contractors, fondly recalled an era in which labor was more secure. He repeated what his father had experienced: "If you were an employee of State Forests and broke this rule or that, you might have to apologize, but then you could always just go to the forester and ask for a different job. They didn't fire you." The forester was a friend, loyal, with resources of wood, meat, jobs, and a listening ear, as well as a patron championing local causes against conservationist or scientist outsiders. How can a figure like this be interpreted in a way that explains a group's common sense and cultural values?

Such figures embody a precise description of a place through the qualities ascribed to them. In his *Arcades Project* (Benjamin and Tiedman 1999), written 1927–40, German Jewish philosopher and essayist Walter Benjamin broke through the way the past was narrated when he described a "dialectic of images" that comes forth through figures. He was writing about the decisive shift to the modern age seen in the arcades of nineteenth-century Paris, where the glass-roofed rows of shops were early marks of modern consumerism. In this work, he taught readers that with the right kind of analytical attention to the figure, as a dialectic of images, the figure can disclose deeper truths about the past and the historical embeddedness of the social, cultural, and political present. An image-based historical sensibility emerges through the figure.

For Benjamin, the *flâneur* ("dandy"; borrowed from Baudelaire's and other poets' writings), the idle wanderer of Paris, could explain the subconsciousness of that city at the end of the nineteenth century, with its subterranean character. In paying attention to the way poets and others used the flâneur, Benjamin explained how the experience of both space and time could be shaken loose from the unconscious habits of a culture. As the flâneur meanders through the space of the arcades, represented as modern, he reiterates modernity's advance by rejecting it.

Like the flâneur, the forester is a figure on the threshold of breaking through a cultural unconsciousness and showing us the cusp of modernity by both rejecting and tempting it. He is between the communist past, with its suppression of ethnic difference and promotion of class consciousness, and the future, with its promise of development vis-a-vis forestry instead of strict nature protection. By paying attention to the set of social and ecological relations that are packed into the forester, we see how and why a figure can smooth over eras that otherwise point to ruptures and divisions between people and between agrarian and industrial society. Benjamin's *Arcades Project* was able to show readers the psychological underpinnings of modernity in the particular place and time he was writing about, and he did this through the flâneur. The forester then is essential to understanding all aspects of local society and the forest conflict. But we need to see what people say and do in relation to the forest as both genuine pronouncements and latent expressions of what is being suppressed.

The figure of the forester, like the flâneur, is an image-based sensibility, even as the two figures exist in very different historical and social contexts. The forester also brings attention to aesthetics. Through the suite of social and ecological relations packaged as the forester, I was able to pay attention to how the forest looked beyond the most widely circulating image—"forest primeval," an ideal that calls forth international values of biodiversity and global heritage and requires the educated urban dweller to consume nature through tourism. An entirely different type of beauty and value was attached to the forest under the forester's care, one that the forester Marek tried to show me on his forest survey. The centerpiece of dead rotting wood, so prolific in conservation literature—those mossy tangled logs that lynx could cross or the leafless desiccated oak keeping hundreds of squirrel-stored fir cones in its grooves—spoke of something sinister to the locals, of their labor ruined.

State Forests lands had many different types of trees and assemblages. There were forest plantations, seeded throughout the 1950s and up until 1990. Then there were stands of mature timber. There were groves of profit-able oaks and swampy alder forest. Local people saw themselves as part of all this, in a personal way, as something that they created. One woman's tombstone in Hajnówka was etched with the pronouncement, "I planted this forest."

This affective response, that "prethought" habituated through decades of their labor cutting and planting trees, combined with strategic politi-cal moves that the forester used to occupy local councils, to block national park proposals, and to keep the network of goods flowing. The local was the world ordered by the forester. And the locals, led by the forester, loved the order of the logged forest. An entire social world—a forest world, one of species that belong, of territory and aesthetics—could circulate back to this figure of the forester.

An Anthropologist among the Foresters

In 1998, the house I rented was a formerly state-owned construction with at least two generations of forestry workers who occupied it before I moved in. It sat directly across from State Forests headquarters in the village of

Białowieża. The owner was the daughter of one of those workers. She had been raised Orthodox. She married a Catholic forester from another part of Poland, whom she met when both were teenagers at the Technical Forestry High School. To accommodate me and a master's student who was renting another part of the house, the owners, Ania and Piotr, installed running water. Ania and Piotr were in their late twenties at that time, just a year or two older than me, and had three children under the age of six. It was hard for me to fathom myself in their position—having three young kids who needed baths, cooked meals, and clean clothes and a house that had only well water drawn with a bucket. They used an outhouse instead of an indoor toilet.

I had to heat with wood through that cold winter, and drafts often blew through the windows. I asked Ania if I could use her washing machine once a week for laundry. She ended up washing my laundry for a small fee. Piotr was rising through the ranks in State Forests. They moved into a forester's lodge, a well-insulated apartment with central heating, a new kitchen, a washing machine, and three spacious bedrooms. They used a small and modest new car to drive the children to and from school. I was glad for their upward mobility.

Because I had an office at State Forests' Forest Research Institute, foresters treated me well. The first time I entered the State Forests offices, two foresters greeted me successively, each lifting my hand from my side to kiss it. I started to chat with one about the water not yet turned on in my house, which diverged into all kinds of other small talk. The other forester, feeling ignored, said "Rzucać grochem o ścianę" (a proverb translated as "throwing peas on the wall"), which didn't make sense to me.[1] Tomasz, with a shiny balding head and long brown beard, jovially tried to explain. "The proverb means he was being ignored." When I still did not quite understand the expression, we switched to English. I had heard that Tomasz spoke flawless English. Switching back to my shaky Polish, I said, "Jestem leniwa na tym sposobem" ("I'm lazy in that way," meaning I will switch to English to source an understanding), to which he replied, "I see you do know Polish, as that's an old theatrical expression." I was a bit surprised by this play of high culture in the forestry offices and a bit unsure if he was pulling my leg.

Tomasz thought it would benefit me to have a letter of introduction from State Forests as I entered people's homes to conduct interviews. I could show the letter to any villager, priest, or official who might need verification of my purpose. With this letter, I entered pathways of exchange. I showed up at people's homes or offices with coffee, wrapped candies, or wine. Local inhabitants shared meals and their concerns: "Będzie las, nie będzie nas" ("There will be forest, but not us"). Foresters brought out huntsman's plates of cured boar and venison sausage. I would sit in foresters' salons, where mounted game trophies stared blankly at us, and imbibe in a few shots of homemade schnapps. Discussing the families I knew in different villages became the currency of exchange. "Oh, so you know Pan Ryszard's mother?" or "How was her honey production this year?"

How different this was than the climate of bureaucratic forestry culture that I came from. When I worked for the US Forest Service (USFS) as a biological technician in the mid-1990s, a forester was not a figure. If there is a figure of natural resource management in the United States, someone whom people immediately recognize in the role of a nature expert, it would be the iconic park ranger with the National Park Service. But a forester was a civil servant in the United States. A forester is an occupation, like a lawyer or a teacher in the United States, not someone you recognize walking down the street and you know who they are because of their uniform, like police officers or park rangers. Unlike Poland, rural US inhabitants did not talk about "the forester" but rather about the agency or simply government agents. The institutional culture I came from centered on rational, technocratic language for managing multiple-use lands; public input often served a perfunctory role in management decisions; and often rural "locals" seethed with contempt when talking about USFS employees.

Instead of viewing the forester as a rational bureaucrat, whose culture of rationality serves to fairly mete out public goods, my comparisons between USFS employees and the forester in Poland drove me deeper into a method for understanding the forester figure in Poland. I had to get to know foresters and tell their history as an institution. But there were challenges from the start. Biologists, including some at the Forest Research Institute where I had my office, and colleagues from NGOs wanted to convince me of the abuses that lurked in this culture of foresters. It also seemed that interactions between foresters and local people were not locations for ethnographic "deep hanging out" (Geertz 1998), or getting to know a group's culture through slow, consistent, and long-term interaction. I could not just wait around in the shop with my notebook recording interactions. I was a US anthropologist, and for many in institutional settings and among villagers, that meant I should be interested in folk culture, ethnicity maybe, and probably language, but what did foresters have to do with my interests? And if I was taking notes, or keeping tabs, didn't that make me equivalent to the former secret police, spying on everyone's business?

I tried to interview foresters in their offices and asked to be taken to the field, which happened only once with Marek, and then on other occasions with groups of visiting international forestry students. I also listened to local inhabitants wax on about the forester as the right kind of expert for the forest. Many people wondered if I was a US agent. Why would I be sent to the border to ask people questions about foresters? I met only a handful of local people who spoke with suspicion about the forester. And they in turn were suspicious of me, looking in my eyes with their brows furled or disclosing how they had been caught poaching in an earlier decade, changing the topic to complain about the price of wood.

Anthropologists know well that the information one receives correlates to one's situatedness (Haraway 1988). In that sense, as a young American woman who had previously worked for the USFS, I was in no position to break through coded language of an organization that some scientists and nature conservationists called "as secret as the masons." But my USFS background did give me some credibility with foresters, as I could talk about variable density thinning and estimate the age of timber. As an anthropologist, I wanted to follow the encounters and discourse; from the local point of view, these were largely encounters in which the forester sent flowers to elderly women whose husbands had once worked for State Forests or the forester ensured that someone would have slightly better heating wood for the winter. For all the forester's hospitality, and for all the foresters I met, I felt that I had a similar set of responses to both formal and informal inquiries regarding forest history and forest policy: foresters were always here, and they had management plans they used to carry out their operations. I searched for a history of the forester that might lend insight into the local people and the forester's self-pronouncements. How was the forester able to make himself a figure in the present? If I could not source this from local people's pronouncements, then perhaps secondary and archival sources could shed light. How could I create strong knowledge about the forester that would distill a supplemental or alternative understanding about this suite of power that neither justified foresters' resource management and control over local society nor dismissed my neighbors' positions in favor of the forester's naturalness?

Transhistorical Time and Transnationalism

When I listened to foresters talk, they spoke of themselves as if they had simply always been in the forest. Michał, a forester from the Browsk district told me, "The forester was an important figure in the village, as important as schoolteachers or priests and referred to as Sir Forester (*Pan leśniczy*). Since the nineteenth century, foresters have been uniformed in their rank."[2] Here again was the emphasis and connection between educated, literate people in the village and the work that the forester has done over long centuries. Priests, teachers, and foresters, in largely agrarian rural society, were the modernizers in nineteenth-century Europe, a time when the ideas of the nation and the ethnic group were being formed and codified and when forestry bolstered national identity (Scott 1998; Lowood 1990; Hobsbawm 1962).

Foresters share an international history and an international model for organization (notwithstanding local, national, and regional distinctions). It is a way of organizing that eschews the unruly and untidy on the forest floor. The idea of a primeval forest arises at the moment when foresters change the aesthetics for the forest and the morality of who can use the forest and for what purpose (Matteson 2015; Oosthoek and Hoelzl 2018). French and mostly German ideas and institutions formed the foundation of the science in the late nineteenth century, and the British Empire took these ideas with some modifications to its colonies all over the globe (Rajan 2006), making scientific forestry an early global technocracy of rule.

The idea of the common good is the basis of scientific forestry itself, with its roots in the German science of cameralism, or how to manage the state's finances (Grewere and Hoelzl 2018; Rajan 2006). Forestry science in its applications by bureaucrats has altered landscapes, changed the relationship of peasants to the state, and allowed for capital accumulation. By virtue of this history, Polish foresters in Białowieża (or US foresters at the USFS) are never fully unique. They belong to a patterned way of behaving and thinking shaped by more than at least 150 years of forestry as an international science and culture.

In literature about foresters in other parts of the globe, the forester is not a uniformly likeable character in the local context. The field known as political ecology and much forest history have countless examples of state foresters imposing order on forests used as "commons," meaning forests with free rights of entry and communal rules for usage. In many examples foresters act as agents of developing states trying to bring the periphery into orderly uses that will yield revenue and make local people into forces for production (Scott 1998) or stop local people from overusing the forest altogether (Peluso 1992). Progress often means moving peasants off the land, away from notions of communal property, into schemes for improving productivity in the forest (Sunseri 2012).

Scholarship on this topic has looked closely at the role of foresters in the colonial and postcolonial settings of the Global South, where there is an assumption that local people had free entry to the forest commons until foresters arrived. Local people often resist incursions and defend their communal rights to the forest (Guha 2000; Hecht and Cockburn 1990; Mathews 2011).

The practical effect in the late twentieth and early twenty-first centuries has been that local people must be presented in development literature as people who can access how resources are controlled, determine how forests are logged, and decide which nonforest timber products can be removed (Sikor and Stahl 2011; Menzies 2007; Carr and Halvorsen 2001; Brosius, Tsing, and Zerner 2005). In that sense, the role of the forester has changed in many locations, Białowieża among them. The forester is supposed to usher in sustainable development and modernize with sensitivity to the local customs.

I conducted research in Białowieża just after the effects of such writings had been felt on an international level. Political ecologist Michael Hathaway (2013) names this form of globalization "environmental winds" to describe the cross-pollination of ideas in places that might seem to have no contact with each other. Environmental winds not only shape but are altered by what they encounter on the ground, whether rocks or open plains—or old women admiring foresters. In this sense, Hathaway's metaphor, drawn from his Chinese counterparts, explains how even areas that close themselves off from the world contribute to the global circulation of ideas and material practices.

Białowieża's foresters used the same language I saw emerging from critiques of conservation and national parks practices, ones where locals are dispossessed of their native rights or natural rights to nature as international agendas supplant local ones. Whether or not they read in this field, I could see foresters' language paralleling the assertion that transnational conservation dispossessed local people who shape nature through using it and suggesting that foresters were obliged to protect local people from this dispossession.

Transnationalism does not just include the flow of goods dissolving old meanings of borders. It involves all kinds of ideas and exchanges, and this case can explain how the forester became the figure he is today. From the mid-1990s to 2014, foresters in Białowieża became interested in the idea that they were local actors, doing things for the local community, as opposed to simply hierarchical bureaucrats imposing their unpopular rules.

Consider a statement that the forester Andrzej made to me in an office interview: "An expanded national park can give people neither jobs nor access to the forest. If forests are contributing to the economy, they're creating places for work. There are products from this forest—wood, blueberries, mushrooms, tourist access—and local people have to be able to develop their own economic activities. Lasy Państwowe oversees all of this. It is their social role." In that sense, the forester had a very clear mission for his moral, civic responsibility to improve residents' standards of living, which is why Andrzej sat on local governing councils. He added, "Our activities as foresters are not just connected to the forest. We need not only to protect the biodiversity of this forest, but we also have to ensure the development of local society. We have this triple obligation then: caring for the forest, using the forest, and advancing local society."

Whether or not this position reflected actual recognition of foresters' community contributions or worked as a kind of political rhetoric for the purposes of retaining power is hard to separate. Since 1990, local foresters and their allies have consistently been voted onto local governing councils, which overwhelmingly advocated for investments, including more tourist infrastructure and attractions and building on the forest meadows that became protected by EU Natura 2000 laws.

Foresters fought against including Białowieża into this legally binding transnational framework. "Natura 2000 is complicated," Andrzej added, "because it addresses sustainable development, like we do, but is overseen by the European Union. This would work fine if we only thought about nature conservation and eliminated people. But because Natura 2000 deals not only with forests but also with the fields around homesteads, what does sustainable development mean? Our [State Forests'] work on sustainable development means ensuring that local people have a voice in sustainable development."

Although many of the foresters I met had lived in the forest area for decades, they were not born there, and this distinction became important as old-time locals called new arrivals *nawalodz*, a derogatory term for "newcomer." Most foresters arrived for work in their adult lives. As I read and researched and compiled a history, I could see that foresters pulled different eras into one: the forester as a continuous presence, defined simply by his management and patron status with locals, but also the forester as the bulwark against EU-led initiatives. The history I sourced showed foresters in complex relationship to outside powers. That history involved local guards in the fifteenth century who ensured that locals would not poach the king's game, Polish Lithuanian gentry who had lost their land under Russian occupation, Russian foresters claiming locals as their serfs, Bolsheviks who led sabotage against foresters, and the institution that represents this transhistorical, figure-driven culture: State Forests.

Foresters in Transhistorical Perspective

Białowieża was part of a quintessential borderland for centuries. In the Polish-Lithuanian Commonwealth (1569–1795), the forest belonged to the Grand Duchy of Lithuania at the border with the Polish Crown. Religious affiliations shifted among Roman Catholic, Uniate, Orthodox, and Protestant. Jews made up more than 10 percent of society. After the Counterreformation (mid-sixteenth to eighteenth centuries), the aristocracy largely identified as Polish and Roman Catholic. Polish magnates ruled over ambiguous peasant populations identified more by religion than ethnicity, and Jews facilitated trade. Scientific forestry begins at this crossroads of history in Białowieża, as does the term "primeval."

On the brink of the Russian partitions that eroded Poland's autonomy, Poland's last king, Stanisław August Poniatowski (1764–95), opened the forest to calculated forms of Enlightenment rationality, including timbering. Aristocratic families accustomed to treating the woods as an extension of their estates had to prove their lease rights. In 1765, Poniatowski sent the treasurer secretary of Lithuania, Antoni Tyzenhaus, to the forest with clerks and scribes to verify what belonged to the crown (Samojlik 2005). Tyzenhaus's efforts were part of a much broader plan to develop manufacturers and industry—his interest in the forest part of his agenda. Tyzenhaus prescribed tree thinning and removed dead timber from the forest. His calculations were meant to wrest power from the hands of Poland's independent and erratic aristocrats. Poland needed a strong state with a large central treasury, not to mention a well-equipped military, to ward off threats from Russia. Despite Poniatowski's efforts to rationalize forest management and streamline the state, Russia, Prussia, and Austro-Hungary partitioned Poland (1772–95).

Polish magnates clung dearly to semi-independence under an initial agreement with Russia and continued exploiting forest resources. In the core of the forest, forest guards prevented logging and poaching. Before the partitions, each landowner would have hired his own resident forester to oversee operations, which mostly produced potash, used to manufacture glass (Schama 1995). Poniatowski's former lover Catherine the Great dispensed the Polish nobility's land to Russian aristocrats and to military personnel, some of them from her own German homeland, further lessening the influence of Polish gentry in the region (Schama 1995, 45–60). In 1795 she turned over management of the entire Białowieża region to Prussian foresters. They regulated the Narewka River to float pine, oak, and spruce as far as the Vistula River, just short of the Prussian border. From the Vistula, timber was hauled overland to the Nieman River and out to Russian ports on the Baltic Sea (Michaluk 1997). Whole units of the forest were cleared for timber and agriculture (Samojlik, Fedotova, and Kuijper 2016). Polish rulers had long maintained a hereditary forest protection unit of beaters and guards, peasants who were free from feudal obligations; however, under Catherine's rule, all beaters lost their rights and fell under the protectorate of Russian and German estate owners (Daszkiewicz, Samojlik, and Jędrzejewska 2012). Russian soldiers and military officers, often with little training in forestry, were appointed as foresters under specialists appointed by Prussian foresters (Hedemann 1939, 142–50; Majchrowska 2018, 326). Despite the onset of logging, the chief forester of the Congress Kingdom of Poland, Juliusz Brincken, described the forest at this time as a "true primeval forest" and published his assessment in French to reach the wider European natural history community (Daszkiewicz, Samojlik, and Jędrzejewska 2012, 179–82).

To counteract the insufficient education of Polish foresters, Polish gentry formed their own forestry school at the newly founded University of Warsaw in 1816. Polish nobility, weary of the new Russian landowners, took up arms and formed an underground resistance movement as part of much larger nation-in-exile uprising. In the insurrection against Russia in 1830–31, Białowieża became a battlefield and a base for the Polish rebels. Hundreds of Polish gentry lost their lives for their insurrectionary roles, with their bodies strung up in the trees. The forestry school in Warsaw cradled patriotism, so Russia closed it down in 1832 and all Polish wardens lost their positions, although Polish nobility continued their forestry education at agronomy schools (Majchrowska 2018, 325–31).[3]

Russian rulers knew that Białowieża was a prime hunting site and that it contained the last wild bison populations in Europe, but it was not until Tsar Alexander II led an imperial hunting party in 1860 that the forest received protection again as a royal hunting ground. Shortly thereafter, in 1863, the Polish territories of Russia became the scene of fifteen months of fighting by two hundred thousand active insurgents (Walicki 1982, 336). After Russia brutally defeated the second insurrections, Catholic churches were destroyed in the forest region, and the population was largely converted from the Uniate to the Orthodox rite as Białowieża became the tsar's private property in 1888 (Kossak 2001, 292). Those who remained Catholic would have their children baptized by priests who traveled through the region on occasion. They kept their religion underground. Although Alexander II did not log Białowieża's trees, he imported wild and exotic game. High densities of ungulates destroyed much of the forest undergrowth. In 1889, Tsar Alexander III ordered the construction of a 120-room palace with sunken Roman baths and English gardens (Bajko 2001). Although mismanaged at various times, forest cover never dropped below 70 percent in the nineteenth century (Mikusinska et al. 2013). In this period, the Polish forester is an undergrounded figure with a messianic vision that Poles would return to the region to restore more just rule.

World Wars and Industrial Forestry

During the German occupation in World War I (1915), the kaiser's Military Forest Administration subjected the ancient trees to calculated exploitation. The administration built networks of railroad lines to transport timber out and set up twenty-four sawmills and a chemical wood-processing factory, using forced labor, in what became the city of Hajnówka (Blood 2010; Sunseri 2012). But at the same time that Germans logged the forest, German nature conservationist Hugo Cowentz, an initiator of a European national parks movement, called for a national park over the whole forest (Okołów 2009, 10). Cowentz called attention to the destruction caused by German army commanders in Białowieża, including the fate of the bison. He formally presented his ideas for a park to the Prussian Bureau for Nature Conservation in 1918 but was turned down (Okołów 2009, 312; Ahrens 1921, 60).

Fig. 2.1. German industrial World War I logging of Białowieża Forest. From Białowieża National Park archives.

German foresters used arguments that they had applied in their former West African colony, Cameroon, to log the primeval woodland (Sunseri 2012, 322). The custodial model, under forester George Escherich, was premised on the idea that old forests needed to be protected from peasants who would misuse the forest's economic potential. Escherich conscripted four to 6,000 able-bodied workers from nearby villages, including Jews and even elderly people. Poorly paid, they labored beside some 2,500 Russian and French prisoners of war to log and process more than 5 million cubic meters from a total of 32 million cubic meters of forest in less than three years under 1,200 German experts. Poland inherited this forest without its famous bison population, the numbers of which dove to extinction, from seven hundred when the war broke out in 1915 to none in 1919. Unregulated hunting by Germans as well as locals decimated the bison (Krasiński, Bunevich, and Krasińska 1994).[4] Poland would put the six sawmills, eighty-five kilometers of narrow-gauge railways for hauling out timber, and many other facilities for processing wood and forest products to further use.

Although war may have ended in 1918 for most of Europe, a brutal Soviet-Polish War started in 1919. Polish territory was not recognized internationally until 1923. Much of the Soviet-Polish War was fought over formerly Russian territory. Poland, under its de facto leader Józef Piłsudski, minister of military affairs, felt it had to move its borders as far east as possible to contain the Soviet Union's territorial ambitions. Lenin saw Poland's regained territory (much of what is now Belarus and Ukraine) as an obstacle to connecting with communist allies in the west. He used the idea of folk culture, including customs, song, and dress, to create nations that would support the Soviet Union, notably breathing life into the identity of Belarusians (Rudling 2015; Hirsch 2005). This tactic was also used by the Germans during World War I (Mironowicz 1993, 23).

In the 1920s, Bolshevik agitators within Białowieża tried to expand the Western Belarusian Communist Party (Komunistyczna Partia Zachodniej Białorusi [KPZB]), founded in 1922, with local KPZB cells active until 1939 (Bajko 2017). During the interwar period, Poland rejected the aspirations of Belarusian nationalists for this reason. The Polish government closed all Belarusian schools in 1924 (Nikitiuk 1958, 55), even as Poland was among the first of eight newly independent states to sign the Minorities Treaty, which constituted part of the Treaty of Versailles (Rudling 2014).

Most inhabitants who would have been recruited for Belarusian schools at that time were illiterate peasants who attended the Orthodox Church. Five years after the signing of the Treaty of Riga (1921), half of the Belarusians within Poland were considered stateless and could not vote. Poland viewed the "eastern" populations around the Białowieża Forest as uncivilized and in need of Polish culture.[5] With KPZB as an illegal organization, those wanting to organize for minority rights formed Hramada in 1925, a legal socialist agrarian Belarusian political party and cultural organization that received support from the Soviet Union. Collectively, these two organizations agitated for better workers' rights in the wood factories and against unemployment (of the majority Belarusian population). Polish foresters curbed free passage to the forest, and peasants had to purchase vouchers for berry and mushroom collecting and for pasturing their cows. Foresters strictly policed people who had formerly been forest guards (Kosel and Pirożnikow 2017, 19–20). The timber economy formed the primary employment in this era. KPZB's tactical strikes created treacherous social relations between the newly arrived Poles (forestry labor and clerical workers for the timber industry) and the Belarusian peasants. In a 1931 May Day march, striking workers and the unemployed distributed fliers that encouraged the creation of "self-defense forces against the police and the forest guards" (Nikitiuk 1958, 50). Purportedly, ethnic Polish workers or Bolshevik activists burned down one of the key forester's estates in 1934 at Zwierzyniec. Wages were severely depressed at this time, and imported laborers often slept in underground dugouts with inadequate firewood for the winter.

Eighty-five percent of the population in Białowieża (then fourteen thousand inhabitants in an administrative district that included Hajnówka) identified (or were identified by census takers) as Belarusian and Orthodox (Statistical Yearbook of Poland 1921). Much of this identification arose during World War I. During the war, the imperial Russian army sent detachments to the villages in Białowieża saying that German troops were nearby slaughtering inhabitants, setting off an exodus. Whole villages were razed, and many villagers fled east. In central Russia, exposed to Bolshevik agitation, the villagers brought back ideas to disperse after 1918 about the necessity of revolutionary politics according to Lenin, including the idea that religion was a form of spiritual oppression. Consequently, Belarusian identity came to be associated with Bolshevism and atheism in Białowieża at that time—or at least Poles perceived Belarusians in this way. Although most peasants were illiterate, those becoming educated utilized smuggled magazines and brochures published by the Soviets promoting Belarusian social advancements (Zieliński et al. 2011). Many ordinary local people came under the influence of Bolshevik ideology and formed or joined the KPZB, the main and stated goal of which was to transfer eastern Polish lands to the Soviet Union (Latyszonek and Mironowicz 2002).

The Polish government encouraged Poles to settle in the borderlands. The arrival of Polish foresters to Białowieża, including the construction of a Catholic church in 1920 (in a place that had never had a Catholic church), began a paternalistic and colonizing relationship of foresters toward Belarusians who would need to realize that they were indeed Polish, that Belarusian was an old language and a regional identity rather than a nationality (Woolhiser 2003), and that Poland rather than the Soviet Union offered a better route to pursue their aspirations (Fleming 2010). Under Piłsudski's military dictatorship, the Second Polish Republic attempted a multiethnic state but was highly contested by rivals such as Roman Dmowski and his antisemitic party Endecja (National Democracy), which sought an ethnically and religiously uniform Poland and would gain increasing political power in the mid- to late 1930s. The Polish government arrested and imprisoned many Belarusian union activists (Chałupczak and Browarek 2000, 114).

As for the forest and its protection in this tumultuous period, Polish botanists, often trained in forestry schools, created the first strict protective measures for the newly formed republic (Krasiński 1994). In April 1919, botanist Władysław Szafer and a team of international scientists surveyed what the Białowieża forest had suffered. Szafer, trained in Munich, Germany, visited the forest to see if any bison were left. Szafer, who later cofounded the International Union for the Conservation of Nature in 1948, had traveled widely to US national parks and on natural history expeditions in northern African colonies. Szafer wrote that the commission found piles of bison bones and skeletal parts strewn throughout the forest but not a single living bison (Szafer 1920). Moved by the unprecedented damage, he gathered support for protecting the area and returned the following year with members of the Polish Nature Conservation Council to designate an appropriate spot for Poland's first national park. In 1921 the first protective reserve was formed, and in 1932 it was officially declared a national park (Szafer 1920). Restoration of the bison began in this era, along with breeding populations using zoo animals.

Between 1916 and 1921 foreign operators cut more than a third of the total Białowieża forest (Kossak 2001, 391–407). Despite the conservation movement, the Second Republic had clear plans for the German industrial forestry equipment to be put to further use. From 1921 to 1928, the British Century European Timber Company logged on contract for the Polish state. Century used and owned the wood, sending the milled lumber back to the United Kingdom. Meanwhile, Poland's new forestry schools organized quickly throughout the country (Broda 2006, 25). Only Polish foresters trained abroad could administer the new Lasy Państwowe, indicating the inadequate expertise of Polish education immediately after the war. State Forests' first director, Adam Loret, soon established an educated cadre that would also have had military training. He abruptly terminated the contract with Century in 1928 once State Forests was firmly established. The break with the British contractor came as Polish foresters (and nature conservationists) sought to end what they saw as another exploitative foreign relationship.

At the same time that Polish foresters returned to Białowieża, their knowledge was shaped with and against that of field biologists from Lviv, Kraków, and other parts of Poland, who extolled the uniqueness and endangerment of the forest. Although foresters and the scientific community could not agree on how the whole forest should be managed, Białowieża's first scientific research institute, the Forest Research Institute, was founded in 1930. It was run by Polish foresters Jan Jerzy Karpiński and Józef Paczoski. Paczoski was Polish by ethnicity but Russian by upbringing and spoke little Polish.[6] He spent years organizing protection for the Ukrainian Steppes and committed himself to nature conservation in Białowieża. Karpiński studied forestry in St. Petersburg in 1915 before the war broke out and, during his time as park director (1929–34), led scientific studies aimed at conservation-oriented forest management, including studies of "virgin" forest and restoration of the European bison. In this way, the Białowieża National Park started as a special unit of State Forests, and its directors were both trained as foresters in Russian administered territories. Paczoski and Karpiński quarreled frequently with foresters conducting timber operations in the interwar period.

World War II brought a period of lawlessness and chaos, including tree felling in the national park reserve (Kossak 2001, 459–84; Kosel and Pirożnikow 2017, 24), but also a seesaw of exploitation and protection. Saddled again with the vagaries of war, Białowieża was first taken under the rule of the Soviets in 1939, who used Belarusians and Jews to identify Polish foresters. Regionally Belarusians and Jews often greeted incoming Soviets with banners, though there is no specific evidence of this in Białowieża. Soviets sent 1,404 Białowieża inhabitants (all Polish foresters and national park employees, including director Karpiński) to work camps in Siberia.[7] They logged in the national park as well (Kossak 2001, 459–84). Soviets executed State Forests Director Adam Loret in that same year (Grzywacz 2014, 98). The Soviets continued logging operations until 1941, taking than two thousand cubic meters of wood and enabling poaching (Okołów 2009, 13), with plans for more than 1 million cubic meters of timber annually (which were never fulfilled) (Kosel and Pirożnikow 2017, 24) and prescriptions for nature protection under their well-established, strict system known as *zapoviednik* (Weiner 2002). Many Belarusians often changed attitudes toward the Soviets during this era after seeing the violence enacted on their Polish neighbors. Belarusians also became targets of the NKVD (Narodnyy Komissariat Vnutrennikh Del; Interior Ministry of Soviet Union) and were executed during the war (Mironowicz 1999, 297).

Five days after Hitler launched Operation Barbarossa against the Soviet army on June 22, 1941, the Nazi flag flew above the Romanov palace. Nazi

Germany occupied Białowieża (1941–44) with Hermann Göring, prime minister of the Third Reich, directly supervising plans for the forest. German soldiers removed all villagers within the forest hamlets to prevent them from abetting partisans. Many foresters who were not sent to Siberia earlier had fought with partisans, living in the forest, through harsh winters and wet springs, supplied as they could by the surrounding peasants and workers. Being found in the forest, no matter who you were, was an act punishable by immediate death.

Logging stopped altogether during the occupation, and Göring contemplated a huge forest protection zone, six times the size of the national park (Faliński 1968; Więcko 1984; Bohn, Dalhouski, and Krzoska 2017, 157–78). Germans eliminated all of Białowieża's Jews (10% of the population at that time) by 1941, executing many onsite in a common grave with Poles and Belarusians. Because of their educated status, Polish foresters served as officers in the war. Many foresters fought as anti-Soviet partisans, and both Germans and Soviets murdered foresters in campaigns to eliminate Polish intellectuals.[8]

Communist Poland

After World War II, Churchill, Roosevelt, and Stalin redrew the map of Poland. Białowieża was split in two (40% of the forest was left in Poland). Because Poland had fought with the western forces, many in the country felt a deep sense of betrayal by its allies. The People's Republic of Poland (1945–89), like most Soviet-led or -backed states, denied national groups their histories. Ethnicity and nation were not to be talked about in reference to the causes of war or even in relation to the ethnic or national populations. Class overrode nation in this new application of ideology. Those who felt themselves Belarusian were given the opportunity to immigrate to the Soviet Union, but only a few did (Wysocki 2010; Wierzbicki 2007; Mironowicz 1993).

In this climate, Poles and Belarusians obtained work in the forestry sector. According to oral accounts by contemporary foresters and their families, some former Polish foresters may have gone to work in their prewar positions, but it is unknown what kind of ties, if any, they may have had to the resistance (Home Army and other partisan groups). Most prewar foresters who had not died en route or in Siberia joined General Anders's army after a British, Polish, and Soviet understanding evacuated

Fig. 2.2. Village women planting trees for Polish State Forests, 1950s. Used with permission from State Forestry Regional Directorate, Białystok.

Polish soldiers held in the Soviet Union. Anders's soldiers returned home to Poland through duties in Iran and Palestine under British leadership. It is doubtful that any of the original foresters returned to the forest. The communist state needed qualified foresters, but foresters likely had "compromised" biographies. This dilemma opened the door to labor migration from other parts of Poland. Foresters arrived from places in the west and hid their biographical details from the party when obtaining positions. Eva Pirozników, daughter of a forester who immigrated to Białowieża after the war and author of a book on foresters in Anders's army (Kosel and Pirożnikow 2017), told me that her father refused to disclose any of his history until she reached adulthood. The Communist Party often anticipated that children would provide details about their parents' true biographies, and so parents withheld this information from their children. State Forests advanced Belarusians through forestry without explicitly acknowledging ethnic identity. Belarusian-language high schools opened in Hajnówka.

Initially, the postwar People's Republic of Poland adopted the prewar organizational scheme. The General Directorate of State Forests administered the Białowieża Forest, as it did all other forested areas, with the Ministry of Forestry responsible for hunting, forest policy, and wood-processing industries. The need for revenue after the war again meant exploitation of forest timber, with a high volume of timber extracted in 1946 and widespread reports of poaching in the chaotic end of the war period (Okołów 2009, 13). After Poland moved to a command economy and central planning (1949), the government looked at State Forests in Białowieża as it did any other state-owned enterprise. The forest was there to serve the needs of industry (Majchrowska 2018). From 1946 to 1975, timber harvests often exceeded 50 percent of the forest cover (Gutowski 2000). Where primary forest had been cut, foresters hired local labor to reseed areas with monocultural softwood plantations. The Ministry of Forestry developed more protective guidelines for the Białowieża Forest in 1975. Shortly thereafter, Białowieża's scientists, including the head of the Forest Research Institute, Andrzej Sokołowski, a botanist trained at the University of Warsaw, called for the expansion of the Białowieża National Park and an end to timber exploitation (Gutowski 2000).

While the communist and postwar policies caused heavy logging and replanting of the forest, they also created social changes, resulting in a blurred identity without subsuming the ethnic question altogether. In this sense, over the course of the communist period, the forester solidified his legitimacy as an expert because he developed trust with the local population, unlike the interwar period when the forester was a divisive figure for Belarusians and Poles. Nevertheless, Poles continued to hold high administrative positions in State Forests (Mironowicz 1993, 154; Fleming 2010, 89; Czykwin 2000). The local population came to see themselves through the lens of forestry as their primary identity. The forester, as a figure belonging to a multiethnic local identity, is rooted in this era.

To date, no independent historical research has investigated foresters during the communist period, either for Białowieża or for Poland generally. Not even my anthropology colleague Agata Agnieszka Konczal (2018), writing her dissertation and then publishing a book on Polish foresters, could find an independent historical treatment of foresters from the communist era. I entered Białowieża when people spoke of continuity, not ethnic conflict, and when people indicated a peaceful coexistence in society, with amiable ethnic relations. I arrived in the mid-1990s and expected the forester to be a civil servant. But with the repeated emphasis on "local," "belonging," and "unity," I felt compelled to find a history that was not being narrated by the people I met, which brings us to the first decade or so after one-party state socialism opened to a different social and political opportunity.

One Can Go Farther if One Remains Silent

"Białowieża carries democratic traditions *because* of foresters' ethos," Marek tried to explain to me in a 1999 interview in his State Forests office. He wanted me to understand that strict nature protection could only be imposed, as Hermann Göring did during World War II: "People live with that memory of being chased out of their homes, forbidden from living in the forest, from going to the forest for grazing, or mushrooms, because Göring wanted to protect nature." He added, "Foresters are a group that never lost their independence, even during communism." He went on to explain how democracy and forestry tradition worked in Białowieża by contrasting Poland with neighboring Belarus. "In Belarus [on the other side of the transboundary Białowieża Forest] you can have this big national park because the residents of that side of the forest all work in the park, but here in Poland we have residents, ordinary people. Those are people who have rights given to them to settle directly from the czars. On what principles could we take those rights away from them? We could change that situation, but that would be communistic. There is a proverb in both Polish and Russian, 'Tisze jediesz, dalej budjesz' ['One can go further if one remains quiet']." His linguistic use was ambiguous both in form and content. It was clearly not Polish (confirmed by Polish colleagues who listened to the taped interview) but perhaps the local dialect or a type of Polish-Russian hybrid. I believe he intended to combine languages, indicating that he could both speak and understand the local dialect, but also there were times when Russian and Polish shared the same deep wisdom. He explained the proverb by adding, "Maybe we will find a method of protecting the forest that will quiet everybody. We don't know how to do that, but we can't do this in a spirit of conflict with the local people. In communist time you could have created this park, and no one would have disputed it. But now things are different, and you must speak up to get what you want."

I was admittedly confused by his logic. The Polish opposition groups had not been quiet during communist rule, and the west recognized them as toppling communism for this reason. Why did people remember nature conservation as being imposed by Nazis but not remember the interwar hostility of Belarusians toward Polish foresters? Marek was emphasizing that foresters were not, in fact, going quietly in the new era. In 1996, nature conservationists had managed to double the size of the Białowieża National Park and had aims for the year 2000 for the whole forest to transfer into

National Park Management, which I will unfold in the next chapter. But foresters would ensure that they spoke against any further strict protection. Foresters earned the loyalty of local people not because they could provide them with jobs in the postsocialist era, as they had in the communist period, but because they spoke as defenders of the local and, importantly, used the power they acquired through actual appointments to local municipal councils or in tight alliances with those councils.

Collapsed History as a Dialectic Image

A figure that can sit on the cusps of eras, ethnic relations, cultures, and modernity is a figure calling out for interpretation. Hints, clues, and summations about the past become the cornerstone of the foresters' power. I have brought these together in a more empirical fashion of secondary sources and a slight touch of oral history.

Walter Benjamin's ideas behind the dialectic image within the figure was that critical scholars must look to the way the image is history, the way the figure is an image. Thinking in images rather than concepts was at the heart of Benjamin's *Arcades Project* (Benjamin and Tiedemann 1999). If modernity conceives of time as progressive and the fate of the world is modernity, then the forester, as a figure, presents himself and is presented as cyclical, mythical, and always on the cusp of developing the underdeveloped, of showing the way so that one day all locals might become foresters or at least have the chance to become one. The neoliberal turn at the termination of communist rule has spelled out the impossibility of foresters modernizing based on the communist-era goal of everyone modern together, everyone securely employed in forestry industries.

If the forester and the forest he creates is an aesthetic image, then the claim to immediacy within the image (the image of the forest as his labor and thus the labor of the community, or, "I see the forest and the forester and know I belong") shows us how power works. Few people can be employed in forestry today compared with the communist era. Modernity, as we see in the next two chapters, is now also claimed by nature conservationists, for whom the ultimate mark of modernity is separating the humans from nature in the national park model.

In the transnational history of scientific forestry, the forester is a rational bureaucrat whose only goal is to apply rules consistently and, in the process, to see the forest as capable of abiding by the rules of science (trees grown in straight rows, timber harvestable in a certain number of years). Yet in Białowieża, the ideal of historical progress, of people socially advancing away from their peasant backgrounds or from their laborer roles and into more bourgeois roles, is held in a kind of suspended time when the forester is a figure. The future of progress will come only when the forester is in charge, but the future is also the past—particularly the past that local people talked to me about as the postwar period until 1989 (as a floating symbol of better times for the villages, what others might officially refer to as the communist era).

Following Benjamin's lead, I am trying to make history from recovered bits, and I am trying to match them with the sensibility of local inhabitants and with histories written by historians or recovered from archives and oral accounts. Historical truth for Benjamin, as philosopher Max Pensky (2004) has shown, was not in the empirical details that a historian might come up with but in the way the bits and pieces get used. Benjamin (1999, 473n9) wrote, "The dialectical image is an image that emerges suddenly, in a flash. What has been is to be held fast—as an image flashing up in the now of its recognizability."

And this is a good place to now piece together ways that scientists, nature conservationists, and local inhabitants deal with the past, ways that will both overlap with and contradict the forester as a figure. It is not surprising that the forester consigns everything to a harmonious past and anything that opposes it to oblivion. It becomes my job both to highlight this process and to unearth the independent history haunting foresters' claims to unity.

Notes

1. Unless otherwise noted, all translations are my own.
2. The Polish language regularly uses the formal *Pan* and *Pani* ("sir" and "madam") in combination with a first or last name. It can also be used in combination with one's occupation, as in *Pan leśniczy* ("sir forester"), which is a higher form of respect, as in *Pan lekarz* ("sir doctor") or *Pani nauczycielka* ("madam teacher").
3. The term "Belarusian" arose in the nineteenth century as a linguistic category. Belarusian was spoken by the Orthodox and Catholic populations of the region. But as Russia consolidated its grip on Poland after 1864, Catholics became Poles and Orthodox became Belarusians (Woolhiser 2003). Mironowicz (1993, 20) describes a Belarusian consciousness for the region developing through the work of Polish Catholic intellectuals at the turn of the twentieth century.
4. The bison populations in Białowieża and the rest of Europe today come from twelve zoo animals used in a two-decade-long rebreeding program centered in Białowieża.

5. The 346 private Belarusian language schools that opened between 1918 and 1919 were closed by the Second Republic between 1920 and 1925 (Rudling 2014). Both Soviets and Nazis promised Belarusians language schools during World War II.

6. Information is per conversations with Paczowski's colleague, Andrzej Sokołowski, director of the Forest Research Institute at the time of the interview on April 14, 1999.

7. Information is per interview on April 15, 1999, with Czesław Okołów, former Białowieża National Park director, who was among the forester families sent to Siberia in those years.

8. The NKVD secretively murdered more than twenty-two thousand Polish officers during the war at a mass burial site in Katyn Russia, an event of extraordinary significance for contemporary Polish society. Soviets denied responsibility for the massacre until 1990. Many Poles consider the act genocide against Poles (Allen 1991).

3

SCIENTISTS AND THE COMMUNIST PAST

Syndromes, Disorders, and a Proper Elite

THERE WAS SOMETHING MYSTICAL AND UNEXPECTED ABOUT MY first meeting with Dr. Simona Kossak. I learned about Simona from US wildlife biologist and World Bank consultant Dr. Steve Berwick in May 1995, when I worked for the US Forest Service (USFS). He told me that Simona was a biologist who lived a charmed life in the woods, residing in a famous forester's lodge without electricity or running water. Exotic and wild animals had run of her house: wild boar ate at the dinner table; she slept with a pet lynx in her bed; peacocks sauntered under the old oaks in her yard; and she bottle fed two pet moose, named Cola and Pepsi. Steve had met and befriended her at an international nature conservation conference in Ukraine in 1993 following the demise of communism in Poland and put her in charge of a World Bank Global Environmental Facilities grant for the Forestry Research Institute, the division of State Forests where Simona was, at the time, an associate professor in the Natural Forest Unit. The grant would ready the institute for scientific research in the postcommunist era, supplying it with four-wheel-drive vehicles, equipment for chemical analysis of air pollution, and other technically capacitating materials. The postcommunist challenge, from the view of the West and funders like the World Bank, was not just to reform institutions responsible for the nation's resources but also to bring these institutions up to speed with modern equipment and facilities.

Just a month after Steve told me about Simona, I left my job at the USFS to undertake my first trip to Poland. I called Simona from a pay phone in Warsaw and arranged to meet her in Białowieża. I was intercepted by one of her students, Małgosia, at the train station in Białystok and delivered directly to her office at the Forestry Research Institute's Czarist-era building, its faded elegance filled with encased beetle collections and sliced cross-sections of logs. After just a short introduction, Simona immediately packed the three of us into her tiny moss-colored Polski Fiat, and we bumped along the pitted dirt road for eight kilometers to her fabled house, Dziedzinka.

That warm June afternoon, we sat on her porch. I remember a peacock hissing at us from the low branch of a pedunculate oak (*Quercus robur*). To the right of the porch, just thirty meters away, I saw the strict reserve part of the national park, which was marked with a red tin placard, "Białowieża National Park." State Forests lands bordered us on the left. Simona chain-smoked her way through our conversation as we dove into the newness of encounter. With Małgosia as our translator, we discussed topics ranging from forest ecology and the Polish pope's (John Paul II) position on women and birth control to her guru, Sai Baba, and how slowly Poland was shedding inefficient and corrupt "communistic" ways of doing things, such as siphoning off materials for private gain or appointing unqualified people.

Simona was forthright, often cutting me off midsentence, even as she spoke little English and I spoke little Polish. Her red wavy hair and petite frame either nodded concertedly in agreement or tensed into a decided "no." With about fifteen cigarette butts in the ashtray, Simona offered to link me to various projects, including a Danish amphibian workshop, a seedling trial at her institute, and a meeting with some Dutch students who also wanted master's thesis projects. The next day she would show me the forest, beginning with a site called Miejsca Mocy, "Place of Power," where I witnessed the way Simona combined her scientific position with mysticism.

That morning we were without a translator. Simona picked me up from the Forestry Research Institute, where I had slept in one of its apartments. We drove a few kilometers off the main road, passed fenced-in softwood plantations, and tucked the car as well as we could off the sandy one-lane track. She indicated that I should walk slowly and quietly. Her first animated narration pointed out the number of trees growing with split trunks from a single base; spruce, oak, hornbeam and others. Then she drew me to an old cracked cement slab etched with an Orthodox cross. A little farther we came to some glacial boulders. "Stonehenge?! Pagan?!" she knowingly suggested. Stopping at the largest boulder, she pantomimed a blessing motion, which I took to mean that the priest would have stood on the flat surface of this rock. Then she picked up a stick from the ground, "Man, come here," and she shook the stick as if it were vibrating, and I understood—dowsing!

She tossed out the words "Notre Dame" and "Grand Canyon" with another pantomime, which took me a while to figure out. She was talking about the earth's magnetic field. Miejsca Mocy shared an energetic quality with other powerful sites.

My position was decidedly agnostic and honored. I did not exactly understand the significance of this place on any level, but I liked the way I felt, as if I had been let into a secret of this place on my first visit. Then, as we were walking away from the site, a red-deer stag bolted out of nowhere and leapt in a large circle around us before disappearing into the forest, spooking me, confirming nothing, and leaving me with many questions about Simona and this forest.

Although I would know her for more than twelve years, until her death in 2007, I never came close to having that kind of surprise and intimacy with her again. I returned to Białowieża in 1998 when she and the Forestry Research Institute sponsored my master's thesis research. She rarely spoke about herself, but everyone else spoke about her, which is perhaps why she retreated into a professional distance. I learned that she descended from one of the most famous aristocratic Polish families of Kraków and was a descendant of Otto von Bismarck, the Prussian statesman who engineered wars that unified Germany in 1871. Her father (Jerzy Kossak), grandfather (Wojciech Kossak), and great grandfather (Juliusz Kossak) painted famously sweeping portraits and panoramas of insurrectionary battles against Russia, the kind where thousands of heroic Polish volunteers defend their struggling nation against well-fortified Russians—swords against guns, peasants praying on a distant hill, corpses strewn on the battlefield. Each generation of painters glorified purebred horses in these scenes. The Kossaks symbolized the original freedom fighters, a family with national status as both intelligentsia and aristocracy, who would lead the myth of an independent nation, free from Russian and German rule, where all would feel enfranchised as gentry citizens.

Simona's mother, Elżbieta Kossak, painstakingly trained her daughter in blue-blooded manners, eating at the dinner table with a book tucked under each armpit. There were Tiffany lamps and a lion skin in the parlor of her childhood home, a home not confiscated by the communists after the war. Although communists seized landed estates and nationalized all housing in Warsaw, Kraków's mansions continued to be lived in by families that survived the war. With a master's degree in zoology from Jagiellonian University, Simona ran away from what remained of the ruins of society life in communist Kraków to take a position as an assistant at the Mammal Research Institute (MRI) in Białowieża. In 1975, Simona left the MRI to take a position counting game animals for State Forests' Forestry Research Institute, where she earned her doctorate in 1991, also through Jagiellonian University. In her three decades in the forest, she accomplished many things, including receiving her habilitated professorial title, professor of forestry, through special appointment by President Aleksander Kwaśniewski (of the postcommunist successor party Akcja Wyborcza Solidarność [AWS]) in 2000 and securing an appointment as director of the scientific council, the advisory board, within the Białowieża National Park in 2005—a position that would bring her into direct conflict with other scientists.

In some ways, Simona remains as enigmatic as she was when I first met her. Then, she was a scientist who dwelled in the mystical, a figure for whom my intrigue was only enhanced by our language barrier. But in writing this book and considering the social structure of postsocialist Poland, she presents a set of tensions that, even if they are not representative, encapsulate the unpredictability of scientific actors and actions that postcommunist politics produced in the forest. Simona exhibited a blend of advocacy for animal rights, love of wild nature and spite for the Communist system, positions that yielded a set of unusual tensions in her commitments to science and managing the forest.

She lived with the artist and photographer Lech Wilczek since the mid-1970s. His albums on wildlife were prized throughout the socialist world, and his uncanny crows and foxes frequently appeared in East German (German Democratic Republic, or GDR) nature publications. He had arrived in Białowieża at roughly the same time Simona did. Both Simona and Lech went to the park director asking if they could rent Dziedzinka, the cottage surrounded by dense forest. Although Lech went to live there first, the director meted out what he thought was a fair decision. They could share the house, which had two apartments. After a cantankerous year of standoff, Simona and Lech knocked down a wall to dwell together. They would be lovers and life partners who never married, which was quite unusual for the village. In addition to taking in injured wildlife from the forest, the Warsaw zoo brought Lech impaired animals to care for, and he photographed hundreds of images with Simona cuddled up or playing with boar, lynx or deer.

Although Simona had many sympathetic attachments to romantic views of nature and had been known to attend deep ecology workshops with "hippies" in southern Poland, she told me in 1999 that she was not

Fig. 3.1. Simona Kossak with her pet boar, Frog, in her cottage, Dziedzinka. Photo by Lech Wilczek. Used with permission.

in favor of the national park promised by the AWS government's 1998 "Contract for Białowieża Forest," which would have protected the whole of the forest from logging. Instead, she preferred a UNESCO "Man and the Biosphere" approach with different zones of protection and use. In many of her writings and public talks, she blamed all of humanity for the forests' destruction, not just foresters. She criticized forestry as it "plundered the remnants of natural old growth" and wrote in her book that "foresters make a fundamental mistake when they look at the primeval forest, a living relic of bygone times, in the categories of a managed forest, planted in rows and maintained in order to yield crop, i.e. high-quality timber" (Kossak 2001, 524). She also sat on a social scientific council of the Puszcza Bialowieska Promotional Forest Complex (a State Forests council) and objected to logging old growth, but her positions regarding the park extension wavered. This would agitate other activists and biologists who worked with her in Białowieża. The Forestry Research Institute always had some researchers who supported the national park expansion and others who supported the forester's approach, but given Simona's passions, I would have thought her to have been the most vocal proponent of the national park expansion. In 1992, she wrote an alarming article in the newspaper

Gazeta Wyborcza saying that the "forest was dying" (Kamińska 2015, 232). Her job and her residence in the forest were both reliant on a good relationship with foresters. Although she objected to hunting—a subject of many of her grandfathers' paintings—she socialized with hunters and foresters and joined the Polish Society of Hunters (Polski Związek Łowiecki), although she never hunted herself.

Beyond this tension between her stances on animal rights and natural wild habitats and her wobbly positions regarding expansion of the national park, Simona inhabited another tension just as curious. Her spite for communism was hard for me to reconcile with her adversarial relationship with other scientists in Białowieża, especially those associated with the MRI, and with the political nature of her appointments. She was active in Solidarity in the 1980s, and in the 1990s, she took the initiative to chair local political action committees for the coalition party AWS. She cared deeply about the course of politics. What most surprised me about Simona was not that she mixed science and spirituality or that she eschewed her aristocratic standards to live simply in the woods but rather that in her efforts to protect wildlife, she baldly facilitated and benefited from behaviors, described as communist, that she herself condemned. Personal influence, corruption and reciprocal exchange—variously referred to as "cronyism," "clientelism," the "acquaintance system," and "bureaucratic power"—that shaped authority and power under the communist system became visible to other scientists, who spoke out against her. Her story is, in many ways, a tale of what happened at institutional levels as certain segments of society tried to distance themselves from communist-era *habitus*. But it is also a story of how the prewar aristocracy, the former communist elite and the new middle class emerged vis-a-vis debates about what counted as legitimate science.

As Simona will demonstrate, the communist past and communist-like power were not just elements belonging to a stodgy old-guard group of apparatchiks. Although Simona and others expressed an extreme distaste for the top-down commands of the communist state, toward the end of her life she participated in systems of advancement based on influence, corruption, and reciprocity that so many people ascribed to the Communist Party. These practices lived on in Białowieża at the cost of democracy and merit-based advancement and were hard to shake at an everyday level. Communism was not just a past system of one-party state control. It appeared in the postcommunist period and formed a sociality that most members of the growing middle class—in this case, key scientists at MRI focused on merit, dedicated to the pursuit of universal scientific truths, and committed to a set of internationally recognized academic practices—wanted to distance themselves from.

Simona's story shows how ideas about communism stuck long after the one-party system ended in 1989 and how they festered and troubled social relations, conservation biology and forest protection. But it also shows that the communist period did not kill the notion that there was a Polish aristocratic elite who constituted a legitimate intelligentsia in the Polish national imaginary and who were more qualified to run the country than communists. When she died suddenly with cancer in 2007 at sixty-four years old, the media lionized Simona, and her legend only grew, meeting the need of Poles looking for an eccentric, self-styled heir of an original Polish aristocracy.

Social Indeterminacy in "Classless" Poland

When I first began reading in the field of postsocialist anthropology, one of the most compelling ideas was that new alliances were forming in formerly socialist countries that blended political and cultural power and that people in formerly rigid social categories might act in unexpected ways to gain legitimacy. As Ukraine declared independence from the Soviet Union, for example, Ukrainians found new categories of "biological citizenship" in the aftermath of Chernobyl (Petryna 2002). Ukrainians highlighted their cultural status within the Soviet Union (e.g., as war veterans) with their diagnoses to claim political belonging in the new Ukrainian state. Janine Wedel's (1998) research showed how Poles receiving US foreign aid in the 1990s had to work between the hard realities of getting things done and the naive expectations of Western donors who thought that grants would equal democratic structures. In much of this scholarship, novel forms of institutional power, often part of the neoliberalization of the state, could be compared against a communist-era habitus (Dunn 2004). Daily life in these accounts was characterized by overwhelming uncertainty, and new institutional responses put forth by the state only exacerbated this uncertainty. From this reading, it would seem that the field for gaining legitimacy was open to opportunists—people tried on roles, repositioned themselves or perhaps gained new rights or privileges during this period of institutional flux. What happened in Białowieża was not that different, but it involved appeals to the universalism of legitimate Western science, the idea that science could transcend politics to produce objective knowledge. There was also an appeal to let the remaining aristocracy and its related intelligentsia provide civic and moral leadership.

The actors in this chapter, including Simona, are largely scientists—namely, conservation biologists—who, in the idealized "Western" world of science, invest in the universality of reason (Lowe 2006). This is demonstrated through certain expert practices, including specific academic achievements, expectations about publishing and funding, and the rhetorical style of meetings. Scientists in Białowieża made the most explicit attempt of any group I encountered to break with the communist past, which meant both terminating the culture of that past and building institutions based on meritocracy rather than the proverbial acquaintance system, which involved calculated ledgers of favors that could be reciprocally requested at strategic moments. Many explicitly differentiated themselves from foresters, whom they perceived to be more institutionally embedded in communist sociality.

Notably, some of these scientists had training and even degrees in forestry, but they were called "scientists," and not "foresters," by all members of the local community. One had to obtain a post as a forester to be called a forester. One had to be pursuing knowledge for nonapplied purposes to be considered a scientist. Scientists attempted to build their legitimacy vis-a-vis claims of the power of science, which would be confirmed by Western grants and Western collaboration. As scientists built institutions and networks, they were also building themselves as the "middle class," meaning a new type of citizen, intellectually comfortable enough to further bolster and reinforce the ideals of civil society but only economically comfortable if one could obtain an occasional Western-located postdoctoral fellowship. Scientists spoke to me of democracy, transition and hopes for a normal future when one reached the middle class not by inherited wealth or allegiance to the old guard but by the integrity of their work and ethos. They actively inserted themselves into building civil society and democracy in the early 1990s and never spoke about class antagonism as an outcome of this process. Civil society discourse hinged on everyone seeing themselves in this universal project (Smoczyński and Zarycki 2017). What postsocialist neoliberal capitalism dangled as a motivating "promise" was that everyone could achieve a middle class standard of living without ever mentioning class antagonism. Class could not exist as a meaningful frame of reference or as a part of science because it belonged to the discredited communist ideology. In that ideology and system, workers and peasants were treated to a type of "affirmative action" that added entrance points to their exams and made the lower classes more competitive in university training and the workplace. All white-collar workers were called "intelligentsia," by the party's logic. Some former aristocrats, like Simona, were spliced into this group.

Simona and her biography demonstrate how ideas about communism, class and science contaminate one another in the postsocialist field of social indeterminacy. On the one hand, some scientists eschewed communist sociality as they built new institutions with the power to anchor society in meritocracy, which should in turn protect the forest from excessive logging and mismanagement. On the other hand, some scientists would not confront the issue of growing inequalities, which, at the national level, led to the kind of nationalist turn we will see in chapter 6. Some people who succeeded in the former system, or at least could get by, descended into poverty in comparison with those who had entrepreneurial skills or could prove their worth, which I will show in the next chapter. As we learned in the last chapter, State Forests in the communist era built up two noncompeting classes: workers and peasants. And although they could not continue to employ everyone, local society still held out the hope that you could socially advance and earn a good income in forestry. In this chapter, Simona's story will confirm that communism did not terminate the aristocracy. A true ruling class, an aristocratic intelligentsia, were still afloat and available to lead society in this imaginary.

As Rafał Smoczyński and Tomasz Zarycki (2017) have convincingly argued, interwar Poland, during the Second Polish Republic, was a kind of "intellectual republic," where a weakened aristocracy began to include more members with less social standing—the "petty gentry," so to speak. This was an outgrowth of a long period of partitions in which agriculture was modernized on large landed estates under three different empires. Many formerly petty gentry, who had managed or worked on the landed gentry's estates, moved to cities; these lesser social members became enfranchised into the intelligentsia during the interwar period. Together, this new intelligentsia, which was still led by the aristocracy, became a "totem" that would claim civic and moral leadership. Smoczyński and Zarycki's sociological studies show that this notion survived communist attempts to erase class consciousness. The hidden script of a proper aristocratic elite saturates Simona's story.

Signals in the Forest

In 2005, ten years after my first visit to Białowieża, much had changed. After spending 1998–99 affiliated with the Forestry Research Institute, where Simona sponsored my master's thesis research, I began another long-term stay for doctoral research. I decided to affiliate with the Polish Academy of Science's MRI, a group of wildlife biologists. The MRI, where Simona had started out in the 1970s, was one of three research institutes in Białowieża (the third being the University of Warsaw's Geobotanical Institute). I wanted an office that provided regular contact with the science community, and the Forestry Research Institute was limited because it conducted applied science related mostly to forestry. To secure the affiliation, I set up a meeting with MRI's director, Jan Wójcik, who threw me off center with the question, "Will you also be working with Simona Kossak?" While he did not go into great detail, he explained that Simona and the institute had a history of legal disputes and that it would not be in their best interests if I maintained dual affiliation. I understood that this was a sensitive topic and had to ask myself if I was betraying Simona. Rather than confront the issue head on at that moment and risk losing an amiable working relationship with conservation biologists in Białowieża, I hastily agreed. I needed a broad perspective and range of experiences to write my thesis. I could not pass up an opportunity because of internal politicking that may have had nothing to do with my research—I would prove to be wrong on this point. Politics between Simona and MRI were critical to understanding how the past functioned in relation to forest protection and use.

At about that same time, Miejsca Mocy became an official tourist destination, part of a wider regional attempt to capitalize on anything that might serve as an attraction. Simona, who had become director of the Forestry Research Institute, was a main instigator of the site's promotion, including its mystical qualities. Tourist brochures claimed that on-site subtle vibrations could improve one's health and enable one to tap into one's own intuition. On my first visit with Simona, it was a mystery site that only a few locals could find, but it made its mark on maps. Road signs pointed the way. Mysticism stood in strange contrast to the public discourse about the sinister and lingering elements of communism.

Poles did not ban former party members from public office after communism ended. Many refer to this as the "Round Table" approach, meaning that both the communists and the opposition sat down together

Fig. 3.2. Polish Academy of Sciences Mammal Research Institute, 2018. Photo by Eunice Blavascunas.

as equals in the discussions leading up to the elections in 1989. Seats in the lower chamber after 1989 were reserved for communists. The postcommunist state gradually implicated communists as a nefarious "other," but this took time.

The first democratically elected prime minister in 1989, Tadeusz Mazowiecki, a Solidarity member, promoted the "thick line" (*gruba kreska*) approach to former communists, choosing not to seek retribution or vengeance toward the previous regime. But by 2005, when the new right wing, Catholic, political party Law and Justice (PiS) won political power, it chose to "out" former communists and secret police operatives in all of Poland's state institutions. Thus, with the elections of Lech Kaczyński as president in 2005 and his identical twin brother, Jarosław Kaczyński, as prime minister, these two former Solidarity members—who would view Solidarity as a compromised organization for collaborating with communists—began to decommunize society. Lech Kaczyński professed in his first public speech that his goal was to "purge various pathologies from our life." Poles clearly understood the allusion to the postcommunist party formerly in power, Democratic Left Alliance (Sojusz Lewicy Demokratycznej [SLD]), which ruled from 1993 to 1997 and again from 2001 to 2005. SLD, like the previous AWS, rejected lustrations and decommunization. As the successor to communist ideas, SLD criticized the course of the economic reforms that Poland embarked on in the first decade after communism. Unlike PiS members, SLD members were not frequent Catholic church attendees, and they opposed religious education in schools. SLD had a wide measure of support in the Białowieża Forest region. SLD's premier, Włodzimierz Cimoszewicz, was an ethnic Belarusian from the region. PiS accused SLD of collective amnesia regarding the communist past. Why didn't SLD openly talk about the crimes the communists committed against workers striking with the Solidarity trade union in 1980s, the beatings and imprisonments, and other oppressive tactics of social control?

With PiS and the Kaczyńskis in power, they made near-daily calls for parliamentary investigations of the entire process by which Poland was transformed into a free market economy. They began to "out" former secret police operatives, serving to stigmatize and prevent many civil servants from future political office. Under political pressure to discover "facts" about SLD, the Institute of National Remembrance, which began operating in 2000, was given the mandate to investigate Nazi and communist crimes against the Polish nation. The institute began to reveal school teachers, principals and even high officials in the national bank. Members of the Catholic Church were not even spared. The archbishop of Warsaw, Stanislaw Wielgus, resigned in an emotional speech at a Sunday mass after the Kaczyńskis' lustration commissions found the bishop's name on a microfiche copy of an original secret police (Służba Bezpieczeństwa) document in 2007. For an almost uniformly Catholic country, this was a major indication of how startling the lustration process was. The Catholic Church was one of the biggest anticommunist forces within Poland during the communist period. Polish priests spiritually led World War II partisans. Pope John Paul II personified national resistance in opposition to communism, and the Church was the place where "truths" could be spoken during that era.

A deep sense of unfairness and betrayal in Poland polarized people who were formerly involved in Solidarity. One the one hand, SLD and many of its supporters felt that participation in the communist system, including its secret police, was so widespread that digging up the "facts" of collaboration was a self-destructing course for the nation. The Kaczyńskis' PiS platform hinged on the idea that former communists who were still in power not only caused harm to their fellow citizens during the communist period but also unfairly profited from the transition at the expense of average Poles. PiS supporters seemed to be saying that good and morally true Poles did not have the means to ascend the ladder of the proverbial acquaintance system (*znajomości*), a well-known facet of how socialism worked in practice—through personal influence, corruption and reciprocal exchange (Verdery 1996). According to many scientists in Białowieża, the whole structure of State Forests was infested with this the acquaintance system.

Communism as a Syndrome

In Białowieża, scientists at the three scientific institutes often shared their views on local and national politics and social relations with me. Pawel was a forest ecologist who shifted among the National Park, the MRI, and the Forestry Research Institute and was also a devout Roman Catholic. He told me that everyone in Białowieża was suffering from a "postcommunist syndrome," suggesting a psychological disorder doomed to be repeated. Pawel welcomed the new "rule of law" that came with PiS and the Kaczyński twins, even if he did not fully agree with their political policies. Simona spoke vitriolically against communism that lingered after the system ended, in a sense blaming Solidarity for agreeing to cooperate with the communists. "That whole caste system of communists, the people of the previous system, [Leszek] Miller, [Alexsander] Kwasniewski, and [Wlodzimierz] Cimoszewicz [all postcommunist politicians on the left]. . . . Poland is still Soviet. They are just lying in wait and the money comes to them. Affairs, stealing, corruption, blackmail, papers in Moscow: We know how Poland is. Solidarity just cannot win! We have the Soviet Union among us, all around us! The red web is all over Poland."

Marcel Mauss (1925) taught anthropologists long ago that all forms of exchange have a calculating dimension; accumulate in order to give gifts that come with reciprocity, but exchange used within the acquaintance system exceeded the moral norms within the idea of the gift. Simona and her colleagues alluded to what anthropologist Katherine Verdery (1996) has called "bureaucratic power," a pervasive and cultural way of operating in communist Europe. In Verdery's groundbreaking model of socialist-era practices in eastern Europe, institutional bureaucracies play a peculiar role in amassing and redistributing resources. It works through personal influence, corruption, and reciprocal exchanges. Bureaucrats try to expand their capacity to give things away, much like some of the Northwest Indian potlach practices Mauss described. In the communist system, people accumulate personal resources, such as jobs and other bureaucratic positions that they can use to hand out apartments, firewood, medical care, permission and funds for publications, and so forth. Verdery broke through the Cold War assumption of Reagan's "evil empire." Communism was not held together through totalitarian top-down control; it was a frail system, constantly undergirded by shortages of raw materials and consumer goods moved around to sustain loyalties. Communism worked through social exchange, by one's ability to put things into the cycle of internal distribution rather than actual outputs. Although "actually existing socialism" functioned in an economy of scarce goods and dossiers, or files kept on everyone, the scientists objected to the sociality of the system of distribution and the ideological obedience expected from foresters.

On a minute, local level, it looked like this. Ursula, an elderly beekeeper, was the mother of a forester. She and her husband had been lowly functionaries in the State Forests system. By sending her son to the Technical Forestry High School in Białowieża and then by his working his way up the system by being loyal, rather than earning more advanced degrees, her son had achieved a high social status while hailing from uneducated parents. Her son's resource for redistribution was firewood, which everyone needed in their stoves to endure the winter. Jadwiga wanted her son to bring her fresh butter from the village nearby, but she said that her son refused because he would have to "give the whole forest away" if he acquired gifts. (Keep in mind this was the late 1990s; gifts might include more manufactured items ten years later.) She was defending the name of her son. Of course, he was beyond bribes in this assertion. But in saying so, she also confirmed what scientists asserted: that gifts, no matter how small, still obtained one privileges from foresters that would need to be met with other paybacks.

Daphne Berdahl's (1999) famous study of the former east/west German border area after reunification points to a tension between the socialist-era expectations and the postsocialist era's disavowal of old patterns. In the former GDR, the goods and rituals that once sustained elaborate social networks drove people in the village apart when communism ended. Something similar was happening in Białowieża.

The scientists most concerned about breaking the culture of bribery and favors felt that they could disembed themselves from the network— that they *had* to disembed themselves—and would do so by pointing to behaviors and language that would make them members of a middle class that the rest of society could emulate. For example, Maciej had just come back from a postdoctoral fellowship in the United States with fresh ideas reorienting his approach to fighting what he called the "last totalitarian organization in this country," State Forests. He started a nongovernmental organization (NGO) on his return and involved himself in breaking up state monopolies on food stores and local newspapers. He told me that in his NGO work, he and other scientists

> dared to question the foresters' approach in the most important forest in Poland (Białowieża). We hit a nerve that had never been hit so far. When you take, for instance, the official magazine of State Forests, *Echa Leśne*, you will find a striking similarity [in] the offensive language and rhetoric to those that could "enjoy" on a daily basis when reading the "official" newspapers in the 1980s about Solidarity. And then there is the nationalist and religious provocation of State Forests, like with other totalitarianisms, used to win the local people. Under the German occupation [1941–45], the Nazis promised the locals independence from the Poles and developed a network of Belarusian schools. State Forests seems to be doing the same . . . when they point at conservationists as their opponents.

Andrzej pinpointed language and rhetoric as lynchpins of the former system, a system that existed strongly in this area because of how Belarusian nationalism was courted by Nazi and then Soviet social engineers. Other scientists decried the nonchalance with which many regional officials spoke of their involvement in the secret police. A prominent ornithologist, Mariusz, who started his own tourist business, told me that locals did not consider communist collaboration a crime: "Secret police could routinely round-up anyone thought to be sabotaging the system, interrogate them and hold them in jail under suspicion. Most local people would openly give information to the secret police. Also, for example, during the 1980s no one was required to march in the May Day parades holding communist banners, but the vast majority of locals came out, lining the streets from one end of the village to the other, whether they were Poles or Belarusians."

Scientists would connect this kind of allegiance to foresters, which we will see in the example below. Independence from this past and being able to recognize the signs and symptoms of communist ideology marked a cultural difference between scientists and anyone who might support foresters. Careers, cronyism, and the state claiming to protect people through intense ideological allegiance were all living symptoms of the communist past for many scientists, wrapped up in a syndrome only broken when you could diagnose that system and then consciously distance yourself from it.

Postcommunist Corruption and New Laws on Nature Protection

The scientists committed to expanding the national park and better protecting the forest identified that the premier example of postcommunist systems of exchange still guided forest politics in the events that transpired between 1998 and 2001. In 1998, with a coalition government of AWS, UW (Unia Wolności), and SLD, representatives of the national government and local authorities signed the "Contract for the Białowieża Forest." This document stipulated that public funds would be transferred to both municipalities and the national park for sustainable economic development of local communities in exchange for expanding the Białowieża National Park over the entire commercially logged forest. (Notably, locally elected authorities were an entirely new concept after 1989.) All employees of State Forests would be given jobs within the expanded national park. The next year, 7.5 million euros (30 million Polish złoty) were divided between the national park and local authorities. The funds went toward building and improving schools, sewage and water treatment plants, and other infrastructural projects.

Nevertheless, local authorities wanted to postpone the park enlargement. When Antoni Tokarczuk, minister of the environment, arrived in February 2000 to announce the national park enlargement, which still needed acceptance by the Council of Ministers, (consisting of the prime minister and a cabinet chosen by the president), hundreds of protesters holding signs in both Belarusian and Polish were there to stop him. Protesters' signs accused three specific scientists of causing poverty in the region. In this case, the protesters believed that scientists engineering nature conservation took away high-paying jobs in the forest, that the European Union was meddling in Polish affairs when Poland was not yet a member of the European Union, and that scientists themselves were not credible experts on the forests ecology—rather, foresters were. MRI scientists repeatedly commented on the novelty of this kind of rowdy populist mobilization in Białowieża. In contrast, the first national park expansion in 1996 was a top-down affair, as nature conservation had always been in communist Poland. Scientists claimed that there were organized bus transports to pick people up from distant forest villages and deliver them to the protests in Białowieża. In other words, this was not a spontaneous social uprising but a staged protest orchestrated by foresters. Protestors threw eggs at the environmental minister. And from that moment, national park expansion began to unravel, and conservationists would never again come as close to their national park ideal for the whole forest.

By the end of 2000, foresters used their connections at the legislative level. PSL (Polskie Stronnictwo Ludowe) legislators introduced a bill, the Environmental Protection Law, that would require the consent of territorially appropriate bodies of self-government to establish, enlarge, or liquidate a national park. NGOs could provide only opinions under the legislation. The legislative proceeding repeatedly referred to the egg-throwing incident throughout the session. The bill passed almost unanimously (fifty-seven to four), meaning that the government turned on its own plan set out in the Contract for the Białowieża Forests. It effectively shut down the Białowieża National Park expansion. Shortly thereafter, the speaker of the lower chamber of the Polish Parliament, Włodzimierz Cimoszewicz (SLD), was granted a forester's cottage on a long-term lease; it was a bit like Simona's cottage, only bigger, with electricity and running water. Because of my involvement with the University Powszechny in Teremiski—founded by a major Solidarity figure and former social minister in the first noncommunist government in Poland, Jacek Kuroń—I met another Solidarity dissident, historian Karol Modzelewski. On his invite, I went to dinner at Cimoszewicz's cabin in 2006. By this year, PiS was in power and Cimoszewicz had just lost a bid for President. He stood strongly against the lustration process in Poland. He had been active in the Communist Party while a student in Warsaw but held no high position in the Communist Party. However, this kind of gathering between former Solidarity members and former communists, in the SLD, so irked PiS.

Modzelewski and Kuroń had also been Communist Party members and wrote a criticism of the party in 1964, for which they were imprisoned for two years. Modzelewski came up with the name "Solidarity." During the informal dinner, Cimoszewicz and I discussed our Fulbright awards. (Critics of Cimoszewicz told me he could have only had a Fulbright given his Communist Party membership.) He and Modzelewski discussed political intrigue beyond my knowledge. After dinner, Cimoszewicz proudly showed me a cleared block of open meadow in an otherwise dense forest, just a stone-throw from the house where he fed bison with hay and watched them from his dining room window. Politicians have long hunted in Białowieża, including foreign dignitaries. It was on a 1938 hunting party in Białowieża that interwar Polish President Ignacy Mościcki and Reichsmarshal Hermann Göring agreed that Poland would not be invaded should war breakout. Hunting has long equaled political deals, whether binding or not. And though bison hunting was illegal in Białowieża, it did not stop Cimoszewicz from identifying as a hunter and a politician at that 2006 dinner I attended.

Cimoszewicz took down a framed image of himself and the king of Spain, Juan Carlos I, so I could get a better look. He explained how the two men were anointing each other on the forehead with bison blood at their kill in the Knyszynska Forest just north of Białowieża. Some scientists I had been talking with wanted me to understand that Cimoszewicz kept close personal contacts with regional and local authorities with whom he regularly hunted. It was frustrating for these scientists that Cimoszewicz supported the park expansion in 1996 when he was premier.[1] He openly opposed the national park expansion in 2000, arguing that if local people did not want the park, he would not support it.

One scientist told me, "Cimoszewicz and foresters prey on local people, who have no tradition of democracy." She was talking about the way foresters convinced people to stand against the national park at a time when scientists were doing the work to build a civil society independent from State Forests. The general director of State Forests in Warsaw imposed a ban on local foresters discussing park expansion. State Forests employees could not talk about National Park enlargement with the local communities, but scientists felt that foresters, in their vast networks of the acquaintance system, were doing just that. Foresters were also organizing "study tours" for groups with political influence, like representatives of the Catholic Church, including bishops (Niedziałkowski 2012, 169).

Representatives of scientific circles and NGOs expressed their criticisms of the 2001 Environmental Protection Law, with its purported ideals of local democracy, that shut down the national park expansion and terminated the Contract for the Białowieża Forest by putting decisions in the hands of local councils. The local governing councils in the Białowieża region were made up of foresters and proforestry politicians. However, to foresters and local people, the legislation represented a victory for democracy and was not a throw-back to the one party system of communism, when national parks could be created at a high administrative level with no consent from local people. For scientists and NGOs, the 2001 Environmental Protection

Law represented clientelism and hidden institutional relationships resulting from the former system because those without proper scientific expertise could make decisions regarding the most important ecological site in Poland and arguably Europe. The Council of Europe decided to suspend its decision to grant Białowieża a European Diploma for Protected Areas in 2007 given its continuous and egregious logging within the forest to the detriment of the forest's biodiversity.

The National Narrative of a "Proper Elite" and Anticommunist Opposition

Talk of communism in Białowieża and throughout Poland depended on the idea that there were legitimate ruling elites in Poland—a gentry, aristocracy, or intelligentsia that would have been more qualified to run the country than communists (Smoczyński and Zarycki 2017). The story of the prewar elite nests within a national narrative about freedom fighters from the nineteenth century who risked their lives in insurrections rather than submit to Russian overlords. Petty gentry and aristocracy formed political cleavages in partitioned Poland, welding national liberation together with modernization of the peasantry and the countryside. After winning national independence at the end of World War I, the state was relatively weak and the intelligentsia was able to impose its legitimacy, insisting that economic capital would not be enough to build the new nation. Many members of these intelligentsia had been trained largely in imperial Austria and Russia. Through the schools and universities they formed under this autonomy, one could build the nation. During World War II, Russians and Germans targeted much of the Polish elite and intelligentsia for destruction. The Polish state and its bureaucrats, teachers, foresters, and scientists disappeared, with a shadow elite surviving outside of Poland in London, Paris, and the United States.

Between occupations by the Soviets (1939–41) and the Germans (1941–45), Polish elites were carted off to Siberia, mass murdered by the Soviet secret police at the site of Katyn, modern-day Belarus (Allen 1991), held in German concentration camps until they perished, or slaughtered in wartime battles. More than three million non-Jewish Polish citizens died during the war, in addition to the three million Polish Jews who would have also made up a large portion of intelligentsia of prewar Poland, especially in the cities. Altogether, 20 percent of the population of Poland died in the war (Davies 1982, 67). The postwar elite—those in positions of power at universities, scientific institutes, forestry offices, and elsewhere—would have been party members in order to obtain their posts at scientific institutes and forestry operations.

Sociologists Smoczyński and Zarycki (2017) explain that communists within Poland initially rejected most cultural aspects of the Polish aristocracy and intelligentsia, claiming that there were only two nonantagonistic classes in Poland, workers and peasants, but there was one further stratum: the "working intelligentsia." The privileged role of the intelligentsia was thus institutionalized under communism (Zarycki, Smoczyński, and Warczok 2017, 16; Zarycki 2012). Surviving members of the prewar Polish intelligentsia had to hide their biographies to obtain work and careers, but in some cases, these people did obtain positions as the working intelligentsia. These former elites viewed communist party members trying to adopt the customs of the intelligentsia as boorish. The idea that a legitimate elite that could be detected through cultural practices was a common belief during the communist period.

The anticommunist movement brought together blue-collar workers with the intelligentsia, which often gets painted as unifying in the Western media. Workers wanted independent trade unions in Solidarity, and the intelligentsia, many members of which had been Communist Party members who were critical of the party, wanted freedom of speech. The participants in Solidarity, who gained political power in the years immediately following the first semifree elections in 1989, had to leave open the possibility of Communists participating in a future government as part of the Round Table negotiations for free elections. Many intellectuals who were part of the Solidarity government in the early 1990s, such as Karol Modzelewski and Jacek Kuroń, believed that democracy had to come from all of society reforming. This would include amnesty for party members. Building a new society, as noted by Danusza Kuroń, Jacek's wife and also a prominent Solidarity organizer, involved using the expertise at hand and not simply purging Communists from the ranks. "Communism had in fact developed some forms of competency," Danusza told me. She and others felt that it was better that the competencies be used in a spirit of building a new society than be wasted through shaming and bans on participation.

Nevertheless, President Lech Kaczyński (PiS) and many scientists, including Simona, disagreed with this position. Simona told me in 2006, "The whole generation, the whole society! Two generations must die in order to let the third generation live. This generation must be trained in the Western university to rule the country. When you kill the last one [from that generation], then a new God arrives." Simona's dramatic statements were visible at the institutional level where younger scientists crafted their institutions with new outreach and new funds. In the early and mid-1990s, well-organized groups of scientists at the Forestry Research Institute, the MRI, the Geobotanical Research Institute, and the national park used their free time to selectively train individuals who would form a society economically independent of State Forests' influence. They hoped such social practices would lead not only to proper interpretations of the correct ecology and management for the forest but also to a well-functioning democratic society that could see the right kind of forest: a forest with old growth, downed woody debris, rare woodpeckers, undrained swamps, and crooked as well as straight trees. Although the scientists involved in these activities did not say so explicitly, they were building a new middle class that was supposed to be the future for all of Poland—and for eastern Europe, according to many Western funders of NGOs and civil society projects. This middle class would neither try to emulate the manners of the old aristocracy nor reproduce the habitus of the communist era.

Building Civil Society and Meritorious Institutions of Science

In Białowieża, the 1990s were a time of political strategizing on the part of resident biologists. Two young researchers, Bogumiła and Włodzimierz Jędrzejewski at the MRI, who would go on to support PiS later, wrote, "The Plan for the Expansion of the Białowieża National Park," in 1992. This plan aligned with the 1998 Contract for the Białowieża Forest, which called for highly curtailed and limited logging to meet local needs alone.

Early on, Simona was part of the agitation for democratic society that cross-pollinated with the national park expansion. With other reform-minded scientists in the village, she would gather at meetings to figure out how to break state monopolies on food shops and local media. Linking ecology to democracy, biologists wanted the forest viewed as ecological processes supporting a host of rare and ordinary wildlife. How could they shape this view without also being elected to local councils?

Although many "gains" were made in opening up free enterprise in Białowieża, biologists felt they were making no headway in terms of their authority to interpret the forest for politicians and locals. They had to scale up their operations with equipment and facilities to speak authoritatively. By the late 1990s, the MRI became the biggest scientific institute in Białowieża. The MRI would take its merit-based turn by doing what Simona, in fact, promoted: connecting itself with the ideal "West," with its objective and independent scientific institutions, in order to be legitimated; however, this approach would also end up absorbing biologists time and make them less prominent in the fight for the protection of the forest.

The MRI went from a cinder-block station of two dozen tiny rooms in 1999 to a mammoth modern facility by 2002 with state-of-the-art laboratories, a well-stocked library, rotunda exhibit space, and offices for all manner of Polish and foreign researchers. It was an "architectural monstrosity," according to Simona. The Forest Research Institute remained housed in the roomy and elegant czarist-era building. Both institutes conducted scientific research, but the Forest Research Institute conducted applied research about managing what was referred to as "natural" forests. For many years, Simona's main research role was counting deer populations so the State Forests offices could determine how many hunting licenses to sell. She earned her doctorate in 1978 from Jagiellonian University in Krakow after researching the foraging habits of deer in Białowieża. In contrast, at the MRI, scientists attempted to model predator-prey relations using both mathematically sophisticated formulas and technologies. However, they also asked important questions for conservation biology: Where were the wolves' territories (in order to protect those territories)? How many deer could predators kill in space and time? Where would the wolves travel to when the population densities of deer were not high enough?

Despite the World Bank grant in the mid-1990s, the Forest Research Institute was fading in prominence, housing only three or four full time researchers by 2005, whereas the scientific staff of the MRI numbered more than seventeen, with dozens of doctoral research projects, a constant stream of international researchers, and a generous administrative staff. MRI scientists published in first-rate, peer-reviewed journals, such as *Ecology*, the *South African Journal of Wildlife Research*, and the *Biological Journal of the Linnean Society*, which led to invitations to international conferences and work opportunities abroad. Globally trained researchers came from Germany, the United States, South Africa, Australia, Scotland, the Netherlands, and elsewhere. Specializing in genetics and evolution, population ecology, biogeography, and behavioral ecology, the MRI also included a historian on staff and supported social science researchers who coauthored articles with natural scientists. This scientific institute would not let communist-era ways of doing things or bureaucratic power interfere with its science and operation and made a point of saying so. This is why, in many ways, I chose to be affiliated with the MRI, but my separation from Simona would soon become clear when I learned about how the MRI's prominence met Simona's stances on animal rights.

Radiotelemetry as Modern Meritorious Science

For biologists at the MRI, an indispensable part of their work included capturing and releasing mammals. Studies began on small rodents in 1952, when the institute was first formed in the science-boosting era of the Cold War. Beginning in 1994 with grants from German and Dutch private foundations and the Polish Academy of Science, the institute acquired and then used VHF radiotelemetry equipment to track the home ranges of larger and small mammals. This change caused a major stir locally in ways that would impact the MRI's effectiveness in interpreting ecology.

Radio telemetry had become standard scientific practice throughout the world by the 1980s (Benson 2010). Biologists would capture a mammal, sedate it, and fit a radio collar with a battery-operated transmitter. Once the collar was in place, it would send out a signal that a researcher could hear with an antenna. The technology tells scientists exactly where animals have been. Telemetry is labor intensive and requires researchers (often young volunteer students) to bicycle or drive at all hours of the day and night collecting data points. Radiotelemetry permitted scientists to track home ranges of mammals and to compare ranges with densities in both historical periods and the present. Patterns of temporal and spatial territoriality proved to be an effective way to see which animals could migrate and genetically interchange from Białowieża to other forests, such as the Carpathian Mountains or Siberia. Use of radiotelemetry transmitters and receivers provided much of the data that helped scientists participate in international mammal science and conservation biology, along with other techniques such as animal census and DNA laboratory analysis. In other words, radiotelemetry gave these researchers international scientific legitimacy that would let them sidestep the entrenched postsocialist forms of behavior.

Local people, however, started to spread rumors about the MRI scientists torturing animals, citing Simona as both their ally and expert source.

Simona wanted nothing more than to bring the use of this technology to an abrupt end. She specifically opposed the use of metal "jaw traps" to capture wolves; she found and kept two of the MRI traps she picked up in the strict reserve in 1993. After Simona refused to return the traps, the matter went to the regional prosecutor's office, resulting in scientists using other methods of capture. But MRI scientists suggested that there was some kind of rivalry behind her antipathy as well as her lawsuits against the MRI, which claimed the MRI was responsible for the deaths of the listed threatened species of lynx in the forest. Simona had first worked for the MRI as an assistant in the early 1971. On her departure, involving a row between her and other staff, MRI scientists reported her claiming to "bring the MRI down," as she changed jobs to work at the Forest Research Institute. Simona, however, explained her objections to the MRI as purely related to her concern for wildlife. "Constant radio signals weaken the animals," she told me. "Can you imagine first being captured with a metal trap, then having a beep sounding in your head nonstop as scientists chase you around all hours of the day?"

When I began my affiliation with the MRI in 2005, many local people with whom I was friendly approached me as if to warn me about the scientists there, as if I didn't know what I had gotten myself into by taking an office with them. People would casually ask me how things were at the office and then start talking about how cruel the biologists were. Simona published in popular books and newspapers that local people read. One family showed me Simona's writings accompanied by gory pictures of mangled weasel strangled by collars. Sawmill owners, cleaning ladies at hotels, and acquaintances buying bread in the shop told me that biologists tortured and unnecessarily killed animals in pursuit of their international careers. Foresters' work, they told me, was not international but rather focused on fitting into the local community. Local people keenly pointed out that they knew the science and ecology of the forest they lived in better than scientists.

The idea of a career, as Ewa, a young administrative assistant of the municipal government (*gminy*), told me, reflects a scaling-up, hiding the mechanisms one uses to get ahead:

> To say you are pursuing a career around here distances you from local society. People in the village hear the word "work" and the relation they have in their heads in to work with the land or work in Hajnówka at an office. But "career"! It doesn't have good connotations. It's very negative. If you are trying to find work, you are improving your life, but career is connected to dirty ways to

getting some higher position. Saying openly that you are working on your career, that your career is really important, means that the only thing you think about is this career. You are not considering family or anything else.

Resident biologists never gained the same kind of respect as foresters, she explained, even after many of them spent forty years or more living and working in Białowieża. Yet Ewa's descriptions of how local society works flips scientists' descriptions of the situation. In this case, it is the scientists who are pursuing careers and wanting to get ahead in dirty ways, and it is the foresters who operate with transparency because of the trust they have with the local community.

One MRI biologist, Bartek, who married a local Belarusian woman, had two children born in Białowieża, and came from a modest agriculture background himself, was highly frustrated with the locals' accusations that biologists tortured animals for the sake of their careers. He explained, "People in Białowieża believe that scientists are coming here for a few years to make money by 'torturing' these animals. They don't understand that they're making degrees and that this is the normal life of scientists. They [scientists] must develop. They must progress. The normal thing is to finish your degree [habilitation]. If scientists are not pursuing their degree, then the director can fire them. This is normal. The people in Białowieża don't know about this. The only thing is that you [scientists] come here to use other people and animals to make money and a career."

Breaking up the social continuity of the foresters and the locals' loyalty and linking oneself to a new, open Europe was exactly what Bartek and others like him were doing. Their regional project, invoking universal Western science, was a wider middle-class project that would not restrict people to geographical, regional, or national identity. As sociologist Tomasz Zarycki (2012, 2) noted, the aspiring middle class in the 1990s and early 2000s was at a disadvantage because members "lack mastery of western culture, intimate knowledge of which becomes indispensable in such a situation." This is to say they had no ancestors or role models within Poland, only the aim of an imagined middle-class lifestyle, as seen through their Western counterparts.

Competing Standards of Science

Locals shrewdly perceived this lack of a Polish-based model of the middle class. Polish biologists could neither belong nor match the legitimacy of

Western scientists. Locals not only challenged biologists' belonging in the forest, but they dismissed Polish biologists' abilities to act like their Western counterparts in this example about improper use of radiotelemetry equipment. A teenage girl, Olga, had me over for dinner one night, and we ended our dinner in front of the television watching the Discovery Channel's "Animal Planet." Olga pointed out that "truly good scientists" did not hurt animals on the shows she watched. They tranquilized them and treated them gently, whereas the MRI scientists did not understand Western standards and clearly "tortured" animals. According to Olga, the Polish wildlife biologists in Białowieża pursued scientific careers at the expense of both the animals they studied and their place in the local community.

Locals also referred to their own understanding of science when they brought my attention to a Yorkshire production translated into Polish, *Tanczęc z wilkami* (*Dancing with Wolves*; 1998) that had once aired on Polish television. The episode circulated hand to hand on a pirated video cassette, which was how I saw it. With the "Western-made" video, they felt they now had evidence of what their Polish biologists were doing in their forest, of things they could not see by simply going to the forest.

In the production, something between reality TV and investigative journalism, a team of British volunteers arrive to help Polish biologists from the MRI. The biologists initially accommodate the volunteers. The film shows Polish biologists training volunteers in how to read maps of the forest and how to use telemetry equipment. As the film wears on, the volunteers discover more and more about the biologists' methods and their disrespect for local culture and customs.

In one scene, elderly locals shuffle against the wintery cold on their way to an Orthodox mass in the Białowieża village. While the choir chants back and forth with the priest in the liturgical Old Slavonic, viewers are indulged with ornate details of the gold-laden interior and icons commissioned by Czar Alexander II. Then the film juxtaposes this scene with the face of a focused scientist climbing a church tower to check the radio transmitters.

What the episode does not say is that the radio tower was located on top of the Catholic church, not the Orthodox church, and that scientists, many of them devout Roman Catholics, arranged to have the tower perched on the church, along with a cell phone tower. The scene makes it look as though insensitive scientists used minority-religion church towers during services with no regard for the sacred space of autochthonous village inhabitants.

From there, the international volunteers want to film the capture of wolves, but the Polish biologists refuse, discussing the safety of wolves and the safety of biologists, who might be attacked if radio collaring is not carried out with precision and focus. Despite this prohibition, the film crew tracks and then sneaks up on the biologists at the capture site, where the biologists scuffle with the volunteers to keep the film crew away from the captured wolf. Yelling and hostility ensue, portraying a biological cover-up of animal cruelty. Viewers see a shaky, zoomed-in close-up of a wolf struggling in a pinned-down net.

The story line then introduces Dr. Simona Kossak, who will sort out the chaos and provide supplementary evidence. Simona is first shown from the porch of her cottage. She gazes off contemplatively into dense forest and condemns the cold nature of biology.

In a shocking conclusion to the production, Simona and Andrzej from State Forests pull a dead lynx from a shed. They explain how a radio collar choked the animal to death. The film's overall message is that Polish biologists are hapless products of the wrong kind of search for modernity in Europe's last primeval forest, which is best left to its Eastern character of Orthodox Belarusian believers and poetic champions of animal rights.

Many scenes from the film showed up as screenshots in the last few pages of an otherwise lighthearted photography book about badgers, published by Simona's partner Lech. Simona wrote an epilogue to Lech's book with the Yorkshire production's screenshot of the wolf pinned in the MRI's net. "Orthodox science wants to pacify and stigmatize their ideological opponents. When others anthropomorphize animals, it is considered the greatest sin," she writes. "Scientists in Białowieża refuse to give animals their own rights. This [the strict reserve] is the one place where the scientists could restore a safe environment where animals are not caught, not crippled, not killed" (quoted in Wilczek 2005, 145).

Janusz, a friend of Simona's, confided that the dead lynx shown in the film was not, in fact, the one originally collared by the MRI. The stiffened corpse shown in the film was Simona's pet lynx, which was killed in a freak accident at her house. The lynx found its way to Simona and Lech for the purposes of filming another nature documentary. One day, as Lech carried a stack of wood from the woodpile to the house, a piece dropped on the lynx's head, and she died soon thereafter. The timing of all this and whether Simona's lynx was preserved through taxidermy was beyond my investigative skills. The short explanation from Janusz was that the lynx used in the

Yorkshire production could not have been the actual lynx radio-collared and found dead in the forest.

Biologists at the MRI hardly wanted to discuss the film with me, mostly because it was not a simple matter, and they did not know if I would further skew their words and actions. They felt betrayed by this film crew, who they thought were legitimate volunteers who cared deeply about their science. Krzystof, a scientist who appeared in the film, agreed to an interview and gingerly explained the lynx death that informed this film:

> The film shows that we force animals. The supposition was that if we use force, this must really hurt them, that they have to die sooner or later. Then they show a lynx who has really died. She had a radio collar, so the conclusion was that it has a radio collar and died. But this picture didn't analyze the reality of this single case. How did the lynx die and when after radio collaring? The foresters found this lynx. It was just by accident, but this lynx . . . it was at least three or five years after radio collaring. This lynx was captured only once and released, and after several years she died. It wasn't that she died because of trapping, because she would have died one or two months later, not several years, and then there's the reason of death. The lynx had visible wounds on the paws. The supposition was that this was because of the snares—it was visible that there were cuts in the skin, but in fact the cuts resulted from the fact that the lynx was heavily infested by mites. The infestation was so intensive that the skin was sick; it was a very thick layer of calloused skin. These kinds of examples are being used by some people to show that radio collaring causes death.

This incident, with its winding tale of scientific rivalries, British sensational media, and local claims of knowing science, is actually a defining story for reflecting on discourses about communism, even though the film itself had no references to communism. With the backdrop of scientists bemoaning the difficulty of conducting "universal" international science in a climate of postcommunist corruption, the question became, Who could be a scientist in the postcommunist era? And who could become middle class in the era, when Poland had only ever known an intelligentsia that descended from the aristocracy and the communist system? How should institutions be shaped to become merit-based in the wake of bureaucratic power? These questions address permeable boundaries between eastern and western Europe, between high and low culture, between what is and is not proper science. In this space, culture does not line up easily along old hierarchies and divisions.

Although the scientists associated with the MRI identified as scientists on the basis of their credentials, methods, participation in internationally recognized forms of scholarship, and so forth, locals viewed them as functioning outside local interests and as incompetent facsimiles of their international counterparts. In comparison to some MRI scientists, Simona hardly qualified as a scientist. To be a "proper" scientist in Poland, one should earn a habilitation (the equivalent of what might be a second major research project with peer-reviewed publications), sponsor doctoral students, and publish in English in peer-reviewed journals. Simona had her professorate (habilitation) appointed by President Kwasniewski (SLD; whom she would openly criticize). She sponsored only one doctoral thesis and had only one peer-reviewed publication in an international journal.

Locals made little differentiation. Simona was a scientist. She was also widely respected in many circles of nature conservationists, foresters, policy makers, and others. But much of her work did not include practicing science as peer-reviewed research. She spent her time making award-winning nature films featuring frogs and butterflies. She produced a popular syndicated daily radio show with thousands of listeners throughout Poland, aired three times a day, with topics like, "Do animals feel?" Her most significant publication was a six-hundred-page fictive history of Białowieża, *Saga of the Białowieża Forest* (Kossak 2001), much of it condemning elite humans' (kings, tsars, state officials, etc.) disrespect for wildlife and the forest. According to MRI scientists, the "nonscientist" Simona Kossak was thwarting their research, preventing radiotelemetry, on nonscientific grounds.

Acquaintances and Performances

Simona received her appointment as head of the Białowieża National Park Scientific Council in 2005 under a newly appointed and widely disrespected park director, Jósef Popiel. Popiel had spent his entire career with State Forests before being appointed. He replaced a widely respected director, Czesław Okołów, who had worked for the park since 1960 and came from a family of foresters sent to Kazakhstan during World War II (clearly a member of the communist "working intelligentsia" who had also been part of the prewar elite). Even park employees, who were often neutral or not in support of national park expansion, confided to me that the new director was a "toady" (*kumoterstwo*) who used the acquaintance system. He invited employees over on Christmas Day and later gave promotions to his guests. Employees told me he created a "boot-licking" (*lizusostwo*) culture at work.

Some also called him a "boor" (*cham*), echoing the notion that there were indeed proper elites and crass careerists.

In the competition for director, Popiel, with a master's degree and no knowledge of foreign languages, outcompeted two other candidates—one of whom was a highly respected national park employee with a doctorate and foreign language skills—who received many more merit-based points for the position in what is a rather public process. Popiel briefly held a position as a forester for the national park before his appointment. In 2005, when Popiel appointed Simona to head the scientific council for the park, many long-term MRI council members were dismissed. The park ended up denying MRI scientists permits to conduct radiotelemetry within the strict reserve of the national park. Animal rights entered the mainstream discourse of the national park, and Simona voiced her sentiments at public events sponsored by the park, including the popular festival Żubrowisko, which she helped organize under Popiel and where her films were shown. Simona opened the festival with the statement, "For too long Białowieża was dominated by science. But science is statistical and cold and the forest is warm and alive. Let's talk about both." In a question-and-answer session, she was also able to impress upon the audience that animals have memory and feeling: "We must observe animals, to bring knowledge of animals together with a love of animals."

Under Popiel, Simona was able to get her emphasis on animal consciousness out to the public, but the culture of institutional favors and cronyism also became evident within the national park. Popiel crassly commercialized the park, installing a billboard advertising bison branded beer (*żubr*) within the 1996 extension to the national park. At a meeting for regional development that I attended in 2006, Popiel introduced cultural practices that seemed out of place for the national park and more in line with the militarization of foresters that harkens back to the interwar period. The meeting began with young male employees, uniformed in formal forestry attire (an almost identical uniform to State Forests) of double buttoned green suit coats, white gloves, and a peaked military cap, ceremoniously proceeding into the auditorium with the Białowieża National Park's newest symbol, the Białowieża National Park flag. The flag showcased a male bison as its centerpiece. Each step of the uniformed employees was measured and punctuated. No such flag existed under any previous park director. At the meeting I picked up a copy of a national park publication that explained the flag's purpose. The new director wrote: "Powerful decision makers in our contemporary times, a moment when the nation is free, look upon the wild herd of bison. This flag will remind us, as it very well should, that we greatly and proudly believe in the survival of bison through near extinction. May we never expire our strength to ensure his [the bison's] survival into future generations." In an accompanying photograph, the new flag adorned with the free bison showed one of the young park employees bent on one knee kissing the flag as the director stood holding the flag.

The audience of local government officials and foresters was asked to rise as the flag was brought in. When the flag reached the podium, the flag bearer clicked his heels, and at the gesture of the park director, the silent audience was now free to sit. As director Popiel stood at the podium with a taxidermy bison theatrically nodding out of the shadows, he proceeded to introduce every government representative and forester present. This was well over fifty names. After the announcement of each name, the audience vigorously clapped. Yet two prominent guests scheduled to speak on the program—Jan Wójcik, director of the MRI, and Stefan Jakimiuk, representative from the World Wildlife Fund—were not announced.

The chief engineer of State Forests, Andrzej, the same one who pulled the dead lynx out of the shed with Simona in *Dancing with Wolves*, spoke a few turns after the director using a discursive style and content more reserved for a political speech as he attacked science itself as a complication in policy: "Scientific experts cannot decide amongst themselves what nature should look like in the forest." Pause. "We can't let their uncertainty interfere with plans for the region." Pause. "What kinds of experts are they? What kinds of scientists? We already have a big protected area in the national park and on the established nature reserves in the commercial forest. Is it going to be necessary to build a fence around each reserve?" And at the end of the meeting, Simona came onstage with the director. The two publicly exchanged token gifts of books and framed photos. The performativity of this meeting highlighted for me both the lived reality of the acquaintance system and the culture of authoritarianism that scientists associated with the communist past.

Fostering Distinctiveness

The MRI held a meeting that same year (2006) for European professors and their master's degree students at a summer biodiversity school. The method of fostering the institute's distinctiveness in the climate of forester culture relied on connecting the MRI with the European Union and international science. Contrary to the institutional culture of foresters, who scientists claim built up their social capital because of what they could give the local population in return for a license to log, scientists located their authority in the world of international science, represented by peer review, grants, exchanges, and international travel.

In the plenary session, Director Jan Wójcik addressed the audience of two hundred students and about two dozen professors from EU countries by stating that the goal of this summer school was the integration of Poland with Europe. Instead of providing a long litany of names, as the park director had done, he proceeded with a list of the institute's accomplishments: twenty-five books and 1,400 scientific papers. He talked about the breadth of the library collection and prepared slides showing the staff's percentages of skills by type (e.g., geneticists, statisticians, small rodent specialists, etc.). The director's burden was to convince international students and researchers that they had come not to the periphery of Europe but to the center of top-notch science. Instead of assuming the audience's support, he felt the need to demonstrate it, which a small group of Dutch and German master's students commented on at the lunch break: "That was strange. Why did the director spend so much time on presenting the accomplishments of the institute?" Another student thought this indicated a "complex" on the part of the institute: "It's as if he had to prove something to us." The students clearly did not understand the postcommunist legacy that produced the need to demonstrate one's value using international standards rather than local ones.

EU officials responded to the strategies of the MRI by funding the summer school; giving the MRI a "Center of Excellence" award; providing western salaries in euros to high-ranking foreign researchers; and sending Martin Sharman, director general for research at the European Commission, to the meeting that day to give the keynote on science and policy. He opened his lecture with the cliché, "Science is independent. Policy depends on individuals."

Sharman bolstered the MRI's goal of obtainable western normalcy through which neutral universal science can be used by policy makers with a conscience, who can stand outside the grip of social conformity to speak in the name of truth. Biologists at the MRI strove hard in this belief, to unveil for me all the machinations of bureaucratic power in their eastern outposts of work and life. In contrast, it seemed that Simona was the one seizing on this belief in the individual while using the system of clientelism to sustain her unique lifestyle and assertive positions that broke from "orthodox science."

In 2006, scientists at the MRI bemoaned Simona's politicking again. She decided to take on a new doctoral student, park director Popiel, whose project idea had been accepted by the Warsaw University of Life Sciences. His project, according to MRI scientists, consisted of counting red deer in the strict reserve. Biologists perceived the director's thesis as simplistic with no scientific depth. Moreover, he used public resources (i.e., park rangers) to drive game so he could count them. Biologists' sentiments hinged on the idea that his doctorate would not be equal to theirs and that Poland still needed to improve the standards in place for earning a doctorate.

As if to vindicate the MRI's charges of lingering favoritism, police dramatically removed Popiel from his office in handcuffs in winter 2007, with his employees watching the arrest. He was taken to the anticorruption department in the nearby city of Białystok. Among the charges were accusations of granting bonuses to employees for receiving bribes, awarding a contract without applying the provisions of public procurement law for the amount of 120,000 złoty, and extortion. After a hearing and confessing to some of the charges, he was released from custody. The charges were later dropped, but he never returned to his position as park director.

In a tragic and dramatic real life twist, the vibrant and sixty-three-year-old Simona was lying in a hospital bed suffering a painful last few months of death due to cancer. Her death was mourned by everyone in Białowieża, even her rivals. But years after she died, many local people lamented that she chose not to be buried in Białowieża but in the Kossak crypt near Kraków. It was also roundly spoken of that she called for a Catholic priest on her deathbed, suggesting her experiment with gurus and her criticism of Pope John Paul II were merely experimental and not reflective of her authentic self.

Having known Simona as I did, as my master's thesis sponsor, through the wild wind of rumor, and as a woman I would admire in some ways but whom I betrayed through my involvement with MRI, I would say that there is no doubt she was an individual, the kind Martin Sharman promoted as necessary for Western meritorious science. Her personality was big, her fight for her causes unrivaled in her passion. But her science was not independent. Her tight relationship with Popiel and her reluctance to support national park expansion by working with other scientists and activists made her look like a product of the local pathways of cronyism in the new era.

In the decade after her death, the media lionized Simona. The attention to her life was part of a much larger fantasy about the Polish aristocracy. Television stations frequently programmed series about the fate of the aristocracy. Bookstores carried countless publications about the different coats of arms belonging to known sets of Polish families. The Association of Polish Nobility formed in 1995, and a general fascination surfaced around the loss of that nobility and the fragments that survived.

A hagiography of Simona's life has grown around this larger phenomenon with a documentary film produced in 2014 (by Beata Hyży-Czołpińska) and a biography (Kamińska 2015).[2] Lech published his photos of their life in a book titled, "Meeting with Simona Kossak" (Wilczek 2011), in which the reader can viscerally relive her March mud-thaw travels from the cottage to work on an old motorcycle or Simona in her twenties in mystical communion with deer emerging from the forest to greet her. The afterlife of Simona seems as important as her life for understanding how discourses about the communist past in a suite of forester power are embedded in totems to an authentic aristocracy in Poland.

My rendition of Simona's story shows that individuals caught in social milieus are unpredictable forces, but her afterlife also points to the ways Poles can excuse the aristocracy, or even adore the aristocracy, for what might seem like erratic or inconsistent behaviors. For all the polarization prompted by the lustration process that reached its peak in 2005–7, we see in this chapter how personal and political interests merge and splinter. There may well have been elites who never supported or benefited from the communist system or from communist-era behaviors; however, in this story, we see Simona as someone who swears against that system but performs the behaviors she eschews while still serving as a heroic public figure.

In 2006 I visited Simona in her office for what would be the last time, asking if I could interview her about her involvement in Solidarity. She was open and cordial but also clearly agitated with me, and it seemed personal. I asked Simona, "Tell me about your involvement in the anticommunist movement and AWS in the early 1990s." She took my open-ended questioning as a lack of professionalism: "I want to see specific questions that show me you know something about this era. Give me a list and then we'll commence." We struggled to make the most of this encounter, she not ready to give away her story and I not wanting to leave just yet. So I pressed, taking her instead to a topic I had heard her talk about numerous times: the problems with the former system. "What direct changes have you seen as a result of your involvement in Solidarity in Białowieża?" She was not optimistic that Poland was on a course that looked much different than it had. She said, "In the former system, you take a folder, because your child needs it in school, and you steal from the country that's stealing from you. It's normal and that's how people acted and in many ways still act. Its starts from people at the top, and nothing has changed. Nothing in our country is transparent. Living for the future was destroyed by the communists. It's a bullying system."

Simona, the true elite who lived close to nature, used bureaucratic power, tied to a version of communist-era behavioral practices, to stop what she saw as animal cruelty. Actors, agendas, and constituencies were skewed in ways that no simple model could have predicted. There was a pastiche to the postcommunist era, so we cannot make sense of Białowieża' conservation politics along simple lines of actors with fixed positions, such as the "elite" or "boors," or pro- and anticommunist political factions. The dominating narrative in a nation with a fascination with its aristocracy and a political faction that wants to expose communists *is* Simona in mystical communion with the Białowieża forest and its wildlife. Any compromising strategies she may have used to secure her life in the forest and make rules about forest use will be forgotten. She is the inspiration for the belief that wild nature is sacred in Poland, which has become apparent in the way nature activists in 2017–18 carried images of her on posters to protest logging.

The Place of Power, the site this chapter starts with, accrued a strange following. Today some locals warn that "bad energy" lurks there. Tourists come away with headaches and bad luck after lured by tales of its subtle vibrations.

Notes

1. Cimoszewicz would later denounce hunting and support a ban on logging when PiS came to power in 2015, after he no longer had a lease on his cabin and moved to the village of Białowieża.

2. An article summarizing Kamińska's biography with Lech Wilczek's photos can be found online; see Kowalczyk (2015).

4

POSTPEASANT COSMOPOLITICS

Man of the Forest

BEFORE 1945, MUCH OF EASTERN EUROPE WAS ASSOCIATED with a large peasantry. The role of the peasant had been fundamental to the cultural identity of the region even as reformers sought to shake loose of the stigma of backwardness through industrialization. From the earliest days of Bolshevik organizing in eastern Europe, reformers targeted peasants as a social group. Inequality, hunger, and poor working conditions—the bane of the industrial proletariat—affected the exploited peasantry, according to Soviet engineers of communism. Executing Marxist-Leninist theory over the course of the twentieth century meant socially advancing peasants—turning them into factory workers and industrial workers for the sake of bringing about a modernity where the workers owned the means of production. This process often involved uprooting peasants and breaking familial bonds in the course of collectivization, the pooling of labor and equipment onto state or collective farms. Peasants across the region largely resisted. Most Polish agricultural land was never successfully collectivized by the People's Republic of Poland (PRL; Polska Rzeczpospolita Ludowa). It stayed in private family holdings. When post-1989 market changes ushered in neoliberal reforms for Białowieża, how did the agrarian structure of Poland compel people to both eschew and celebrate peasants in the forest region?

In 1988, 38 percent of the Polish population (approximately fifteen million citizens) lived in nonurban areas. At this time there were around two million individual farms in Poland. More than half did not exceed five acres and only 6 percent had more than fifteen acres (Halamska 2016, 35). Most had mixed, small-scale, animal and crop systems worked with family labor. Even more people grew their own food without counting statistically as farmers.

When Poland joined the European Union in 2004, EU agricultural policy did something that no other institutional or border change had done previously: it eliminated the peasant as a category in Polish society through subsidies and structural pressures, making way for the professional farmer. From at least the sixteenth century, when the principles of serfdom were laid down, the agrarian question (i.e., how to modernize peasants) had loomed large for Poland. Its agrarian structure with its many small and "inefficient" farms kept Poland both socially conservative and "backward" by the standards of modernizers, including Prussia, Austro-Hungary, the Soviet Union, and members of the Polish elite. Supporters of nature conservation and forestry in the present portrayed the Białowieżan peasant within their own discourses about what it meant to be modern vis-à-vis the forest. What follows is how one such "post-peasant" can tell the complex story of the peasantry for Białowieża, where people farmed for centuries in the shadow of the ancient forest.

Man of the Forest

When Leszek woke up every morning, he saw the capercaillie (*Tetrao urogallus*), an extirpated bird of the forest. Its image was torn from a glossy wildlife calendar and pinned to his wall. The wood grouse seemed to flutter off the page. When I met Leszek in 2006, he told me that his good friend Adam Wajrak (an environmental journalist) took the picture: "We go to the forest together, not to hunt but to take these photos."

Born in 1953, Leszek lived in one room of a subdivided wooden house. There was an aluminum wash basin under the bed. His house had neither a bathroom nor a shower, just a small sink with running water. His clay-tiled stove in the corner was a testament to an era when everyone heated with wood, when almost all residents worked for the Białowieża State Forests district on an as-needed basis and produced most of their own food on two- or three-hectare farms. Such people were classified by PRL as "worker/peasants." His small electric heater warmed his one small room on cold days. Because his brother Mirek used wood to heat his subsection of the house, and his aunt did the same on the other side, Leszek could concern himself with other matters.

I would visit Leszek often, seeking him out for mushrooms. Leszek harvested and sold boletes, honey mushrooms, chanterelles, and other edible fungi at purchase points in Hajnówka or through his vast networks of acquaintances. He supplemented a monthly disability payment by selling his harvest for cash. "Why should a man find a job when he can live for free off the forest?" he asked.

Leszek embodied the quintessential "free man" of the forest, a man with few possessions but a cultivated knowledge from a lifetime of experience in one place. "I know every inch of this forest," he said. "If they dropped me in the forest from a helicopter in the middle of the night, I could tell you exactly where I am. That's me, 'Man of the Forest!'" In his fiery explanation, I never knew who "they" were—as in helicopter operators or a command person—but it would not have surprised me if Leszek knew someone with a helicopter. He had all sorts of friends. Leszek's local friends and family gave him the title *czarny bocian*, "Black Stork," because of his long wiry legs and dark hair. His equally tall younger brother Mirek, also a bachelor, was called *Biały Bocian*, "White Stork," because of the red boots he wore as a child, which resembled the spindly legs of the white stork. Black storks live and breed within the riverine forest habitat. No one has seen one in the past few years in Białowieża. White storks are birds of the meadow. Few remained after the decline of peasant agriculture in Białowieża. As soon as Leszek introduced himself, always using his title, you knew what he wanted to be called, and it wasn't Black Stork: "I'm Leszek Szumarski, Man of the Forest!" Yet knowing his title did not mean you always knew who or what the "man of the forest" was. He would defend the forester one day and speak with great loss about the old trees on another. What kind of relationship between the agricultural clearing and forest had there been to create such a man of the forest in Białowieża? And what kind of forest was Leszek the man of?

It was hard to generalize about Leszek. Adam Wajrak, his journalist friend, a generation younger than Leszek, gushed that he was "a living legend of this place." Other neighbors told me that he was "a drunk" or "a guy who gets around," but that "everybody likes him." His positions regarding the forest's protective status were never clearly aligned with any one faction. He "hated ecologists," particularly because they advocated for a forest with downed woody debris, and in his version of the forest, nothing went to waste. At the same time, he insisted that the forest was now a "lost *puszcza*." He told me, "Forty years ago it was a real wilderness." He said, "Now, it is potted. It's an unruly thicket, cut out, chopped down, mangled, and the forest is just like the woods you find around Warsaw or anywhere." I interpreted his multiplicity of positions to mean that he did not want to work but was nostalgic for a working forest. He hated ecologists but was best friends with an ecologist. He lamented a forest with smaller trees but did not like the dictates of the new laws requiring downed woody debris to be left on the forest floor. His positions were not his alone. Leszek, like everyone, existed in a cultural and historical context.

His persona of Man of the Forest could have arisen only through the legend of local people *in place,* a people who formed as "elusive woodland inhabitants," as described by historian Simon Schama in his classic treatise, *Landscape and Memory* (1995). The book's staging arguments, set in Białowieża, tell us that memory resides in landscape and not just the other way around. Through an 1821 visit, nineteenth-century Polish German forester Baron Julius von Brincken described these woodland people. Schama takes the license of paraphrasing what the Baron saw: "For the forest people with their nut-brown weather-beaten faces and short fustian coats were evidently not true serfs, whatever their official legal status. They conspicuously disdained the drudgery of the field for an Arcadian life of hunting and gathering, much the same, he supposed as their pagan Lithuanian ancestors" (49). Leszek knew only a few strategic phrases in English. Although I never inquired, I doubt he had read Schama, but he cultivated his Man of the Forest image in storied proportions for anyone who would listen, seeming to echo von Brincken's summations: "I'm an Indian because I live here. They will have to give me a fine, but I'll be the one giving fines because this is my land"; "If there are mushrooms, I'm in the forest from eight in the morning until sunset"; and "The greatest tragedy I ever had in the forest was with a moose. It was a hundred meters away. He stood there as I was collecting bison grass [a sweet grass used to flavor vodka]. Instead of him escaping from me I had to escape from him. He tried to make me a *kotlet schabowy* [breaded meat cutlet] with his antlers."

The man of the forest was not a wild man. Unlike North American perceptions of "wilderness," the primeval forest and civilization were not antithetical in the local and Polish contexts. Conservationists and Leszek acknowledged that humans had a history of managing the landscape for hunting, beekeeping, grazing, charcoal production, and, more recently, forestry. Leszek planted thousands of spruce, pine, and oak seedlings, working seasonally for State Forests, in the 1970s and 1980s and watched them grow. "I have a right to what's mine," he said, referring to the dead wood rotting on the forest floor.

Fig. 4.1. Leszek Szumarski with calendar photo of a capercaillie on the wall, 2011. Photo by Jodie Baltazar. Used with permission.

Although I never saw Leszek in "fustian," a coat made of linen, he did bequeath me his handmade, long-haired goat vest. He made it for himself decades ago from brunette-haired goats raised and slaughtered on his family's farm, goats that probably grazed in the forest before forest grazing was forbidden in 1978. With this gift, I became one of Leszek's friends.

Cultural Broker in an Iconic Forest

Anthropologists try to interpret their friends (Abu-Lughod 1986; Rosaldo 1989; Briggs 1970), which is often an awkward thing to do. Wasn't I also egging him on in the process? And as Leszek shared more of his persona and history with me, did he want me to include him in a story that would reach a wider public? Leszek helped me think about both the difficulty and integrity that it takes to be rooted in a formerly agricultural and forest-based community inundated with tourism and new money. He helped me think about how people negotiate the past, both their personal pasts and a kind of historical past, to build the space of the present—to use those elements to creatively form oneself and one's possibilities to inhabit a new position.

There is a long tradition in anthropology, stemming back to the colonial era, of anthropologists questioning whether their informants are authentic enough for ethnographic description (A. Zimmerman 2001).

Anthropologists, who frequently worked for colonial governments, had to find "savage" representatives who could ensure that people were not just performing for the anthropologist. Such representations went on to support notions of cultural evolution proposing that all societies and cultures would move from savage to civilized. Finding "backward" representatives of "mankind" validated the rule of the "civilized" colonizer. Conservationists and other people, like myself, interested in Leszek navigated similar terrain in postsocialist Poland. Because Leszek promoted himself as Man of the Forest, Leszek raised the question of authenticity but also the question of the *lumpenproletariat*, meaning the type of individual who can easily give way to ideology or whoever is in power. Was he trying to craft himself as authentic for an audience like myself, tourists or nature conservationists? Could I trust him for credible accounts given his range of opinions? Could Leszek be representative of a local person or a representative of a peasant past that the nation of Poland had a complex relationship with and that he was running away from or creatively reforming? I gravitated toward Leszek in the research and then the writing because of his generative power, the way he fed me a steady stream of evocative pronouncements about himself and his social relations, and because of his cultural creativity with the idea of the free man of the forest.

His long-term neighbors and family either worked seasonally for State Forests or for a few local sawmills. The men at the sawmills often labored on the black market. A few found jobs in construction or carpentry for new home construction in Białowieża. The majority of Leszek's companions were unmarried and spent their free time drinking heavily on porches or in front of the local shop. I chose to focus on Leszek because he was a cultural broker, but like Simona in the previous chapter, he was not exactly representative of a whole social class. With one foot firmly rooted in the local and one in the world of newcomers, Leszek was interesting for me because he was not "corrupted" by contact with the new era, what Leszek condemned as an era of "money, money, money" (he often used the English word in quick repetition). He did not try to sell himself for ecotourism, as a kind of attraction.

The Man of the Forest persona was certainly created by the opportunities of capitalism, an era of changing morality and reciprocity, but Leszek retained significant artistic license. He invented himself as Man of the Forest and that meant taking his intimate and community knowledge of the agricultural fields and forests and using it, or at least the appearance of that knowledge, to earn credibility in the new social and economic structure of tourism and conservation politics. I say the appearance because he boasted about his knowledge as much as he demonstrated it. Many of my attempts to bring Leszek into the forest were short-circuited by his social encounters in the village, especially in front of the small shop in Teremiski, where he purchased beer and cigarettes.

I first met him there. In a hamlet of sixty inhabitants, the shop was about the only public gathering space left in the hamlets of Teremiski and Budy. Unlike the bustle of Białowieża (seven kilometers away), Teremiski and Budy tended to be quieter, with fewer tourists and no administrative institutions. With my bread roll and herring for lunch, I sat down on the bench where Leszek smoked, and we struck up a conversation. "You see this hand?" he started in, baiting me. His curled hand, swollen and gnarled, looked like an advanced case of rheumatic arthritis. I chewed and murmured, "Mm-hmm?," smiling politely but guardedly. "This is because of my karate days," he said. "This hand is beaten up. A brick was thrown, and I broke it in half with my hand. I was part of a security bureau." A fantastic tale, I thought, but I wanted to know more. He boasted about a Berlin filmmaker who came to Białowieża and chose Leszek to star in the lead role of a film called *Reality Shock* (2005). "It's about Poland's first day in the (European) Union," he said.

When he dropped the director's name, Stanislaw Mucha, I paused and put down my bread roll. Having just read an academic article by University of Vermont colleague Adrian Ivakhiv (2006) about Stanislaw Mucha's eastern European border film *Absolut Warhola* (2001), I immediately probed further, "Stanislaw Mucha!?" Leszek continued casually, "Yeah, Stanislaw Mucha. He paid me 30,000 złoty [US$10,000]. I've got the sequel all figured out. In the next movie, I go to the forest, and find a young boy that no one has ever taught. And I teach this child poaching, like Tarzan. I teach him and then when he's grown, we go together and there we are, 'son of the forest' and 'man of the forest.' I've agreed to thirty thousand more from Mucha. He says we don't have the money, but he's agreed to it." I stopped the flow of his narration with astonishment: "Really, you worked with Stanislaw Mucha?"

Leszek's prompted me to take note of the way he endeared himself to those who could circulate his image. I asked Leszek's friend Adam Wajrak, the journalist who was also my neighbor. Adam put Leszek in the media spotlight as well, including Leszek in his television appearances. Their relationship began, as Adam, tells it, when Adam first moved to the village of Teremiski in 1999. Leszek approached Adam. He asked Adam if he wanted to see a wolf. Adam said "of course," and so he went with Leszek to the forest. "He showed me first the raccoon dog tracks [an invasive tree climber from Asia]," Adam told me. "I laughed, then he showed me others, but nothing was a wolf." But then Adam asked him about the scars on his hands, and Leszek led him to a trap where he had released the lesser spotted eagle. Adam could see feathers all around the metal snare and knew that Leszek was not making it up. "And from that time on I liked him."

His friendship with Adam Wajrak got him into the most trouble with Leszek's extended family in the village. They referred to Wajrak as *wariat*, a pejorative sounding similar to his name, meaning "madman." Leszek's relationship to Adam facilitated the growth of his reputation and his opportunities to seed his image more broadly.

In 1995, when Adam was in his twenties, he moved to Białowieża (later to Teremiski). With no formal education but a love for wildlife, he started writing articles about Białowieża's animals for *Gazeta Wyborcza*, Poland's leading liberal newspaper. Television stations soon gave him airtime for wildlife shows, such as *Wajrak on the Trail*. In a decade, he was the most famous environmentalist, nature writer, and photographer in Poland, with a huge following of readers and viewers. *TIME* magazine named him one of "25 European Heroes of the Year" in 2005. In the same year, he helped stop construction of a major EU highway slated to run through the pristine Rospuda Valley. He traveled on nature expeditions to Spitsbergen (Norway), Greenland, throughout the United States, and elsewhere, but mostly he stayed in his modest house in Białowieża going to the forest every day, then writing posts for the newspaper about birds, bison, fox, and other animals. He used his forest knowledge to lead a campaign to stop logging in the Białowieża forest. He also spent lots of time with Leszek.

The two seemed like uncanny best friends, and this came through in their media relationship. In a 1999 classic appearance for the series *Animals*, the two men sit together on a bench trimming the dirt off their mushroom harvest. After Leszek laments the disappearance of the big trees he knew as a boy, Adam chimes in to confirm. "And that's how it is, ladies and gentlemen, the forest dies, and politicians don't give a damn, and as the wild forest dies, so do the authentic people who live here, the people of the forest, and Leszek is probably the last of them." Leszek's neighbors would never let him off the hook for what he said on television.

EU Regulations and Conservation of Peasant Agriculture

Leszek could not have been the Man of the Forest without people like Adam, Stanislaw Mucha, or even myself. The Man of the Forest persona required the attention of others looking for a man of the forest or maybe a "people of the forest," yet Leszek, unlike his neighbors, was ready to perform other people's expectations. In playing to the public, as well as to his neighbors, he became his own creation. An economy of appearance (Debord 1967) went along with the capitalist era and ecotourism, in which marketing and images were used to sell products and experiences and consumption was supposed to individuate one's self, as Leszek seemed to know so well.

The postsocialist era used images for profit-motivated needs in an expanding market that drew urban Poles to the country's "backwater" to see Europe's last primeval forest. These images were the all-too-familiar trappings of tourism, contaminating the "purity" of the place with busloads of people looking for the authentic. Many Poles I met came with a copy of a guidebook titled *Exotic Poland*. And before the market for these images of wooden architecture, storks, and Orthodox churches was created, conservationists were ready to prime the image of a local forest peasant.

The right kind of peasant/freeman was a target creation for a conservation agenda after 1989. Leszek adapted accordingly, not as the "correct" version of the conservationists' agenda but rather as a sui generis local person who was ready to engage and play with that image. He made almost no money from it, which did not support the conservationists' agenda.

Conservationists, mostly Poles, intended to improve local residents' lives and stimulate a new tourist economy while retaining living traditions. Initially, "saving the *puszcza*" would be linked to celebrating small-scale agricultural production. And for much of the first two decades after 1989, tourist businesses advertised and promoted authentic rural traditions. Eventually, the traditions themselves became so obsolete that marketing took a fairly predictable turn toward satisfying bourgeois urban tastes for spas instead of swamps, barbecues on lawns instead of bonfires in the forest, and coiffed hostesses instead of "real" farm producers. But before things went in that direction, the conservation community made a concerted effort to save and promote agricultural traditions within the forest hamlets.

Farming was never easy or practical in the middle of a large forest. Potatoes and beets needed to be guarded all night against wild boar and bison. Wolves might eat young calves if the deer population was overhunted, especially when cows grazed in the forest (until 1978). And if you did not keep close watch, hawks often flew off with hens in their clutches. But for several centuries, if you lived in the forest, you had to produce most of your own food under these conditions. Even in the mid-1990s, shops sold little in the way of eggs, meat, or vegetables. Small-scale extensive agriculture shaped conditions favorably for white storks, lapwings, fire-bellied toads, and many orchids. These flora and fauna were highly prized by conservationists and rare in the rest of Europe.

When Poland joined the European Union in 2004, people in Białowieża began to sell off their milk cows. They ate the last pig and downsized their fields to small vegetable gardens instead of planting rye and flax with horse-driven ploughs. New EU regulations required capital investments if one planned to sell food on an open market; these included cooling equipment for milk and barns that separated pigs from sheep and cows from goats. Concrete had to be laid over the mud floors for sanitized hose-downs of animal feces. In Białowieża, as elsewhere, it was simply cheaper to purchase milk and meat at the shop than raise animals in the forest meadows.

Tourism, connected to promoting the primeval forest, needed the appearance of peasants—hearty and generous, knowledgeable about the forest and fields—to sustain the industry in its infancy in the 1990s. Conservationists acted strategically to bring local people into tourist enterprises that celebrated peasant life. World Wildlife Fund (WWF) Poland hired cheerful Poles, often attractive women, to go door-to-door surveying residents about their openness to hosting tourists in a spare bedroom of their houses. A World Bank Global Environmental Facilities (GEF) grant supported researchers at Polish universities who studied forest biodiversity protection, documenting not just movements in the forest but plants and animals associated with peasant agriculture. Other groups, like the small, seven-member Society for the Protection of Białowieża worked individually with people by suggesting things that ecotourists might like, such as types of food and room arrangements. A multimillion-złoty Danish grant also provided startup funds for bed and breakfast entrepreneurs. Meals made at villagers' farms were supposed to be central to the tourist experience. Villagers would become well versed in trails and natural history, according to conservationists' visions.

Conservationists pinned their ideals on more than just supporting a local economy. They hoped that agrotourism, with its bed-and-breakfast farm stays, would develop democratic society from the legacy of socialist behaviors. Foreign and Polish NGOs, despite different ideas of forest protection, enriched this vision with financial support. Creating entrepreneurs from peasant-workers required education. Education would come through tourism workshops and contact with outsiders, both international and Polish, who would share their love for the old-growth forest, while urbanites, both foreign and Polish, would be enriched as they experienced living traditions.

Any control over that image soon slipped away from both conservationists and actual residents as hotel chains and other entrepreneurs cashed in on Białowieża's status as Europe's last primeval forest. By the year 2000, three 150-plus-room hotels had opened in a village with only twelve hundred residents, scattered in seven village settlements. Ubiquitous billboards for a midsize pension featured a bleached blond young woman sitting dreamily in the doorway of an old wooden cottage, her above-the-knee dress resplendent with the green and red colors of Belarusian folk costumes. The hotels initially staged historic gentry and peasant scenes in their exteriors and interiors with features such as thatched roofs and staff dressed in billowing blouses or dress suggestive of folk. Much of it had no original basis in local history.

Many villagers opened bed-and-breakfasts at conservationists' urgings. They were drawn into trainings, workshops, and grants that would afford them free fax machines, discounted solar panels, and sometimes cash or small loans.[1] The new entrepreneurs soon realized that it was easier and cheaper to buy all their meal items for guests at the attractive German owned *Kaufland hypermarket* twenty kilometers away in Hajnówka than give them their own cured meats and homemade jams.

Villagers who no longer needed barns for animals used their newfound incomes to retrofit these buildings for tourist rooms. Bed-and-breakfast operators found ways to maximize their profits by charging 100 złoty (US$33) for a bonfire; 60 złoty (US$20) for each bed, sometimes with four beds to a room; and adding more and more beds to each room, with five rooms to a house or barn and multiple buildings on one property and each generation owning a different building to evade taxes. Many residents, but not all, went from being poor farmers and forestry workers in the mid-1990s to middle-class entrepreneurs ten years later, owning new cars and SUVs, remodeling the interiors and exteriors of their houses. Both villagers and hotel operators used the peasant image, but villagers flat out rejected being the peasants in a new tourist economy. Many displayed their old ploughs in decorative garden arrangements at the front of the house. Anthropologists Richard Handler and Eric Gable (1997) refer to the phenomenon as "nostalgia progress"—you take elements of your past and relegate them to artifacts to neutralize that past. But larger political and economic structures determined where peasants-turned-entrepreneurs could take their traditions.

EU environmental protection laws—namely, NATURA 2000—prevented villagers from developing infrastructure on their meadows, some owned privately in part and others communally. The meadows were part of a buffer zone adjacent to the park with bird habitat shaped by age-old practices of hand scything and pasturing old breeds of milk cows. Farmers could apply for EU agri-environmental subsidies to retain these traditions.

In short, conservationists wanted a "peasant" who was committed to conservation and slightly tidied up for tourists. Capitalism overwhelmed the image of that peasant. It took a misfit like Leszek to throw these images into relief, to take some creative license over history and do what no conservationist expected: link the freeman-peasant image with a version of nature that neither his neighbors nor the conservationists would fully understand. In playing to multiple publics, Leszek took his Man of the Forest persona, drawn from lore, and married it to the socialist past, to State Forests, and to communist Poland.

Newcomers and Changing Aesthetics for the Village

Leszek worked with and against this currency of the peasant image as he networked to create himself, for it was the reminder that a large group of tiny family-farmed subsistence plots meant underdevelopment in the region. This stigma moved many forest residents to appropriate the peasant image for new goals. They used underdevelopment to develop, or they used the peasant image to sell a leisure package to newfound consumers. The future all over Poland involved rural development, just as had happened throughout Europe following World War II.

A man who was opening up a bed-and-breakfast centered around the production of traditionally fermented bread asked me, "These newcomers say they like the village, but do you think the village likes them?" He referred to the influx of people from the cities who would purchase the land in Białowieża's hamlets. Newcomers to Leszek's village of Budy and nearby villages admired the forest in aesthetic ways. Dead trees in the forest were beautiful. Stumps and straight trunks were not. They tried to create or recreate some vestiges of village communal structures, such as starting theaters in old barns, but not like the "disco" where Leszek once played drums for all his friends during the socialist era. Often the new projects were didactic, meant to recruit villagers or educate villagers about the importance of their own past as a means to create a good future for the village. But villagers did not want to become that version of cosmopolitan, with its national park interests and views of wild nature. There were no common work projects that bonded newcomers with inhabitants who had been there longer, working and farming. Some newcomers mingled and others kept to themselves, but their presence and influence was felt nonetheless by people who had been peasants.

Adam and his Spanish wife, Nuria Selva, a wildlife biologist whom Leszek helped with her zoology doctorate on carcasses, lived in Leszek's walkable universe of the Białowieża forest. A man from Switzerland perched an elegant multistoried wooden house nearby. The former chief of police from Hajnówka built a retirement home, and well-off pension owners resided there. In other words, there were postsocialist newcomers to the village who pulled their incomes from arts grants, online work, large tourist operations, or retirement. These were people with multiple connections to the intelligentsia of Warsaw, Białystok, and beyond. This gentrification and urbanization of the village allowed Leszek to craft his image through these people.

He did so in such a way to make everyone believe that he was a kind of superman of peasant origins who didn't really like farming. His brother, Mirek spoke more often of the farm he and his brother *had* to work on with their mother throughout the 1980s and 1990s and how Mirek was the one to milk the cows and pasture them when Leszek went off to work in the Polish German borderlands for a tourist agency, then lived in Warsaw with a girlfriend, and joined a circus as a carpenter where, in his own rendering, he briefly took up a knife-throwing act until he nicked the wheel-tossed lady in the ribs. Leszek finally returned to Białowieża in the mid-1980s never to leave the forest again because "a man who is born in the forest should die in the forest," telling me how much he detested urban life.

Both of Leszek's pseudonyms, Man of the Forest and the Black Stork (a bird of the forest bogs), spoke to Leszek's belief that the forest and not the fields was his true home. In a different way than the entrepreneurs, the bed-and-breakfast owners, and the big hotels, Leszek found a niche to rework the freeman-peasant image in a way that did not involve consumption. Leszek was trying to convince his friends and acquaintances, such as Adam; the director of the Warsaw zoo, who he spoke with on his visits to the bison reserve; and even Lech Wałęsa (as Leszek insisted) that he should be known and recorded for his intimate knowledge of the forest. He would sometimes guide people to the forest, but he did not advertise or work through a tourist agency. If he was home and Adam brought someone to him, he jumped on the chance to be in the forest with visitors, but on days he was too drunk to work or too ornery to socialize, he kept to himself or socialized on his porch with neighbors.

Leszek and Mirek told me their mother was Belarusian and came from a nearby village. Their Polish father moved to Białowieża from central Poland to work for the railroad after World War II, maintaining the narrow-gauge rail system used to haul out timber. Leszek was the eldest of five children. The three sisters left for work in town. The family's fields were not just behind their house but along the Łutownia River several kilometers away and near no actual houses. This was common with property ownership in the Białowieża Forest, given centuries of partible inheritance. Leszek remembered winding rivers in his boyhood, before the county municipality drained and straightened the wetlands and rivers in the 1970s—a move enabling the growth of more spruce and pine in the forest and more arable land in the meadows. In those wetlands and rivers Leszek caught fish "with his hands." He loved to snare animals (illegally) with his father and uncles.

Although conservationists started out wanting to help and protect people like Leszek and Mirek who farmed and knew the forest, they later realized that people who farmed had a "peasant mentality" that would prevent changing their mind-set to understand the necessity and beauty of a self-willed forest, unplanted by humans and unmanaged by the forester. The forest of conservationists' dreams was encapsulated in the strict reserve portion of the National Park. Polish conservationists were not just a globally connected group; a distinctive Polish historical narrative shaped their expectations about peasants and the Russian past in Białowieża. The figurative Polish peasant served the conceptual needs of the nation—a nation working for its independence from imperial powers, its freedom from communism, and its protection of natural monuments.

Farming after 4:00 p.m.: Two Visions of Białowieża's Peasants

It took many years of living in Białowieża for me to understand two competing cultural versions of the peasant. In one version, the peasant represents a universal image, a person living close to nature, rich with tradition, generous, and not compelled by the logic of modern capitalism. In the other version, local peasants of the Białowieża Forest "outgrow" their peasant status much earlier than the postsocialist break with the past.

In the "outgrown peasant" version, the local people are a rough-hewn working class always subject to the patronage of the forester and to the industry of logging. They have a backward peasant mentality whereby nature must be put to use for practical human goals, but they can always be accused of not being real farmers, of "farming after 4:00 p.m."—that is, after work. In this version, the peasants were already becoming a kind of proletariat, knowing industry better than nature.

In the "universal peasant" version, the imaginary peasant figures into a Polish national narrative because "peasant" has been a category within a specifically Polish experience, one explained through exile and where Polish lands sat on the periphery of three empires as industrialization developed much of Europe in the nineteenth and twentieth centuries. The peasant category explains the persistence of small-scale farming in Białowieża, as elsewhere in Poland, long after peasant farming ended in the rest of Europe.

Annales school historian Witold Kula (1983) documented how Poland ended up so agrarian by the twentieth century. For much of the early Renaissance, Polish feudal enterprises focused on supplying grain to western Europe; this approach set the stage for fewer cities, with their focus on consumption over production. In these circumstances, tradition overtook market logic. Polish gentry began reforms to change the conditions of the peasantry and modernize agriculture, but as they came to legislative reform, stronger powers took over the country. During the more than 120 years that ethnic Poles fought and died for the return of their nation to the maps of Europe, expatriate nobility presented a unified relationship between Polish landowners and peasants in which both classes were deprived of freedom (Kieniewicz 1969, 79–81). Emancipation of peasants from the feudal system and ousting foreign occupiers had the potential to throw class difference aside and begin real institutional reform for a modern Polish nation.

Genteel Polish men, classes of lesser nobility and magnates, left the unscrupulous business of trade and lending to Jewish merchants while they sought dignity in the arts and sciences.[2] Among Jewish merchants, peasants, and the nobility (many petty nobility had almost as little as peasants except in title), only the nobility advocated national rebellion for the sake of all "Poles" (Opalski and Bartel 1992).

Peasants, the group of unfree laborers under the feudal system, barely saw beyond their own local condition. If ethnic Polish peasants participated in insurrections against Russia, they likely did so because their landlords pressed them into service (Nagengast 1991, 41–43). Inequalities between serfs were based on land ownership and labor obligations. Landlords could exert all kinds of demands to influence stratification in villages, including evicting families and commuting labor to other serfs. Conditions in each of the partitioned parts of Poland differed radically, as attested to by the different dates for emancipation of the serfs: Prussia in 1807, Austria in 1848, and Russia in 1861. However, Polish romantic writers living abroad, such as Adam Mickiewicz, Juliusz Słowacki, and Zygmunt Krasiński, painted the portrait of a peasantry that was sturdy and deterministic, qualities they ascribed to the Polish national character even as peasants within these lands spoke different languages; belonged to the Orthodox, Catholic, Baptist, Calvinist, or Old Believer rites; and might identify with other ruling ethnicities or empires.

Poland regained its independence in 1918. But after the end of World War I and then a bitter Polish-Soviet War (1918–21), class differentiation was still intense. The nations' lands emerged from the ruins of defeated imperial powers. Some fifteen million peasants, 3.5 million of them landless, lived in Poland. Only 43 percent of these peasants owned their own homes (Nagengast 1991, 67). These were conditions of abject poverty tied to ignorance and "primitive mentalities" that the Second Republic of Poland (1921–45) had to overcome through modernization. The agrarian question of whether peasants would ally with socialist revolutions, especially those in the eastern provinces, loomed heavily. National consciousness among Polish peasants appeared only with the war with the Bolsheviks in 1920 (Halamska 2016, 30).

Agricultural reforms in the interwar period (1919–48) attempted to distribute 2.6 million hectares to peasants with little or no land, but almost a third of farmland remained in large estates. Numerous peasant parties in this era took the lead on "political agrarianism," an ideology glorifying

Fig. 4.2. Traditional architecture in Białowieża, 2010. Photo by Janusz Korbel. Used with permission.

people who worked the land, backed by theorists who suggested an ideal type of peasant consciousness and personalities formed by peasant agriculture (e.g., Prime Minister Władysław Grabski, 1920, 1923–25) (Halamska 2016, 31).

Poland missed out again on modernization for the countryside in the years after World War II. This was a period of intense recovery after 22 percent of Poland's population perished in the war, including 90 percent (three million) of its Jewish citizens (Buchowski 2001, 16). Poland lost most of its eastern territories and minority populations by the war's end. However, land redistribution from rich to poor and often to landless farmers briefly quelled discontent. In the years 1944–48, almost ten thousand landed estates totaling 3.5 million hectares were socialized, and of those, 1.25 million hectares were parceled out to peasants (Halamska 2016, 31). Collectivization drives in that period tried to get farmers to pool their lands. Peasants' refusal to collectivize in the 1950s did not result in an application of force and massive starvation, as it had in Ukraine under Stalin's mad pace to collectivize the Soviet Union between 1928 and 1933. Three million Ukrainian peasants starved to death because of forced collectivization (Graziosi 2014).[3] Instead, private peasant landholding, meaning land producing on-farm consumption, was tolerated on this "uniquely Polish road to socialism," as the authorities called it. Life in both rural and urban areas improved, with electrification for the countryside and modern infrastructure for urban areas. In 1956, Party Secretary Władysław Gomułka officially ended the collectivization drives, three years after Stalin's death (and three years after Leszek was born). State policies intended to slowly modernize by preserving the output potential of individual farmers but subordinating them to the centralized method of the whole economy.

Where nonagricultural industries did develop, they drew their labor force from the "surplus" rural population. In Białowieża, timber and small manufacturing such as furniture making (in Hajnówka) provided employment for people who grew food for themselves and sometimes sold a bit of milk or grain to the state. Leszek trained as a carpenter in a technical forestry high school. Peasants, like Leszek's family, often fed their urban relatives desperate for staples in the shortage economies of socialism.

The intelligentsia throughout the late socialist period viewed peasants dualistically. On the one hand, they were a class of persons beyond capitalist and socialist logic. On the other hand, they could be used to support the Solidarity movement by joining the larger national project for better working conditions and intellectual freedoms. In Poland, the state's inability to collectivize peasants as a class was matched by urban perception of rural people as citizens with more goods to exchange and give away than "culture." By the 1970s, the state's policy on small farms changed to favor more specialized farms (*farmerzy*) in a push for further integration of the peasant farm into the communist economy, including loans for farm collectives to purchase machines and pensions for farmers for the first time ever in Poland's history (Korys 2018, 289). However, food shortages in the 1980s demonstrated the system's chronically unmet demand. The shortages forced many urban people to rely on their rural relatives for basic food items. As the alternating dependencies and rifts grew between urban and rural, urban Poles in Solidarity accused their rural counterparts of not thinking of the common good. Even as a small number of rural inhabitants participated in the rural Solidarity wing in the momentous events of 1980–81 (with almost no farmers taking part in this movement in Białowieża), peasants served the conceptual needs of the anticommunists far more as a figure that successfully resisted communism (anticollectivization; i.e., supporting private property) when it first took root in Poland rather than as an active political force for social change during peak moments of resistance in the 1970s and 1980s. The anticommunists wanted peasants to stand in as sentimental embodiments of their cause. Their narrative admired peasant virtue and

independence while castigating peasants as backward and narrow thinking. In other words, peasants considered only their immediate gain and
not the nation's well-being in relation to anticommunist resistance. Farmers who participated in Solidarity lobbied only for more assurances that
they could keep private property, with favorable terms for loans to purchase
equipment (Hann 1985).

But this notion that the definition of the peasant is someone who cannot be duped by the state's logic is one lodged in multiple historical and
sociological debates (Scott 1985, 2010; Taussig 1980; Netting 1993). This
idea is perhaps most attributed to the early twentieth-century Russian
economist Chayanov (1966), who theorized the peasant as a social class
for postrevolutionary Russia. The Chayanovian image of the peasant was
one in which the family farm formed the basic economic structure of the
village, and by keeping family labor for the farm (i.e., for subsistence),
peasants cannot give their labor to the state for modernization projects.
In the Soviet Union, Lenin wanted to move peasants into history, meaning
the future of international communism with its proletariat workers and
collective farms, but Chayanov advocated retaining small holders in post-
Revolutionary Russia, against Lenin's prescriptions. As peasants became
proletariat, by taking roles in industrial or urban workforces without
abandoning their commitments to the farm, they could still be "advanced"
by the communist system, as was the case in Poland and Białowieża. The
historical genesis of the postsocialist idealizations of the peasantry for the
purposes of making conservation work properly in Białowieża is tied to a
long agrarian history.

Never "True" Peasants

However, Białowieża was eastern Poland, and for many in the nature conservation community, that meant Białowieża residents were always under
suspicion for their sympathies toward Russia and communism. Defining
Białowieża as eastern Poland, and a royal forest, adds yet another layer
to this "true" peasant depiction. In the deep historical time of the royal
Białowieża forest, peasants were never true peasants because they were
given land title by Polish and Lithuanian royalty for their service as beaters
in the hunt and forest guards. Undoubtedly this relationship is complicated,
but it explains what Leszek was doing with his Man of the Forest creation.
Leszek was a Man of the Forest on a stage that had been set by the rules of

empires, specific to Białowieża in its high status as a royal hunting preserve or source of valuable timber.

Catherine the Great's Russian rule took Białowieża villagers' land ownership rights away in a single 1795 document, with the tsarist seal robbing all beaters, wardens, foresters, and beekeepers of their unique status in feudal Poland. Villagers went to work for mostly German, private landlords. The way this sweeping history looks if you identify as Polish today is that Polish royalty provided unparalleled freedom for villagers compared with the rest of feudal Europe. Tsarist Russia took that freedom away. And in the communist period, the anticommunist resistance would see communism as always being Soviet-imposed.

Communist Poland's goal of attempting to get peasants to join industrial projects succeeded in the Białowieża Forest. In Białowieża, foresters enrolled local people in forest planting and other work such as clearing brush. Men often worked for State Forests as salaried employees in addition to farming. Women and children cleared branches after a felling operation in the winters, purportedly doing so voluntarily. People would go to the forest when the forester required help, earning a day's or week's wages. There was not much to buy. The shop might have two pairs of shoes and cheap cigarettes.

Many local people who lived through this period, including Leszek, remembered the communist period fondly. I have yet to meet a village inhabitant with ties to forestry or farming who scorns the communist period for its hardship or social tension. Communism gave people homes. It let them control on-farm production, deciding what to plant and how much. The system kept villagers hopeful about reproducing themselves culturally in the village. Villagers talked about the hardships of that era as signs of a populated village (in comparison to today's emptying out).

In 2012, for example, when Leszek, Mirek, and their aunt shared three "apartments" in the house of less than eight hundred square feet, they all spoke about the past as a time of abundance. In the 1970s, seven people lived in Leszek and Mirek's part of the house and five in the aunt's part of the house. During communism, everyone had the dual life of work in the forest and work on the farm. The village was growing back after the ravages of World War II. The village was an intensely social place, with feast days, marriages, births, and work exchanges. And every June or July, when it was dry enough, villagers went together to the meadows to cut the tall grasses for hay. Where people went in the fields, the storks followed.

White Stork in a Field of EU Regulation

In the 1990s, 25 percent of the world's breeding white stork population nested seasonally in northeastern Poland. The Białowieża Forest region was renowned for its hundreds of breeding pairs. No other bird today is as synonymous with the Polish village as the stork. The Warsaw airport sells stuffed stork toys and other trinkets next to folkloric plastic dolls and hand-carved jewelry boxes. A stork nesting on a roof, barn, or nearby telephone pole brings human fertility and good luck. Throughout the heat of the summer, the birds will arch their long necks, nearly touching the crown of the head to the spine, and let out long clicking sounds like the release of a ratchet winch. Although the birds seemed to show up in the spring one at a time, their late-August departure was collective and dramatic. A thousand or more storks would gather in one farmer's field for over a week before departure and then take off on their migration together in a cloud of flapping wings.

Without peasant agriculture, the storks began to disappear. Villagers lamented that the breeding pairs, mated for life, produced fewer and fewer offspring each year. They blamed it on their own exit from farming. "The birds don't have anything to eat," eighty-year-old *Pani* Nina told me. "It all lies fallow." White storks eat grasshoppers and frogs. If the shallow ponds get choked with vegetation because there is no grazing and cool a few degrees because they are shaded, no frogs lay eggs. And the frogs and grasshoppers rely on a cow's hoof depression in the wet meadows, creating a cool protective microclimate to hop between ponds and forest. White storks, traditional farming, grazing cows, hand scything, and the liveliness of the village were all intertwined in residents' landscape memories.

Much of the transition from 1989 to Poland's entry into the European Union in 2004 undermined the continuity of life in the Polish village by targeting this system of extensive smallholder farming, not to mention eliminating two thirds of jobs for State Forests. Budgetary logic demanded the agricultural changes. The European Union subsidizes its farmers generously. But French or German farmers make up only 2 or 3 percent of the French and German populations, as opposed to Poland's 14 percent in 2017 (Statistical Yearbook of the Republic of Poland 2019). And the 1990s EU subsidies to farmers under the Common Agricultural Policy took up more than half of the total EU budget. If Poland and other postsocialist economies were going to join the European Union, then structural demographic changes would work to reduce farmers. More capable and younger farmers would purchase their neighbors' farmland, grow commodities, obtain equipment to increase the scale of production, and rival their competitors' output. Others would move to the city or grow the tourism sector. From 2003 to 2010, there were 30 percent fewer farmers in Poland, with almost a million farmers transitioned out of farming (Eurostat Statistics for Poland 2012). Those dynamics were at work on the larger national scale but not at the scale of the Białowieża Forest, where small fields were hemmed in by the great woodland.

Outside of the forest's borders, entrepreneurial farmers could purchase bigger parcels of land. They could apply chemical fertilizers and herbicides, which were to be banned from the critically sensitive habitats of Białowieża. Although the amended sandy soils grow beautiful garden vegetables and grain was always part of the fields in Białowieża, the extraordinary cost of purchasing your neighbor's land and the value of that land for tourist enterprises were the biggest reasons why farming disappeared in the hamlets of Białowieża.

The European Union designed programs to subsidize small-scale, low-tech, old-breed farming in areas with high natural value, such as Białowieża. Agri-environmental subsidies for EU farmers worked hand in hand to protect lands designated in the EU-mandated NATURA 2000 program. All EU member countries must set aside their best ecologically valuable habitat for nature protection, with high penalties for noncompliance. For the first decade of EU membership, I did not hear of anyone with land in Białowieża who signed up for agri-environmental funds. But by 2014, almost everyone who owned meadows received the subsidies—still at 20 percent less than EU subsidies for competitors in France or Germany—but no one was actually farming. The municipal administrative offices reported two cows on the village record in 2012; the cows were gone in 2017. Villagers could say on paper that they were still farmers, but they did not cut the meadows themselves. Białowieża's "farmers" hired equipment operators from outside of the area who drove their mowing machines to the fields and were paid a set rate to mow. Bison began to use the meadows devoid of humans. In some ways, these nature management practices benefited storks, which returned in higher numbers following the return of mowing.

Conservation organizations hope the EU policies will bring the number of white storks back into a total portrait of meadow and forest. There have been early signs of breeding success combined with a grant-funded con-servation project that digs and maintains frog ponds. There is less urgency than in the early 1990s about saving peasant farming but more programs to pay for managing nature.

Reality Shock: The Postpeasant in the European Union

When unsuspecting people are confronted by the complexities of the European Union, they tend to develop an ambivalent relationship with the idea of Europe, which is what Stanislaw Mucha's film *Reality Shock* is about. Leszek's appearance in the 2005 production implicitly engaged this European peasant legacy, much more than the film would explicitly let on. *Reality Shock* is far from a film about the peasantry or human/nature relations in the Białowieża Forest region. But it gets its audience to think about how the European Union's arcane bureaucracies and mandates for everything from education to farming drive local cultural response, the kind that I saw with and through Leszek. *Reality Shock* was made in the meadows and forest outside Leszek's house and in the nearby logging town of Hajnówka.

This film is absurdist. It starts with a model airplane buzzing over a map (think *Casablanca*) and the narrator announcing (in German) that they are headed to the Polish *Urwald*, translated in the English subtitle as "jungle." We learn that this old forest, in some obscure representation, might be telling of a relationship between the west and the "rest" on the first day of entry into the European Union. The characters, including Leszek, contest contact in the new era. Although many locals from Hajnówka and the Białowieża Forest region appear in the film, Leszek is clearly the star. Mucha gives Leszek improvisational space to talk about his Man of the For-est character. Leszek guides the film crew into the forest to look for bison, and all they find is a person dressed in a shabby white bear costume lazily holding the EU flag over one shoulder, kicking down scrawny birch trees. Later, Leszek wears a business suit and leans against a pile of stacked logs in the forest describing his work in a circus. Often Leszek shoots guns and sets off grenade explosives. The viewer is left to interpret what seems to make little sense on the surface. Leszek sits in a field at a table, for example, listen-ing to a Russian punk jazz ensemble, with the lead singer belting out grav-elly tones while a lollipop-sucking Catholic priest is tied to a tree. Leszek drinks shot after shot of a light purple-colored cleaning alcohol, *Denaturat*, throwing pawns from a chess set at the priest. This scene conjures a murky portrait of Russian history, drinking woes (where poverty drives people to ever cheaper highs), and contempt for Polish moral authority in the hinterlands.

Residents of Hajnówka and the villages of Białowieża told me the film mocked them when it veered from Leszek performing his character, which they loved, to "reality." In such a scene, a farmer guiding his one cow down a dirt road talks about a UFO sighting from thirty years ago. There's a drunk man with an eye patch blabbering on nonsensically while hanging out with gravediggers in Hajnówka, and a "gypsy" reads fortunes about Poland's future in the European Union, which is eerily foreboding. *Reality Shock* does leave its viewers "shocked," maybe because of the film's brazen rendering of real village and small-town people stylized to make the point that the European Union might not know who all its new members are.

The village, the forest, and the postsocialist industrial logging town also mock back in the film. They mock the EU capacity for unification. Rural tradition gets left behind and distorted in an encounter with the European Union. Never nostalgic for tradition, the film, which starts with thousands of geese bursting out of an industrial holding facility, concludes with Leszek killing the film crew. He uses an old peasant well with a weighted drop bucket as cover. As the crew collapses in feigned death, a startled white stork flies out of her nest. Shortly thereafter, the director returns to Leszek for answers. Mucha asks, "Leszek, how will it be in the new Europe? Do you have a vision of Europe?" "It will be worse than it is," Leszek responds sadly and blankly in the most candid moment of the film. The long-held image of a subdued Leszek is the one we are left with.

In all the years that I knew Leszek, he was never more bitter about a social encounter than that with Mucha. Before Leszek saw *Reality Shock*, he spoke of the casting and film shoot as if he were on his way to the life he wanted and deserved. But once he had seen it, on a DVD copy, long after its premier, Leszek never passed an opportunity to cast his derision at Mucha. Leszek told me that Mucha appeared at a screening in nearby Białystok (eighty kilometers away) and didn't invite him. He didn't even send Leszek a copy of the film. All Leszek had to show were some promotional shots from the film, which he often thumbed over when I drank coffee at his house. "If I see that guy again, the knife will open on its own in my pocket," he threatened.

Mediating History and Image

Because of the popularity of *Reality Shock* and my fondness for Leszek, I jumped into this mix of people who wanted to give breathing space to the Man of the Forest. There was more to tell, more for Leszek to tell than Mucha or Leszek's short appearances in Adam's shows. I wanted a format to disrupt tourist projects while speaking to those with a desire for the peasant image. But making a film and pointing a camera at your informants is different than situating yourself in the village as an ethnographer and slowly and strategically asking questions over a period of years. Making a documentary film turned me into a "predator," in Leszek's eyes. He grinned when he called me this and notably referred to himself as a predator as well, which I took as a sign that I was not totally out of bounds.

In 2009, I returned to the Białowieża Forest with my video-making equipment. I learned to operate the equipment on the fly and followed Leszek around. Leszek was beautiful, usually in good form, but often criticizing me for not staging and directing more of the shots. The footage was shot with a handheld camera. The sound was poor. Other people in the village, including Mirek, the White Stork, told me to turn off the camera, questioned my motives, or said they would speak but allow me to record only their voices. They wanted the viewfinder off.

Marek, a sawmill owner asked suspiciously, "What is this film about?" Without waiting for an answer, he said, "I don't want to be in it." He and others thought I might make them appear as *Reality Shock* had, as a parody of themselves, even as I tried to use my long-term relationships as an insider/outsider to involve more people in what I said and believed was a "community-based film." Without funding and now four months pregnant, I paused the project until I was back in Poland on another research grant in 2011. At that time, I engaged professional feature film maker Jodie Baltazar. We fundraised US$8,000. Leszek and Mirek were each paid US$500. The shots became staged with a boom microphone hovering just outside the frame of every scene. Baltazar was looking for a character story, which I did not necessarily object to, but I wanted to tell the story of the two brothers, the Black and White Storks, and how their lives paralleled the lives of the namesake birds. I wanted to show entanglements between the forest and fields and the difficulty of knowing the "truth" about these men and about the forest. And I wanted to do this by being present to document what unfolded without prompts. Any intimacy I had developed or ideas about a "man of the forest" that I wanted to present could not just be staged for the camera.

Given our equipment rentals and other people's schedules (not to mention my then one-year-old child and my filmmaker having to fly back to the United States as her mother was dying), we could stay for only a few short shoots. Without Leszek or Mirek owning phones, we could not just call the brothers to tell them we were coming by: "Are you ready for the shoot today?" Nor could we rely on them to be home when we scheduled times to shoot. Sometimes they were too hungover to get out of bed. But we obtained 23 sixty-minute cassettes of footage, not all equal to the story I had intended. Worst of all, for the goals of the film, we could not get Leszek to go into the forest with us much. He experienced intense cramps in his leg, which made walking difficult.

Within a year we had a rough cut. On another trip to Poland, I took the cut to Teremiski for an exclusive screening with people who appeared in the film and their families. About sixty people showed up. When the conservationists appeared in the film, the villagers booed. They laughed at Leszek and nodded in agreement at their own accounts about the forester being the proper "boss" and "expert." After all their reasoned objections to being on camera, some took offense at their cameos: "Why didn't you show more of me in the film?" Then at the film's end, Leszek stood up and got everyone talking about the number of trees they planted in the forest, who had planted more, as if he were the leader of a memory brigade. He seemed to do this to divert attention from the film's portrayal of Leszek with Adam Wajrak, which might call to mind that infamous episode of the *Animals* television series in which they had appeared and he had seemingly condemned logging. Before a longer dialogue could unfold, we were cut short by the start of a 7:00 p.m. soap opera that everyone wanted to return home to watch. Leszek told me he approved of the film and assured me that I had his permission to take it to Cannes. *Black Stork White Stork* is on YouTube today (Blavascunas and Baltazar 2014).

I cannot be the judge of how I improved on Leszek's Man of the Forest rendering. But the attempt provided a self-reflection of how Leszek pulled me and the other image makers into his universe and how Leszek, by being unrepresentative of any kind of average villager, was still operating in a cultural milieu. I, too, like the conservationists, was asking Leszek to reorganize himself for ecology, using the peasant past to do so, using film to draw him into a cosmopolitan world that he used his agency and character to shape. We were partners, although not equal, in shaping Białowieża as a cosmopolitan place where one looks for the authentic.

Beyond the Mud: Postpeasant Possibilities

Leszek bridged roles and relationships, remaining materially poor throughout his life. Even his right to ride his bicycle three kilometers to the nearby store was taken from him when police caught and fined him 1,000 złoty for riding drunk. The court ordered a punishment far exceeding the "crime," taking away his bicycle-riding privileges for a year and half. Adam paid Leszek's fine. And Leszek sometimes defiantly took to the road. But in immaterial ways, Leszek maximized his social capital in this new world hungry for an authentic forest dweller.

Leszek died in 2012 of tumors in his lungs and kidneys, like Simona, a victim of virulent and unexpected cancer. He did not just walk into the forest and lay himself down to rest, as Leszek or Adam once projected he would when he was still strong and entertaining, "For a Man who was born in the forest should die in the forest. And I would even *want* to die in the forest!" (emphasis in original). He died in a hospital in Hajnówka, the pain dulled by morphine, and they buried his body in a Catholic cemetery near the village *Zabłotczyzna* (meaning "beyond the mud"). Within a week of his diagnosis he was gone, fifty-eight years young. Adam emailed me with updates and then the news of his death and funeral, which I could not attend because I was in the United States with my young daughter. I learned that Leszek asked Adam to make copies of *Black Stork White Stork*, the rough cut, so he could distribute them on CD to the doctors and nurses at the hospital. This was the greatest gift Leszek could have given me, an appreciation of our relationship through the years of friendship, research, and filming. But I wonder if I let Leszek cross over to the place I knew he wanted to go. Did I let him become cosmopolitan through his Man of the Forest persona? Is he part of a national longing for the figure of the peasant, where the figure is already safe in the past and Leszek on his way to the future?

Leszek brought together a surprising range of identities. He was an artist, creatively borrowing material that belonged to everyone to individuate himself. He was the village drunkard. He represented the past of a forest-dwelling freeman. He ran from the idea that he was a peasant.

I knew a few things about Leszek for sure. He consistently shared certain positions. He did not want an expanded Białowieża National Park.

Fig. 4.3. Leszek Szumarski with Adam Wajrak, 2011. Jodie Baltazar. Used with permission.

He wanted friends, and he wanted a forest that he could spend much of his day in and that felt like the forest of his youth, with logging *and* with many old trees. Leszek did not want to conform, to be like his neighbors and open a tourist business. He never wanted to be a farmer. He wanted to be a "legend of this place." But oddly, he could only be the representative Man of the Forest because people like me, and Adam, biologists, restaurant owners, and countless other people who used and interacted with Leszek wanted a "man of the forest"—a funny guy, a friend, and a knowledgeable expert about the forest and its history.

The postcommunist moment of nature conservation tensions was one in which most urban Polish tourists, and a small number of foreign nature lovers, came to see the primeval forest. This forest had come to most tourists' attention only after the fall of communism. Tourists, especially Poles, came expecting images of eastern, peasant, rural Poland. But a growing clientele did not enjoy the mosquitoes and mud. They spent more time in the spa-like hotels, themed around bison, than actually going into the strict reserve national park.

In this world of themed attraction tourism, Leszek made himself into a fantastical character. He used and manipulated the moment of people looking for authenticity in the forest, cloaked in tourist kitsch, to really become someone who would speak to many people. And I do not believe he was being false or fearful when he said something that Adam and his friends liked, as in Adam's TV show appearances, and another when he claimed that "he hated environmentalists." We all wanted Leszek and he wanted us, and when I say "us," I mean anyone who cared about the forest as either a logged forest or a national park—anyone looking to stabilize the forest's meaning in terms of which pasts matter.

Notes

1. One bed-and-breakfast owner reported an 80,000 złoty grant in the late 1990s to start her bed and breakfast (US$20,000 in the year 2000), amounting to two or even three years of salary for many employed Poles at that time.

2. By the end of the seventeenth century, nearly three quarters of the world's Jewish population lived within the borders of the Polish republic, and Poland was described by Jews as a haven in a world of persecution. Class relations during the partitions were highly fraught with differences and contradictions. Classes rapidly disintegrated as new social classes formed and took shape in each partitioned area. Yet Jews did not participate in farming, whereas some Polish petty nobility farmed (Abramsky, Jachimczyk, and Polonsky 1989, 1–5)

3. Known as the *Holodomor*, or "terror famine," in Ukraine (see Graziosi 2014).

5

BORDERLINE ENGAGEMENTS

Relict Forest, Relict Communism

Ambiguity at borders is both commonplace and unsettling, especially for nations like Poland with shifting twentieth-century borders. The reason for drawing the border is suspended in an anxiety about what might erupt from history. Since 2004, Europe's last primeval forest has straddled the border with the European Union. It straddles the border with one of the last European dictatorships, Alexander Lukashenko's Belarus. It was the Soviet-Polish border until 1991. Before 1945, the area was briefly the Second Republic of Poland (when the border of Poland was much farther east) and, before that, the Russian Empire (1772–1918). Together, a relict forest and a relict of communism created an imaginative geography on the Polish side of the forest. Landscape aficionados and tourists animated the forested border as a site of progress against Poland's communist past.

Because the Białowieża Forest is a space of multiple representations covering valuable timber resources and primeval woodland, it became a flexible idea in the postsocialist decades—an idea through which Belarusian and Polish as well as European relationships were imagined. Its ambiguity within different interpretations lent the forest a kind of unruly power that debating sides harnessed for their own ends and that refracted perceived differences between Poland and Belarus and between Poles and Belarusians. Under a Polish imaginary of relict nature and relicts of the Soviet, Russian, and communist pasts, the forest became an object that was supposed to usher in a new type of normality for an EU member, a normality in which some relicts were treasured markers of continuity from the past and others useless appendages, better amputated for the sake of the body politics. How did this happen as marginal rural residents became intertwined with the aspirations and consumption patterns of tourists and landscape aficionados?

The communist past afforded new opportunities to act out identities at the forested border. Themed hotels and restaurants, with campaigns to "save the primeval forest," became the sites of taming and negotiating the forest's and the border's ambiguity. Polish tourists and landscape aficionados played with and in their forested border with Belarus. Traveling to the forest, including its tourist attractions, seemed to arouse the creative powers of these Poles to transform their relationship with communism.

"Play" figures prominently in this geographic and ethnic imagining of east and west as a way to escape the more burdensome parts of Polish and Russian history. In play, people come dangerously close to encounters that do not happen in everyday life (Geertz 1973). By engaging in these potentially risky encounters, they reaffirm their status. Meaning is shaped in the encounters of play as people engaged in play also know the seriousness of not playing. At times, for example, ethnic Poles inserted their own images into legends and the romance of the past for the purpose of enjoyment. Certainly, politics intruded on fantasies as soon as they were animated, like the Belarusian government's jailing of Polish media during the 2006 presidential elections in Belarus (BBC News 2016). Nonetheless, real-life politics did not stop those who would use the past's reenactment to affirm their own identities in the present.

In this context, I borrow Clifford Geertz's (1973) well-known concept of "deep play" to explore Poles' antics at the forested border, such as hiding from park rangers or feigning one's signature on fake Communist Party membership forms. Deep play is the idea that people activate meaning in play form. Geertz developed it from his fieldwork observations of an illegal cock fight in Bali in the 1950s. "Playing" during the cockfight and as those betting ran from the police enabled Geertz to see how the cockfight, including its illegal nature, reflected as much about the people "in play" as it did about the actual cockfight. The cockfight was a series of "texts" to be read and interpreted for the anthropologist. But Geertz imbued the cockfight with the deepest meaning of all: culture, in the grand sense. The cockfight *is* Balinese culture, as it is also play. Deep play does not threaten culture but rather enriches it and is not ordinary play. Deep play is deep because the stakes are actually high.

In that sense, how are Polish tourists and landscape aficionados—meaning people who love the look and feel and history of the landscape—

activating meaning in the forest in relation to communism? How are they doing this as a faction of Polish society eschews the lingering communist "taint" in society and politics? The forested border with Belarus became a place to explore and internalize the communist past for these groups, not abolish it.

Geertz wrote about culture in the static sense, as a series of attributes belonging to a particular group. Thomas Malaby (2009, 207) reminds us that Geertz saw games as appraisals of unchanging social orders, which is why anthropologists need to look at the experience of games as something open ended and indeterminate: "Viewed this way, games assume a powerful relationship to human practice and social process. What is more, this view allows us to see how games may be related to a particular mode of experience, a dispositional stance toward the indeterminate. This is an aspect of experience that disappears from view when practice is left out in favor of materiality or representation." As I use the notion of deep play, I zero in on the question, "Why play?" in the postsocialist era—agreeing with Malby's assertion that play becomes play because of its unknown outcomes.

The Schengen Area, the European Union's open-border policy for twenty-six EU member countries, might indicate that the border at the edge of Schengen is a strict site of opposition, just as it was in the Soviet era.[1] Play is not officially encouraged, and the European Union and Belarus continue to strictly police the border. Importantly, the Białowieża forested border delimits the Schengen Area. Schengen formally included Poland in 2008. A large barbed-wire fence prohibits the movement of animals and people. Soviets erected the fence in 1981, at the height of the Solidarity movement, when they feared political unrest spilling over the border.

Equally if not more significant, the Soviet Union came to an official end in the forest. In 1991, in what is today the Belavezhkaya National Park at the Viskuly Estate hunting lodge, the Belavezha Accords provided autonomy to nations within the Soviet Union. Three of the fifteen Soviet Republics— Belarus, Ukraine, and Russia—signed the agreements December 8, 1991. Shortly thereafter, in 1994, former state farm manager Alexander Lukashenko became the first elected president of Belarus. He eliminated term limits, stayed in power for more than two decades, and made the Viskuly Estate one of his personal homes. Yet, not once did I hear anyone speak of or reference the famous accords in Białowieża, Poland—not those living in the forest who considered themselves Belarusian nor foresters, conservationists, or tourists.

Instead, I followed years of discourse about the "exotic" Belarus (from everyone except the Belarusian minority), referring both to the neighboring country and to Belarusians within Poland; Belarus created the conditions to become "other." In many ways, Belarusians' inability to embrace democratic norms turned them into objects of Polish play. What was as a stake?

Imagined Geographies

"Othering" can occur anywhere. You take a place and its people to whom you feel superior and cast them as your alter ego (Buchowski 2006; Zarycki 2014). Where you are "modern" or "rational" or "developed," they are "soulful" and "deeply cultural" and also always "backward." Edward Said (1978, 3) famously elaborated on the use of othering in *Orientalism*, when he wrote, "European culture gains strength and identity by setting itself off against the Orient as a sort of surrogate and even undergrounded self." Proverbial western and eastern Europe did this with each other for much of European modern history. Western Europe was synthetically associated with rationalism, progress, and invention, and eastern Europe mapped as a fiction of romantic nationalists fighting for unobtainable democracy in otherwise inefficient peasant lands (Wolff 1994).

As the European Union admitted new member countries in 2004, Poland and eight other countries joined but not without loud discordant factions. "Marginal" Europeans continued to feel marginal, in many senses of the word, more than a decade after entry. Citizens of what is now more appropriately referred to as "Central Europe" still feel ignored in their historical interpretations, economic opportunities, and cultural contributions. But culturally, they live within notions about competing territories, unjust international treaties, and whether or not being within or without certain borders makes them peripheral or central.

As for Schengen, a Europe without borders did not let Central Europeans dwell in a melancholic romance about the virtues of being a country that suffered. How to remember the communist past was an issue of borders. If Poland wanted to be a good member of the European Union, of the "legitimate" west, it had to remember communism as a backward system with backward cultural roles (Dunn 2004; Mark 2010; Buchowski 2006; Wedel 1998) and eliminate the habitus that sustained its own peripheralism (Berdahl 1999). Poles not only had to reform their legal codes but also had to behave as if they had conquered any vestiges of communism.

Svetlana Boym (2001, 241) has argued that the Iron Curtain that separated East and West served to let people find their alter egos, for which an encounter with difference is necessary. The imagined Western "rational man" needed the soulful feminized East, with her suffering intact. An important part of the love affair for those trapped in the East was the power and freedom they dreamed about if only they could acquire the means to purchase more items signifying comfort and status. Obtaining material comfort would not diminish their souls, as it had in the west.

An array of scholars documented the disappointing results of real encounters in a "united" Europe (Rakowski 2016; Knudsen and Frederikson 2015; Dunn 2004; Kideckel 1993; Pine 1996, 2002). Some countries fared better than others, and class divides grew in all countries. Nevertheless, on all global indexes of a country's economic health, Poland always stood out in the media and official International Monetary Fund (IMF) reports as the shining example of a sturdy growing economy, even after 2008, when many European countries suffered through imposed austerity measures and economic downturns. But these reports often underestimated the rise of inequality. The top 1 percent of Poles captured twice as large a portion of the total income growth as the bottom half (Bukowski and Novokmet 2017). Visit most ordinary Poles in their homes and, even with remodeled apartments, flat-screen televisions, and other markers of a robust economy, the differences between an eastern and western European standard of living are pronounced. Many educated Poles such as schoolteachers and public servants reported to me that they earned less than US$1,000 per month.[2] A park employee working for nineteen years in the Białowieża National Park told me she took home US$500 a month in 2017.

Playing with the communist past stems from this mixed anxiety about purchasing power—having more but not enough. For intellectuals, as Boym (2001) has argued, nostalgia for the communist past also lies in the purity of youthful struggles, when the border was guarded by Soviet tanks. They can be nostalgic for the receding moral purity of communist-era struggles, at least for those who partook in youthful resistance to authority. The result of such nostalgia was a type of border confusion, albeit mediated by the forest itself through its very ambiguity.

When I write that the forest mediates nostalgia and othering, I mean that the forest is a type of slippery object in this play. Even as the competing groups argue for different forest management and pronounce the forest's known qualities through science, the forest necessarily remains unknown. Białowieża is both the last primeval forest of Europe and a commercially logged woodland. In other words, it is both "pristine" and "imperiled," "already ruined," and the site of best hope for knowing a "wild European forest." The forest's ambiguity is compounded by Polish tourists and landscape aficionados in association with things Belarusian. Moreover, the forested border has a shape and form unlike a border at a river crossing, where you can see the other side, or the mountain pass with its demarcated ridge. The Białowieża Forest is a tangled, overgrown barrier and enabler between Poland and Belarus.

Poland joined the European Union with a series of national axes to grind about history. The Poles emphasized their legitimate place in the west, especially in contrast to Belarus, a nation without a strong, coherent national narrative (Hirsch 2005; Rudling 2014). In addition, according to many people I spoke with in Poland, Belarusians had not done the collective work to secure their democracy following the revolutions of the late twentieth century. Next to Belarus, democratic Poland envisioned itself as Europe proper. It was self-determined and sovereign.

President Lukashenko's political moves, such as jailing opposition candidates, befriending and selling weapons to former Iranian President Mahmoud Ahmadinejad, dissolving parliament and then hand-picking replacements, played into Poles' ideas about themselves, the Belarusian minority in Białowieża, and their Belarusian neighbors. Poles wanted to help free Belarus by exporting their history of anticommunist organizing, as demonstrated by support rallies and frequent newspaper coverage sympathetic to the Belarusian opposition around the elections of 2006. Poles aligned themselves with harsh western criticism of Lukashenko.

Through promotion of Poles' own accomplishments since the free elections of the 1990s, Belarusians appeared to be trapped by their own stereotypical predispositions. In the Poles' course of development, the forest embodied ideas about an expanding Europe with entitlements for Poles and a regressive east, whereby Poles could redeem their place in democratizing Europe through assisting the Belarusian underground. The appearance of Belarus as a holdover from the communist past and the forest as a timeless object outside of politics did more than just let Poles "save" their Belarusian neighbors or generate stereotypes. In Białowieża, Belarus enabled Poles to play—but maybe you can only play when you feel confident and believe you have a good chance of winning.

Keeping the Present at a Safe Distance

The deep ecology activist, photographer, architect, and journalist Janusz Korbel opened his home to hundreds of activists and scholars, both Polish and foreign, who arrived in Białowieża needing a guide to politics and culture. In his humble cottage, they listened to Janusz marshal heart-felt and persuasive evidence of why the forest needed better protection.

Along with his love of the forest was a love for authentic regional distinctiveness. When he first arrived in Białowieża in 2002, after living most of his adult life in the mountains of southern Poland, he had already spent a decade organizing protests against logging of Białowieża. He filled his house with old regional antiques. He hung hand-embroidered decorative linens on the wall, the outline of a girl jumping rope. He laid out simple, long floor mats, assembled from rag fibers, that one can no longer purchase or make. And he fed two clay-tiled stoves by hand through the long winter, in the poorly insulated rooms of his house.

Janusz's sensibilities condensed into a nostalgia-based activism to protect the forest's heritage and its distinctive local culture. When I first met Janusz in 2004, through the scientist and animal rights activist Simona Kossak, he subscribed to the notion that Belarusian culture was somehow humbler than Polish culture.

A slightly hunched yet sinuous man with long gray curls framing his face, Janusz possessed all the radical sensibilities and energy of his younger counterparts. In 1994, Janusz led one of the first protests against logging of Białowieża with his group Workshop for All Beings (Pracownia na rzecz Wszystkich Istot). Together with friends, he found a semitruck driver willing to haul an oak stump, several hundred years old, from Białowieża to the parliament in Warsaw to show the world the injustice of logging ancient trees. Janusz also exhibited maturity, thinking beyond his younger colleagues about the need for planning and design according to historic patterns of settlement. If one were going to save the forest from logging, one also would have to save the villages from brazen modernity.

Janusz felt no embarrassment about being a hopelessly unreformed romantic. He tried to keep the more tawdry components of the present at a safe distance. He loved the bricolage of artists who could take traditions and breathe new life into them, such as his friend Todar, a rock musician from Belarus who created revamped tributes to the ancient Slavic gods, in an open-throat voice. But foreign architectural elements

Fig. 5.1. Janusz Korbel. Photo by Agnieszka Sadowska. Used with permission.

pained Janusz. Plastic siding, oversized pillars, bright red aluminum—these did not belong.

Although trained as an urban planner, Janusz spent most of his life in villages. Like a docent at a museum, he rarely let an opportunity pass to draw his guests' attention to the arrangements of space for the village. Houses on many streets were built close together because of the Russian taxation policies of the nineteenth century. The gingerbread ornaments on the cottages were an early twentieth-century addition to the houses when exiles returned through Russia. Fields and meadows abutting forests created a synergetic living architecture with the lapwings and bison.

For Janusz, the Białowieża Forest was not simply another place to appropriate rural traditions. He was returning home in 2003 when he relocated from the mountains near Bielsk-Bialo—home to the region of Podlasie, where his grandparents and parents were born and where he spent much of his childhood on the family estate. He was reared in a family that lost almost everything in World War II except their manor house. In the new era, his cousin transformed the manor into a commercial tourist operation called "The European Stork Village." His boyhood retreat now lured tour groups that came to see an unnatural conglomeration of stork nests. More than twenty pairs of storks returned to the manor each year and were fed sausages, among other things, by his cousin. The staff helped to clean and maintain the nests. Janusz remembered cranes from his childhood, not storks particularly. Janusz grudgingly accepted that some form of tourism would irrevocably alter the mood and feel of his childhood landscapes, but he did not exist easily with the upheavals threatening an authentic relationship with the region.

Janusz took to fighting battles that would keep the garishness of modernity at a distance. He worked to suspend objects and landscapes in this spiritual realm, as a living presence beyond their usefulness in a productive economy. He saw Belarus in the landscape as an old regional culture that felt rather than showed, that extended back much further than the Western Belarusian Communist Party or Lukashenko, and that included a range of cultural experiences during the communist period.

Every one of Janusz's campaigns centered on halting development— or, rather, developing without added attractions. He fought to remove an adventure train ride and beer advertisements from the Białowieża National Park. He foresaw that tourism would drive up real estate values and build on the communal pastureland no longer in use, so he marched into the municipal offices and demanded land-use maps, rallying people to change zoning against development. He organized public debates with the department of roads to stop the cutting of corridors of old trees that protected agricultural fields from high winds. Importantly, he worked with Belarusian and Orthodox intelligentsia, local people from the nearby logging town of Hajnówka, to form the Society for Landscape Protection. That organization connected longing for these cultural details with concrete actions for protecting nature and landscape. In multiple ways, the society fought to keep the region free of commercialization. Commodification of the forest region favored space as a functional receptacle for consumption rather than being a place of dwelling.

In 2000, the world's largest hotel chain, Best Western, franchised the former state-owned hotel Żubrówka, named after the fragrant sweet grass on which the woodland bison grazed. Visitors paid to park in Żubrówka's gated lot. The hotel opened the village's first nightclub, the Czar's Boudoir. Male waiters wore skin-tight black pants and billowing silken red shirts. Just down the street from the Best Western, the Soplicowo hotel opened in 2003, themed around Adam Mickiewicz's 1834 epic poem *Pan Tadeusz*. As Poland's national bard, every Pole understood the Mickiewicz references within the architecture of the hotel.

The former railway station, originally commissioned by Czar Alexander II, now housed the Carska restaurant (Czar's restaurant). All trains had stopped serving Białowieża by 1993, because of budget cutbacks, and the sagging, moss-roofed building signaled a sumptuous, forgotten era that seemed like it would never return to Białowieża. Yet, in 2005, a Poznan entrepreneur meticulously restored the building. Soon it became the destination for local elites and Warsaw businessmen. By the early twenty-first century, the Białowieża village—next to the national park primeval forest—was fast becoming a stage on which to perform historical notions of both proper gentry and peasant relations and Poles' relation to former Russian domination, reflecting a more pressing obsession with communism. Within five hundred meters of the Carska restaurant, neighboring Belarus was drawn into a type of nested orientalism, like the famous Russian stacking *matroszka* dolls, where valorized essences about east and west were kept intact even as territories changed (Bakic-Hayden 1995). Janusz selectively embraced some of these tourist developments and rejected others.

For Janusz, the past at these hotels and restaurants lived in a kind of Polish chauvinism about the ascendancy of a legitimate ruling class over the rest of society, a landed class with estates and formal manners that was much diminished through Russian and later communist rule. But they also represented brazen profiteering and the soullessness that meant joining the west as part of Europe Union expansion. Perhaps because of his own elite background, Janusz found the chauvinism of the hotels and restaurants at odds with his vision of blending with the landscape and being "native," a point he emphasized repeatedly. Those who were not native tried to over-write history. He exhibited what Nietzsche (1995) called "a true historical sensibility." For Nietzsche, who distinguished the ways in which Europeans use the past to further their national history and their goals of finding meaning in the past, a true historical figure finds happiness when he knows that "one's existence is formed not arbitrarily and by chance, but that instead it grows as the blossom and the fruit of a past that is its inheritance and thereby excuses, indeed, justifies its existence—this is what today are in the habit of calling a true historical sensibility" (104).

In this vein, for example, Janusz criticized biologists' attempts to narrate the past, particularly some scientists at the Mammal Research Institute who were trying to write an environmental history of the Polish royal era. Polish royal history excluded the Belarusian minority and their identity vis-à-vis czarist Russia. Janusz scoffed at another scientist's idea to supplement the museum of Belarusian culture in Hajnówka with a museum of Polish culture to be located in Białowieża village.

In part, Janusz relinquished claims to any Polish gentry entitlement he might have inherited and instead chose to align himself with a heritage he understood as Belarusian, becoming a columnist for a Polish-Belarusian cultural monthly and bringing Belarusian musicians to Białowieża. The Belarusian language, for Janusz, was an old, pan-cultural element of the region where, in the relative liberal democracy of the nobles, diverse ethno-confessional-linguistic groups cohabited and often used Belarusian as the common language.

Janusz exercised his historical entitlement to the region by being the arbiter of taste. For instance, he and his member organization, the Society for Landscape Protection, supported the initial restoration of Carska and looked down at the hotel architecture. The owner of Carska, Michał, played only Russian ballads, especially those of Zhanna Bichevskaya, whose songs are prayer-like compositions written by an orthodox monk-poet, Yeromonach Romanon. Michał found period furniture; paintings of Czar Nicolas II, who had commissioned the station in 1903; and other fine details that marked the restaurant as historically accurate. The Best Western, by contrast, hosted car shows, and its female employees donned dresses that looked slightly like Bavarian *dirndl* while its male employees wore crisp, white, buttoned shirts under maroon vests. These costumes bore no resemblance to the area's historical dress.

Deeply embedded in Janusz's aesthetics was an embrace of things Belarusian because of their historical facticity. Belarusians belonged to the forest region, because of Russia perhaps, but not everyone knew this history as well as Janusz claimed to. He even chided "the Czar," as regulars soon called Michał, for not understanding the Russian of Bichevskaya's songs. "It's a little bit funny," Janusz told me, "because she sings an Orthodox song about people who only drink and eat and these people don't see what's going on outside of the restaurant because they lost God. But 'Czar' doesn't understand Russian good [*sic*] enough."

Border Crossing for an Imagined Geography

One of the important battles that the Society for Landscape Protection lost was the opening of a border crossing through the middle of the Białowieża Forest to Belarus in April 2005. Given the proposed role of tourism as the economic alternative to logging, one might think that Janusz, and the Society for Landscape Protection more broadly, would welcome new possibilities for exchange and for tourists to see this famous UNESCO World Heritage Site. On the Belarusian side, the whole forest received "protection" as a national park. The border crossing, for foot and bicycle traffic only, was supposed to direct tourists to the primeval forest zone dividing Poland and Belarus. The border opening could be interpreted as an apolitical act of cooperation in a tense political climate between the two countries. During the communist era, when Poland belonged to the Soviet Bloc, the border was virtually closed, with extremely limited cross-border contacts between relatives. Viewing "nature" did not challenge the Belarusian state's control. Like many transboundary nature parks, where crossing lightly manned stations signifies peace in an otherwise tense political climate (Buscher 2013), Białowieża was meant to be an open space for the free movement of people. But landscape lovers like Janusz believed that the crossing spelled further incursions into animal habitat and fragmented the forest.

Furthermore, the thick layer of asphalt indicated a road suitable for heavy car traffic. The European Union, concerned about guarding its new external frontier, financed a large, two-story, border-crossing facility; cleared a hectare of forest; and built a large parking lot. Moreover, Janusz and his associates, such as Olga, organizer of the Orthodox choral music festival, and Daniil, web designer for the city of Hajnówka, saw the border crossing as a bad political alliance between Lukashenko and Polish foresters.

For Polish tourists, however, the excursion to Belarus became an adventure into the Polish romantic past in which the Belarus of old, multi-ethnic Poland figured prominently. My own "adventure" at the Belarusian border might explain this. In 1998, before the Schengen Area and seven years before the crossing opened, I bicycled with a Polish American friend to the border gate. During Soviet times, there had been limited crossing for residents who had family on the other side of the border. When we arrived, it was not an open border-crossing era. To our astonishment, a Belarusian soldier rolled open a two-meter fence on the Belarusian side and began walking toward us. We had expected an empty border and a glance in the direction of Belarus. However, friendly looking civilians accompanied the guard. Two men and three women carried baskets of mushrooms and wildflowers. They walked leisurely in our direction, stopping exactly on the official line about twenty meters from gate in front of us. The Belarusians, with their easy and inviting manner, called to us in lilting Polish, "Dzień dobry!" ("Good day!").

They motioned for us to come over. With an ill-conceived impulse, I said to my friend, "Why not?" She had been born in Poland but was also unfamiliar with border policies. "I'll hold the camera and take a picture," she said, cautiously encouraging me and snapping one of the Belarusians as she said so. Since a Belarusian soldier was there, I assumed it must be an innocent and friendly gesture. Just as I ducked to go under the gate, a Polish soldier who had been hiding in the forest watching the entire encounter ran out yelling, "STOP!" I froze in my tracks. The Polish soldier then explained that it was a setup. If I inched any further toward their outstretched hands, they would pull me into their territory. For my illegal infraction, a large fine would be levied and possibly a few days' stay in a Belarusian holding facility before diplomatic resources could be marshaled. It was unclear to me if this situation was common. I don't know if the Belarusians had intended to pull us over the border, for they surely must have known that Polish border guards watched their side. However, Polish and foreign tourists relied on the unpredictability and unknowability of the forested border for their fun.

In Soviet times, everyone knew the potentially fatal consequences of more than hand waving at the border, of dashing toward the other side. Though people attempted to cross to the "West," few people felt motivated to jump to the Soviet Union or to Poland. No one would be waiting on the other side of the border to shuttle them to safety. Moreover, the threat of state power deterred anyone from trying. One could be arrested, imprisoned, or shot, among other fates. The People's Republic of Poland and the Soviet Union used inconsistent applications of power in that era to effectively sustain the unknown. Those in power felt a smug superiority over those who did not know what would happen to them.

In the late 1990s, before the border opened to tourists, an adventure train ride through the commercial forest featured a scenario in which the train stopped dead. "Soviets" hijacked the train and "rough-armed" ticket holders into joining the Communist Party, supplying membership cards with an early Soviet-era painting of the operation's owner, Wojciech Rynarzewski, patting Lukashenko on the back. At the end of the tour, participants went to the owner's bar in Hajnówka called U Wołodzi (meaning "At Włodzimierz," referring to Lenin's first name). There, in the bar's small shack, Rynarzewski encouraged people to dress up in Soviet soldier uniforms. He freely mixed images of Lukashenko with those of Lenin and Pope John Paul II on the interior walls. The bar stood at the edge of the open-air

Fig. 5.2. U Wołodzi bar, Hajnówka, owner Wojciech Rynarzewski. Photo by Janusz Korbel. Used with permission.

market, and frequently Belarusian petty traders drank at tables next to Polish tourists.

The flip side of this play was that it was hard for tourists to fathom this neighboring country that so routinely violated human rights. Disparaging news of Belarus made the Polish headlines weekly. I spoke with Polish tourists who had crossed the border. Responses varied: "Taka bieda!" ("Such poverty!"); "The tour guides won't let you out of their sight. You can feel the KGB"; "I think it's a military zone"; "But what a beautiful forest. You just can't see the same thing on the Polish side"; "I wish we could have traveled off the pavement though and really seen the forest." As Polish tourists experienced it, the enterprising, draconian Belarusian government that strictly policed tourists' whereabouts in the forest appeared to Poles as a failure of "European" modernity. This became especially clear from narrations about the tour's end point, home of the Belarusian Santa Claus (*Ded moroz*).

At this highly ornamented, ginger-bread-like house, an actor playing *Ded moroz* greets tourists year-round. After your visit you can pick up your

Fig. 5.3. Father Frost exhibit in the Belarusian side of the forest. Photo by Janusz Korbel. Used with permission.

Christmas gift of gingerbread at the tourist shop from costumed and bored-looking clerks with little inclination toward friendly service. All of these elements combined to provide self-recognition of what the Soviet Union was like twenty years before these tourists had the means to visit—and what Poland did not become in the present.

Kresy

Most of the tourists I spoke with returning from the Belarus tour were urban. They took advantage of new leisure time and disposable income. Polish tourists brought their imaginations about the *kresy*, or the eastern province of what was once the Polish Lithuanian Commonwealth. This land is highly mythologized in literature but also a factual political territory that included lands that belong today to Belarus, Ukraine, and Lithuania. When Poles use the word *kresy*, Belarusians and others, such as Ukrainians, Lithuanians, Jews, Cossacks, and Tartars, appear as colorful characters of the former commonwealth. They are there to support Poles in a messianic vision to restore an ancien régime of Slavic unity.

This kresy imaginary arises partly through nineteenth-century romantic novelists but also through geographer and historian Wincenty Pol, who coined the term in his 1854 novel/poem *Mohort*, relating to the times of Stanislaw August Poniatowski before the Polish partition. *Kresy* means outback, periphery, or frontier. Poles endowed the term with emotional associations about the splendors of the former republic. Writers Henryk Sienkiewicz and Adam Mickiewicz, both native sons of the kresy, wrote about the kresy as an idealized portrait of a multicultural Poland. Kresy was the eastern part of the Second Polish Republic (1918–39), constituting nearly half of the territory of the Polish state. The postwar myth of the kresy imagines a peaceful, idyllic, rural land. Schoolchildren in Poland to this day are required to recite lines from national bard Mickiewicz's most famous epic poem, *Pan Tadeusz* ([1834] 1992, 152), which intones in book 4,

> Comrades of Lithuanian kings, ye trees
> Of Switeż, Kuszelewo, Białowieża
> Whose shadows once the crowned heads did cover.

Mickiewicz wrote the poem in Parisian exile after the failure of the November 1830 uprising against Russian rule. "Crowned heads" in the poem double as the tree canopy and royalty in the tale of feuding Polish landowning families. Against the background of idyllic depictions of provincial life, the landed gentry come together in conspiracy aimed at exploiting Napoleon's conflict with Russia to restore Poland's independence. Russian encroachment on the gentry's rights unites the families in a forest hunt. The poem inspired the Soplicowo hotel, named after a disputed manor in Mickiewicz's work.

The Soplicowo Hotel opened in 2003 (and burned down in 2010), not far from the new border crossing to Belarus. It had an ostentatious design, but I heard no comments from tourists comparing the hotel on the Polish side with the Belarusian Father Frost exhibit. To my eyes, there were many surface similarities, particularly as Poles and Belarusians engaged with the idea that the primeval forest needed themed attractions for tourists. Poles believed that Father Frost could never count as a historical original, whereas Soplicowo, even in kitsch form, set the stage for historical reenactment, including the accompanying Jankiel's Tavern, named after the Jewish tavern owner who eschews European secularization in favor of

Fig. 5.4. Soplicowo Hotel, 2005. Photo by Eunice Blavascunas.

the "backward" shtetl, out of loyalty to the Polish landlords (Opalski and Bartel 1992, 90).

Soplicowo was a two-storied, thatched-roof manor with thick colum-nar pillars supporting the awning to its entrance. Tourists could enter-tain their impulses to engage some of the class elements of this period at a rotunda diorama exhibit in the parking lot. There, they could peer into a shrunken poacher's cottage, with an unmade bed, snare traps, and a jug of home-distilled vodka. Live rabbits filled one of the display cages to ani-mate historical fiction. The hotel that attempted to recreate Mickiewicz's *Pan Tadeusz* flattened and simplified Mickiewicz.

Mickiewicz was an internationalist emigrant, a poet, an essayist, a bard, a professor of Slavic literature, and a political activist. He was Poland's Byron or Goethe. Surviving Russian imprisonment for founding a secret patriotic society, he criticized the despotic tendencies of czarist Russia and traveled in intellectual circles throughout Europe. In his epic poems, dra-mas, and essays, he developed a messianic vision about the universal salva-tion of mankind that was much influenced by French thinkers interested in religious and spiritual renewal as well as socialism. Mankind needed a millenarian redeemer who would free the world from suffering and offer new revelations to bring about the Christianization of social life and rule of moral principles in international relations (Walicki 1982, 239). Just as Christ had to be crucified to redeem the world, so did Poland for the future of a brotherly union of all nations. "The most developed spirit," Mickiewicz wrote, "has a natural duty to lead the less developed ones. This is the chief dogma of Messianism" (quoted in Walicki 1982, 258). Mickiewicz embodied a borderland citizen. Born in Nowogródek, Lithuania (today in Belarus), he always thought of the region as his home. He married a converted Jew (a Frankist) and spoke Belarusian, the language of the Polish gentry in Lithuanian lands at that time.

In the nineteenth century, when Mickiewicz was writing, many Roman Catholic gentry spoke the Belarusian language. Mickiewicz sentimentalized a partitioned Poland as the "Christ of nations," with each of the powerful neighbors—Russia, Prussia, and Austria—"crucifying" Poland for the redemption of Europe. Mickiewicz's texts played an important role in developing Polish messianism, where he contrasted rural, patriarchal Poland (losing its wealth but not its soul) to the west, contaminated by the sinister forces of money.

The Mickiewicz-themed Soplicowo hotel meant that the forest with a Belarusian minority (the Polish side of the forest) was fast becoming a stage on which to perform notions of historical class relations. The themes of the hotel strongly inferred that the lands in Mickiewicz's work would remain "eastern" in the ethnic Polish tourist's imagination. In other words, Mickiewicz fought for the Polish national cause (not a Jewish, Ukrainian, or Belarusian cause); however, at the same time, national consciousness was nascent in the nineteenth century but not yet spread widely through peasant masses, who more often identified through confessional rite (Hobsbawm 1990; Hroch 2000; Gellner 1983; Jedlicki 2014). Through forest tours and in the hotel, tourists symbolically championed the Polish cause, the kresy cause, as the way for an undemocratic Belarus. Once minorities see their own interests in the larger Polish interests, they stand a chance of redemption, according to both Mickiewicz and the tourists' projections.

Polish hotel investors and tourists wished to play out the fantasy of uniting with their Belarusian brethren, who were still under the yoke of Soviet-like oppression. Polish tourists came to possess knowledge about the draconian Belarus of the present by engaging these distant ideologies when

Poles suffered for other nations. Through Soplicowo and the act of crossing to Belarus, Polish tourists exercised European citizenship, but also, through Mickiewicz and the messianic ideology, they feel that Mickiewicz's legacy protects them from vapid consumerism. Belarusians have now become their alter ego. Instead of Poles needing to turn solely to the west to prove they are better than Belarusians, they turn to their own nineteenth-century history and bard. The people who engage in the fantasies of the Soplicowo hotel, or any of the themed tourist adventures that draw on the kresy, exercise a new-found yet historical entitlement to this heritage of making Belarusians an internal "other."

An important feature of this European identity for Poles is the ability to travel, not just as migrants looking for work (e.g., going to Ireland to work as a plumber) but as tourists. The nineteenth-century romantic literature on the Polish east always provided its readers with the vantage point of gentry who returned to these lands from exile for spiritual renewal, traveling between Paris and the kresy (Eile 2000). This point would have been especially valuable during the socialist period, when people read Mickiewicz's and other popular works sentimentalizing the kresy to remember the Polish national cause of independence and to travel as a reader to faraway lands beyond their reach. The new Polish leisure class exercised its right to travel freely beyond the borders of its own state, but this is also an exercise in nation building to the internal and unexplored frontiers of its own country. In effect, Polish tourists to the forest gentrified and tamed the borderland. They moved it out of its peripheral status to a pilgrimage site to see the small patch of what they were told is "primeval nature" (the initial tourist draw) and to be in the Polish memory of the kresy. Those geographical imaginings are very much a part of the ambivalent project of Europe-making at Poland's scale of the kresy, which wishes to bring Belarus into the sphere of "democratic" Europe (Polish style) while wanting it to remain "other" so that urban Poles can have a positive identity by comparison. The primeval forest also does this.

Tours of the Forest

I had many occasions to walk among the old trees in the Białowieża National Park strict reserve. I sometimes entered with Janusz, who sat on the scientific advisory board of the national park and had a special pass. Many times I went with tour groups, both Polish and foreign, and other times with scientists to collect data. One cannot enter the strict reserve without a trained guide or special pass. Tours of the Polish section of forest designated as the Białowieża National Park Strict Nature Reserve (9% of the Polish forest area, about five thousand hectares), provide the cultural transmission necessary to sustain ideas about a primeval forest. The required guides serve a powerful rhetorical function in promoting Europe's last wild forest, especially when nature elsewhere, as in the commercial forest, is set as a comparison. Nature of the commercial forest materializes as young and humanly touched. The primeval is not as obvious. Roads transect the forest in even quadrants, where stacks of sectioned logs and educational signs enforce the idea that the Białowieża Forest relies on the forester's care. But in the commercial forest, tourists can have bonfires and walk at their leisure. The strict reserve tours require listening to the tour guides' pronouncements about nature and history.

A tour begins at a large oak gate three meters high. "We are now about to enter the primeval forest," the tour guide often begins. The guide recites from memory words written on a large poster behind her: "UNESCO World Heritage Site"; "Europe's last fragment of primary forest"; "A Man and Biosphere Reserve"; "A Natura 2000 site." Once past the gate, tourists hear about the founding fathers of the park, botanists Jan Karpiński and Władysław Szafer, whose names have been inscribed on granite markers. These tours last two to three hours and cover a well-worn loop, much of it on an old royal hunting road rutted by horse-and-cart tours. The guide draws attention to particular trees to authoritatively teach the workings of primeval nature, such as the role of dead wood in the forest and why all nine species of European woodpecker breed in the Białowieża strict reserve.

When I traveled to the strict reserve with Janusz, the forest often became the site of subversion, outside the eyes of didactic authority. Our excursions relaxed me. We shared a quiet appreciation of the same details, and we frequently exchanged quiet smiles when we saw a similar kind of beauty in these details. But there were also times when I could see how the forest became the place for Janusz to enter a kind of themed past where the "free space" of nature enabled him to be immersed within ideology about the forest.

For instance, I traveled with Janusz by bicycle to the strict reserve in September 2005. We met in silence in front of his house, got on our bikes, and rode quickly. We were going to listen to deer during mating season, and dark was coming on. The whole journey had an urgent and secret feel to it. Once past the gate into the strict reserve, Janusz motioned at the tumuli, the ancient graves of tenth-century Slavic tribes, without saying a word. These graves formed huge loaf-shaped mounds under the leaf duff. He took me to a carved-out trunk of a centuries-old pine; its top had fallen decades ago, and all that remained was a hollowed-out area about six feet high under which you could find cover, if needed. "This was probably where the bee-keepers kept out of the rain," he speculated in a whisper, curving and stooping his body to try it out, recalling the era in which local residents tended hives in the czar's forest.

We finally stopped to listen in stillness to the deer calls. Their voices shot out of their throats in agonizingly low groans. We sat directly on the forest floor, two hundred meters off the path. An owl screeched. Then it was almost completely silent, but as I listened, I could detect small forms of life settling in the leaves. The night was certainly too cold for insects. These were not mice, just the sound of things settling, small little cracks and pops in the foliage. It grew darker and darker, and the buck calls accelerated into even more ghastly cries. Soon I could not even see Janusz, who remained perfectly still. I felt awkward rustling or changing the weight of my sitting position. The moon did not come out early that night. A bicycle light suddenly cut through the blackness. Earlier on our excursion, Janusz said that he had met men in the forest the previous night as they counted deer for the park director's doctoral thesis (see chap. 3). This must be one of them I assumed. Park rangers are often seen as lesser foresters, not as protectors and interpreters of nature.

I suddenly felt like a partisan during World War II who must cover his tracks and learn the ways of the forest in order to evade capture. Janusz made a small hand motion in my direction for me to remain still and silent. After the light was at a safe distance, Janusz whispered that these were indeed the same men as last night. From the numbness in my legs, I was sure that Janusz would also be growing cold and uncomfortable. But Janusz asked me to stay for another hour. He did not want to leave before the deer counters did because the men were surely scaring away animals: "You see, we heard that owl before they came in and a few others birds, but now the forest is silent." An hour passed without us exchanging any more words. When the cyclist returned in our direction, he directed his light almost at us, but we were already lying low and the light did not catch our bodies. We waited about ten minutes after the man passed, and Janusz said that maybe now we would begin to hear some animals. We rode out slowly, but no more owls or deer made a single sound.

When we reached the gated entrance, the entourage of about ten park rangers was waiting. Park rangers were not the "friendly public servant" of the US imaginary, but a type of lower paid guard, more interested in catching people breaking the rules than protecting nature per se. I could only make the men out initially by the burning ends of their cigarettes. Not until we were right upon them did they emerge as human figures. They stared at us, yet said nothing. I attempted to broach this divide, wondering if I recognized some of them by saying politely and softly "good evening." They mumbled back indiscernibly.

I could not help thinking that there was something similar about our encounter in the forest and tourists' play-acting in the hotels. Michael Herzfeld (1997, 2004) asks anthropologists to adopt a combined "top-down" and "bottom-up" approach in what seems personal and intimate. He encourages anthropologists to theorize how spaces that seem free are, in fact, the loci where we most need to consider culture as a national and individual project. The anthropologist takes the stance of cultural relativism while maintaining her own cultural and moral beliefs. The culture of our hiding on the forest floor was based on rueful self-recognition between Janusz and the park rangers (and myself). There was a sense of complicity playing hide-and-seek in the forest, where the park rangers, affiliated with the suspicious park director Popiel (see chap. 3), were agents of a corrupt society for Janusz; we were the nature lover and the academic, both perfectly within the codes of who could enter the forest, but also encountering others in opposition.

"Cultural intimacy" is often reduced to a single plot. Herzfeld (2004) coined the term to explore how social actors often recast official idioms in pursuit of highly unofficial personal goals or enterprises but how, in doing so, they constitute national identities or official state ideologies. He encourages anthropologists to probe behind facades of national unity to explore the possibilities and the limits of creative dissent. Social actors strategically adjust to the demands of the historical moment. In this case, the plot is that national memory of communism can be played out under the cover of Białowieża's trees. The themed hotels and crossing to Belarus are enacted as a form of national memory. Janusz and I, and the park rangers, in contrast, each take stereotypes into the forest as we move across its space and conspire against one another based on simple views of good and evil. We have an imagined national community (Anderson 1983) based on exclusion, not affection.

Janusz's identity rested on fighting commercial forestry and commodification of the villages and forest. He was not like the biologists described in chapter 3, who were motivated by perceived Western meritocracy and rationality. Janusz was sustained by the "good" fight, arguably one of the kresy, where the landscape and the forest were to be the living receptacle of multicultural memory. He drew his love of place and Orthodox culture together with his deep ecology philosophy, but how unlike a romantic nineteenth century poet was he, searching for spiritual renewal in a national park. Neither soulless Western consumerism nor scientific detachment or the authoritarian habitus of communist cronyism would temper Janusz's fight for the region.

I agreed with Janusz that tourist development took some kind of life force from Białowieża. It seemed harder and harder to move about Białowieża in any quiet way, as when I first arrived. More cars, more bonfire parties in the forest, new hotels, and new money contributed to the cacophony. However, Janusz and the tourists, as well as the tourist industry, relied on the image of the forest as primeval, even if it was just the idea of the primeval and not the actual contents of the forest itself. Communist-like neighboring Belarus was a necessary component of the primeval forest for tourists and landscape aficionados like Janusz. The Białowieża region, with its intimidating and corrupt climate, was "little Belarus in a pill," as one activist decried.

Belarus: A Hard Pill to Swallow

When Janusz articulated his concerns about the landscape of his youth receding behind the economic reality of the present, he condemned the culture of foresters, Polish chauvinism, and the dictatorship in Belarus. On many occasions, he and other conservationists exasperatedly joked, "Why don't we just move to Belarus," as if conditions in Białowieża were no different from those in Belarus. There appeared to be family resemblances. Intimidation characterized the tactics of communist dictatorships and local politicians. For example, the mayor from a nearby town who was also the former head of the Secret Police (Służba Bezpieczeństwa) during the communist era bused in dozens of uniformed foresters to what was supposed to be a small meeting between the Society for Landscape Protection and the mayor to address the society's concerns with regional development. In another instance, I witnessed the same official subtly intimidate Janusz. Janusz had emailed the Soros Foundation just after it awarded the mayor an honorable distinction. In his email, Janusz informed the foundation that it mocked democracy in its choice of recipients. Someone at the Polish wing of the foundation tipped off the mayor, who took Janusz aside and warned, "You should keep track of who is using your computer. A very strange message came from it." Belarus symbolically existed in Poland in the mind of Janusz and his activist friends, with their correspondence surveilled and their opposition activities silenced through official, rough-arm tactics, such as NGO environmental group members finding their tires slashed when legally monitoring logging in the forest.

When Belarusians from the other side of the border actually came to visit their Polish colleagues, it was sometimes difficult to determine who might be a spy. Vassilii, a forest activist from Belarus, wrote to Janusz asking for a meeting on his visit to Poland. I was with Janusz in his house for several hours waiting for Vassilii to arrive, but he never showed up. Friends from Hajnówka returned Janusz's worried phone calls saying they had led Vassilii to the main street and pointed him to the bus station hours ago. Finally, three hours after our scheduled meeting, Vassilii rang Janusz and said he got lost in Hajnówka (a small town with two main commercial streets). "Could we come to Hajnówka for the meeting?" Vassilii inquired. We agreed and hopped in Janusz's Renault to drive the twenty kilometers to town. On the way, Janusz laid bare his suspicions. Vassilii must have been a spy—why else would he have gotten lost for hours without calling?

We met at a restaurant beneath the Belarusian cultural center and museum, where the journalist Adam Wajrak was waiting. We found Vassilii, and over potato pancakes and *kartacze*, a boiled starchy dumpling with bacon in the middle, compared the political situation in Belarus and Poland. The conversation proceeded in a mix of Polish and Russian—Vassilii spoke in Russian:

> VASSILII: I have not been allowed to go to the *puszcza* [old forest] for two
> years. Lukashenko owns the forest and told me it is forbidden to
> go [because of his activist work against current management of the
> Belarusian National Park]. But the forest is big, and there are other
> ways to access it. [He grinned with sly satisfaction.] After this ban, I
> organized a press journey of both the legal and underground press.

We were all organized and planning to leave. At 6:00 a.m., they [KGB] called me and told me, "You have seen enough of that forest!" They didn't allow me to go and took the press on their own tour of the forest. You are lucky to have a better situation on the Polish side.

JANUSZ: I'm not so optimistic.

VASSILII: If we change the democratic situation in Belarus, we can change the situation in the *puszcza*. Most of our problems will vanish with democracy.

ADAM: Don't you understand! The Białowieża Forest region is little Belarus in a pill. The director here can do whatever he wants. Białowieża Forest received the European Diploma [a designation from the European Council of Protected Areas]. Instead of this, they should have given Poland a sawmill diploma.

[Janusz chimed in that he no longer felt welcome in the local library because of his activist writings.]

VASSILII: Oh, that's bad bureaucracy.

JANUSZ: No, that's politics. But it's specific to this region. The rest of Poland is not this bad.

ADAM: It's a Belarusian trait.

JANUSZ: It's not Belarusian. It's local!

In this conversation, Janusz wanted to divide things Belarusian from the corrupt local politics, but he struggled with what was locally bad and locally good, what was Belarusian, and what was undemocratic. Clearly, these discourses are not easily separable. Cultural difference may as often be consensual as conflictual (Bhabha 1994). To see cultural differences, such as what is Polish and what is Belarusian, is to see strategies of representation within the shared identities of what Vassilii, Adam, and Janusz had in common.

The immediate "danger" of the geographic Russian/Soviet/communist past in the present shaped the desires of Janusz and those of tourists and other forest activists. They wanted the forest to be a kind of free space, free for democracy and nature. They also needed corrupt politics in the forest and the dictatorship in Belarus to sustain their identities and causes in the present. The confluence of interactions, like this one between Vassilii and the forest activists, hardened the categories that created conditions for an imaginary world of play in Poland.

When Janusz and I lay motionless on the forest floor in the middle of the night or met with Vassilii, there was as much playful conspiracy in this as for the tourists staying at Soplicowo or going to Carska restaurant. Everyone knew how to relate to one another in terms of the activity flow. The edge activities, such as being surprised by the park rangers or willingly participating in what you assume is a draconian tour of a forest in Belarus then returning to Soplicowo, gave people a chance to see what their culture was about and to contemplate the underlying rules that conditioned their lives. Both cozying up to a potential spy *and* taking a borderland train ride where you are hijacked by Soviets let Poles reenact dramas from the various points in the historic past. This opened them in small ways to the sites of the unknown, to ways in which the play begins with certain understood roles but the possibility of a different future; not knowing the winner or the outcome entices Poles to return to the game.

Communist-style corruption in Belarus symbolically seeped into Poland, and forest activists and tourists found their positive identities in this way. The *puszcza* became the great hope of freedom for Poles wanting to support Belarusian oppositionists, but Polish activists and tourists also needed the alter ego of draconian Belarus to create themselves in the images they performed.

Janusz never decided whether Vassilii was indeed a spy. The meeting ended with pledges of cooperation to publish a booklet about abuses on both sides of the border.

Tutejszy—From Here

Are Belarusians in the Białowieża region just props in this world of Polish play? In an interview, Belarusian identity activist and author Sokrat Janowicz from Krynki (outside the forest region) returned to a distinction I understood well from fieldwork in Białowieża: there are two types of Belarusians in Poland—those who call themselves Belarusians and those who call themselves *tutejszy* (from here).[3] The ones calling themselves *tutejszy* possess a bit of false consciousness from Janowicz's perspective. They should recognize that ethnic national minority status as Belarusian offers them a common history, minority voting rights, and funds for language and culture development.

In Białowieża, those who call themselves *tutejszy* use the term with the effect of resisting the idea of borders. As Adrian Ivakhiv (2006) suggested, the term arose as armies and borders crossed people who remained in place.

It is a protoethnic identity receptive to the ebbs and flows of borderlands. Yet Belarusian identity activists, along with some conservationists and foresters, often failed to embrace the creative potential of a hybridized subject, instead finding a dormant consciousness among the *tutejszy.*

"I don't speak Belarusian. I speak *pa naszemu* [our own]," one young shop attendant, who attended the Orthodox Church, told me, "but when those Belarusians come to play music here and sing in that language, I feel like I belong to that culture." Musicians from Belarus seemed to be the only type of Belarusian one could visibly identify in Białowieża after Schengen shut out the petty traders. A few years earlier, before Poland's entry into the European Union, Belarusians frequented the streets of Białowieża, selling merchandise out of the backs of their cars or going door to door asking people if they needed cigarettes or alcohol. Schengen brought Belarusians to nearby Białystok as shoppers, where it was cheaper to purchase consumer goods, such as clothes, bedding, car parts, and kitchenware, than in Belarus. Just after Schengen, Belarusians arrived in Białowieża as folk groups wearing traditional costumes; as choirs filling the churches with their liquid voices; and, in several cases, as oppositionist ethno-rock bands. Any nearby location might be a suitable place for such concerts. However, the growing importance of Białowieża as a "must-see" tourist destination, combined with an assortment of EU funds to support "neighborly" relations in the Euroregion of Puszcza Białowieska, made Białowieża an important site for Belarusian music that, like all things in the area, worked its way into the national park debate.

Urban Poles found it ironic that the most "Belarusian" parts of Poland turned a blind eye to Lukashenko's regime. Belarusian oppositionists found a supportive base in Warsaw for their anti-Lukahsenko campaign in 2006, but in the Białowieża Forest, the Belarusian cultural center and museum in Hajnówka declined to show human rights films focused on Belarus in its auditorium. Museum officials responded to the festival organizers by claiming that one of their employees, who appeared in the film, was unfavorably portrayed. In this official climate against criticizing Lukashenko, forest activists sought to shake up local politics. They invited one of the most popular underground musicians from Minsk, Todar and the WZ Orkestra, to play a benefit concert in support of the Białowieża International Solidarity Network (BISON), a grassroots conservation group.

Janusz and other conservationists acted strategically when they brought Todar into their campaign. First, Todar sang songs in Belarusian about "the independent bison," a symbol of both the *puszcza* and a free Belarus. And second, all proceeds went to rebuild the elementary school that burned in a Christmas Eve fire. Rumor among the conservationists said that foresters accidentally started the fire after renting the school for a party, with the suggestion that alcohol was involved. Foresters steered clear of the concert, but many villagers made an appearance. In the "free space" of ethno-rock music, shop clerks, bed-and-breakfast owners, tourists, field biologists, and even elderly ladies gathered. Todar created a climate where people did not think they were attending a "political" event, even though the motto "Dzikie jest piękne" (wild is beautiful) framed the stage and the concert wrapped up an international day of action to protect the forest. One of the concert organizers shared his strategy with me: locals would participate as long as they could see themselves in the music, which people could understand linguistically, rhythmically, and locally, as Todar sang about the animals of the forest in which they lived. Their strategy was to gently coax the minority-local to their side of the debate by way of a concert benefiting the community.

People who might call themselves *tutejszy* would not consider themselves passive. The word *tutejszy* referenced but did not directly correspond to Belarusian nationality for them. Historian Per Anders Rudling (2015) describes Belarusian national consciousness as limited but with considerable suspicion and resistance to nationalist messages. Historian Eugeniusz Mironowicz (1993; see also Łatyszonek and Mironowicz 2002) explored the struggle for an independent Belarusian identity both within the postwar and communist period (1945–89) and in the Third Republic of Poland (1989 to present). No matter the historical interpretation of Belarusian ethnic and national identity, Belarus is one of the few central/eastern European countries to be cast as indifferent to nationalism.

In Białowieża, identifying as *tutejszy* acknowledged that you could be some combination of Orthodox, Roman Catholic, Baptist, Russian, Belarusian, Polish, Ukrainian, or otherwise but that you came from a family that settled many generations back and that you spoke the local dialect. It also meant loyalty to place superseded loyalty to nation. When I asked questions about nationality and place, locals often demurred, saying they were of a "spokojny naród" (peaceful people) and indicating that they did not want to involve themselves in something political. Notably, several villagers brought my attention to the US wars in Iraq and how "Belarus" never invaded other countries.

Tutejszy was not a term one brandished with any pride. It simply filled in when people wanted to express neutrality on the part of their allegiances. Saying you are *tutejszy* is a response to the question, "Are you Polish or Belarusian?" People usually used it to deflect further questioning.

In these people's suggestive self-description by way of redirecting questioning, a strong identity and political position about the border and forest politics was not so much absent as it was implicit. There was a sense of encroachment in these claims, so *tutejszy* do not draw borders, perhaps do not possess the power to draw borders, and they distinguished themselves from me (the American anthropologist) and ethnic Poles, both of which encroach on other nations' autonomy.

What troubled Janusz about people who answered this way was the beaten-down sensibility of local rural Belarusians, or *tutejszy*, even as he himself published a number of short pictorial booklets echoing this *tutejszy* sentiment. He wanted Belarusians to bring their own past to life in his publications and concerts and cultural events, yet they rarely joined him in this pursuit, with the exception of a few young high school students and urban Belarusian intelligentsia in Hajnówka. He also saw the term "Belarusian" as a stand-in for a "Homo Sovieticus" identity, but this was the fault of the Soviets in Janusz's rendering and not an inherent defect. I was with him one day as we struck up a conversation with people who might be *tutejszy* in Teremiski on election day; "What was, will be," was the dry pronouncement to Janusz's friendly nudge that they go to the polls and vote. Another elderly woman on the bench admitted that "no one has ever voted in Teremiski."

Janusz saw his cultural work as bringing Belarusian culture to life and not just cocooning Belarusian/Orthodox culture into a representation. He and I met Belarusians who had benefited from social advancement during the communist period, people who were now school teachers and dentists and scientists at the Mammal Research Institute; however, Janusz also saw such people as a minority. He wanted to use his historical and aesthetic sensibilities to animate the regional living architecture of people and landscape. Janusz brought the past to life, but the past was perhaps his own alter ego.

Notes

1. Three Schengen Area countries do not belong to the European Union: Norway, Switzerland, and Iceland.

2. Since 1991, Poles' annual income increased from US$2,300 to US$13,000 (Sharma 2017).

3. The term *tutejszy* is used by a vast number of rural inhabitants of the Ukrainian, Polish, and Belarusian borderlands (Holm-Hansen 1999; Ivakhiv 2006).

6

RESURGENCE

Outbreaks of Bark Beetle and Right-Wing Nationalism

A S I LEARNED ABOUT BIAŁOWIEŻA OVER THE YEARS, it had always been peripheral to the Polish imaginary in the postsocialist period. Situated as it is in the eastern part of the country, it was part of an imagined Polska B: largely undeveloped and less urban than Polska A in the west. It was Belarusian in character, a quality (as I discussed in chap. 5) that rendered it "exotic." This sense of it was further enhanced by its identity as both a one-time imperial hunting ground and a tourist destination in the "backwater" of Poland. Other nature sites in Poland, such as the Carpathian Mountains, served as repositories of national identity, but not Białowieża. Białowieża's foresters, accused of acting like "communists" (see chap. 2), were not the best representatives of Polish national interests, at least by conservationists' standards. And then the story changed. Beginning in 2015, an elected right-wing government, PiS (Prawo i Sprawiedliwość [Law and Justice]), centered on Białowieża, both materially and discursively, and crafted a nationalist narrative around it and the forester.

On the ground it looked something like this: A spruce bark beetle out-break threatened the commercial forest. To control the bark beetle (*Ips typographus*) and manage the forest and its commercial resources, the PiS government prescribed a salvage logging treatment. A new type of nature conservationist, the forest activist, established encampments in the forest to block a planned three-fold increase in logging the Białowieża forest. The forest activists, nonlocal and sometimes international, used radical ecology strategies and citizen science to block logging. State Forests mobilized a paramilitary unit of foresters to stop the activists. PiS mobilized a whole set of stories and myths about Białowieża, Polish forests, and Polish foresters, who would become the emblem of a nationalist resurgence and of Poland itself.

Since 2015, Białowieża has become central to defining what it means to be Polish and identifying where Polish authority resides in relation to experts deemed not Polish. Heavily logging Białowieża under the pretext of a bark beetle outbreak became a way to challenge the supremacy of the European Union and secular environmental activists. It became a way to securitize belonging in and to postsocialist Poland. This nationalist turn affords us the opportunity to think through how the forest and its ecology, suffused with agency and agents (e.g., the bark beetle), creates rupture and shapes politics; how nature might help us to interpret postsocialist turns; and how ecology can help us apprehend a world that is unfinished, ongoing, and always becoming, rather than strictly ordered by well-defined eras. Many infrastructures—for example, research institutes, communism, capitalism, the European Union, local residents, and all kinds of experts—shape and have shaped what can and cannot survive in this forest. But we must note that the forest has also compelled a change in politics. A highly unsuspecting agent, a "rewilding agent"—the bark beetle—has played a key role in shaping which myths, stories, and histories would be patched together with forest expertise to imagine Poland's future. What kinds of pasts, and thus futures, were imagined with and without the spruce bark beetle? What kind of forest would Białowieża be? What type of forest could it become, and what type of Poland would it be emblematic of?

This book has been about how people in the ancient forest are entangled in repressed histories that resurface in unsuspecting ways. It offers a narrative that begins with the end of communism, at least in terms of my ethnographic presence, but ends with resounding evidence that communism has not disappeared. As ideas about the unfinished nature of communism swirl in the ideological discourse of forest politics, far larger ecological and political phenomena enter the story—namely, climate change and European disintegration. Climate change poses numerous challenges to and unknowns for wildlands, weather patterns, species, and population. Euro-skepticism and separatist movements challenge a Brussels-run European Union with German and French interests claiming center. Right-wing nationalist movements, led by white supremacists, claim that European nations are losing their cultures because of the arrival of immigrants and refugees and that this is facilitated by such extranational formations such as globalization and the European Union. But even if the EU separatists prefer borders, bark beetles and climate change have no respect for lines drawn on maps. Both climate change and the turn to insular nationalism in Europe undergird the nationalist turn for Białowieża.

The spruce bark beetle population has defoliated spruce and spread throughout the Białowieża commercial forest and national park related largely to climate change. The PiS administration planned a three-fold increase in logging the forest to address the bark beetle problem. It also used State Forests to insist on Polish sovereignty, for that was the moral ground many Europeans wanted to stand on in their eschewal of EU power and global regimes that cast "global" interests in the name of world peace and environmental protection. Poles in government rendered themselves "reasonable" in contrast to those representing the interests of such internationalisms as the European Union or globalization, which were unfair and factually incorrect about matters that should have been left to the expertise of the Polish forester. Poland should not sacrifice its prized managed forest (Białowieża), they argued, to a shallow and distant understanding of the forest's ecology as primeval or wild and that subordinated humans, never mind sovereign Poles, to nature. For PiS, State Forests, and the foresters, western Europe's history of marginalizing Poland meant that the European Union could not see its own arrogance and thus had no basis for counseling or chastising Poland in relation to its sovereign interests. Ecological activists—mostly Polish speaking, although many were not—congregated in the forest, calling for a terrestrial politics over and above nationalist politics. In this sense, they mocked PiS's position. Białowieża Forest took center stage in debates about the meaning of the nation, whether the nation would use Białowieża in a muscular defensive against the foreign, and why the nation was even necessary for Białowieża.

Viewed through a Polish nationalist lens, the claim to Białowieża is unfinished. This region was Lithuanian during the Middle Ages and the Renaissance. After existing as Russian territory for more than a century, Białowieża did not become fully Polish, despite the attempts of ethnic Polish foresters in the interwar period (see chap. 2). The forest region was not one where all citizens had the same memories, loyalties, languages, and mutual rights and duties. A constellation of ultraright ideological groups seized on ethnic/national difference in the region and brought it into play on the back of an insect "enemy." Forestry treatments to control bark beetle were intended to irrevocably transform the ecology of the forest so that nature conservationists could never again claim the commercial forest as part of the larger primeval icon that was the Białowieża Forest. Nature conservationists became "pests" and "ecoterrorists" in pro-logging discourse and were construed as threats to national unity. Foresters could not afford to have them portrayed as a party with equally legitimate knowledge. Not only did foresters deny the legitimacy of the forest activists' knowledge, they used violence to stop the activists, much like they did against the other enemy in the forest, the bark beetle. In denying the legitimacy of the terrestrial politics of the forest activists, PiS also denied the legitimacy of the bark beetles themselves. There is no role in PiS forest ecology, which has long been the management espoused by foresters, for bark beetles or forest activists, even as the bark beetle is native to the forest. Logging for the PiS government was a short-term prescription for the bark beetle but also served as a performative act. Polish forests are national constructions, according to PiS and other ultra-right-wing political forces, and Białowieża is the forensic for this assertion.

Between Postsocialism and Posthumanism

As fields of inquiry, both postsocialism and posthumanism help us apprehend a world that is unfinished, ongoing, and indeterminate. They refuse sharp, tidy distinctions between eras and historical agents, and they point to processes of contestation and negotiation in the production of knowledge and counterknowledge by various agents. Postsocialist scholarship examines the past thirty years of "transition," mostly in eastern Europe, from state socialism to the retreat of the state under neoliberal forms of capitalism. This scholarship has also theorized what appears to be the interminable state of postsocialist transition for some countries and the stigmatization of those countries that did not succeed in mirroring the West economically (Knudsen and Frederiksen 2015; Rakowski 2016). Posthumanism notices how nonhumans shape historical outcomes. It questions the hubris of anthropocentrism, for instance, challenging the assumption that humans are the only species deciding what survives in a forest made up of different assemblages of plants, animals, bacteria, and other influences, none of which are entirely separate (Latour 2018; Smart and Smart 2017). Examining Białowieża Forest through the lenses of postsocialism and posthumanism means perceiving it as both a site of ongoing contestation about the future of postsocialist Poland and an agent shaping debates about what the forest will, should, or could look like.

Postsocialism and posthumanism refute determinacy. Postsocialism rejects both the inevitability of capitalism's triumph and the endurance of a communist mentality, sometimes personified as Homo Sovieticus—a person frozen in the communist habits of everyday life (Verdery 1996; Humphrey 2002; Buchowski 2001, 2006; Dunn 2004) and often mobilized to explain the "failures" of transition. Posthumanists refute the idea that humans alone are afforded a rational consciousness that distinguishes them from other species and defines them as individuated actors solely capable of political authority (Wolfe 2003; Latour 1993). They call attention to the ways in which other technologies and, indeed, other beings make us human, and in doing so, they offer an implicit challenge to the type of ethnocentrism running through postsocialist nationalism (Haraway 2016; Tsing 2015).

The end of one-party communist rule challenged ideas about the nation and the state and raised questions about who the polity was in new territories and republics. In nations that were denied their national histories under communism, nationalists revived stories about great moments in the nation's past or about martyrdom, even as postsocialist scholars demonstrated the diverse ways people both lived the communist past and recreated the nation in an era of neoliberal capitalism. Taken together, postsocialism and posthumanism offer a framework for rejecting the idea that one culture, one nation, or one species will determine the ultimate outcome of ecological assemblages or political futures.

The way in which posthumanism and postsocialism call attention to issues of temporality—namely, the ways people experience time—is also important for understanding the nationalist turn in Białowieża Forest. Posthumanists posit modernity—marked by the creation of highly specialized groups of people who eschew backward, rural, small-scale production in favor of technological and national progress—as a radical temporal break. This temporal break informs the hubris of anthropocentrism: the modernist faith in progress informs the belief that humanity has learned from past mistakes and, through technology and rationality, will become more individuated and thus able to always see humans as separate from other species. In contrast, posthumanists insist on the ongoingness of processes among species, ideas, and things. This sense of temporality is crucial for accounting for the role of the bark beetle in both the ecology of Białowieża and the concurrent nationalist turn.

In postsocialist anthropology, attending to how people experience time means situating what our informants say in the present and the interests represented in their statements within a wider, temporal, historical frame. In Białowieża Forest, the condition of postsocialism—the recovery of formerly suppressed national histories—has created an experience of time directly tied to both the communist past and the nationalist future. Situating present statements made about and in the forest within larger-scale processes, especially in the era of climate change, is extremely important. The biophysical phenomena of climate change compel scholars to reexamine how industrial modernity created nations—for instance, nations that put national interests above class interests or nations that now care more about securitizing borders (often in the face of climate refugees) than addressing the terrestrial problem of climate change.

In summarizing the two fields, postsocialism refutes the determinacy of one type of cultural experience or temporality for people living in the region that "finished communism," and posthumanism refutes the determinacy of the human as the main type of interpretive and agential actor. Considering these fields together provides more than flat realism of what happened historically or what a forest is or should be. Environmental change and history are grafted together. There has to be an account of Białowieża that is simultaneously material, political-economic, and ecological because nationalism and communism are material, political-economic, and ecological.

Communism and ultraright nationalism have had a recursive tension in Europe, but neither has been thought about as ecological. Slavoj Žižek (2001) complicated classic notions of fascism and communism as competing totalitarianisms by highlighting liberalism's role in bringing together right-wing nationalist fundamentalisms and radical-left emancipatory projects. This insight is crucial for thinking through how liberal politics and policies in postsocialist Poland created the conditions for the marriage of nationalism and forest politics in Białowieża. As Žižek (2001, 58) writes, "Freedom is ultimately nothing but the space opened up by the traumatic encounter, the space to be filled in by its contingent/inadequate, symbolization/translation." For Žižek, in his psychoanalytical overview of the time after communism's official end, an enigma will break through determinist projects. Białowieża Forest—both logged and protected, borderland and national territory, primeval and modern—is, in my interpretation, Žižek's enigma. It is ambiguous as a borderland. It is both logged and protected. It is often purifying for different political agendas and in need of purification. And it is a forest on the cusp of the future if only one can understand its unfinished and resurfacing pasts. It threatens the thrust of determinist projects to foreclose other possibilities and buttress such "truths" as "the forest is Polish" or that "communism ended."

Both right-wing nationalism and communism are ecological and transformable. They are not ecological in a sociobiological or evolutionary-psychological sense that they are natural behaviors. Rather, they are ecological in the way that philosopher of science Isabelle Stengers (2010, 34–35) speaks of when she writes that "ecology is then, the science of multiplicities, disparate causalities, and unintentional creations of meaning. . . . Human societies are always susceptible to producing a justification for what they undergo, of transforming their inventions into norms, and forgetting the price paid for their choices." Understanding right-wing nationalism and communism as ecological means tending to how they inadvertently create meaning when they cannot create the future as intended. But Stengers intends to use ecology as its evolutionary explanatory knowledge system to include humans and their histories. Why is Polish nationalism an invention for this forest then, especially given the history of Poles dying in the forest for the sake of the nation? Ultraright nationalism spread throughout formerly communist eastern Europe after communism suppressed such nationalism. During the interwar period, Poles attempted to make their mark—their national mark, customs, and culture—on Białowieża. Communists terminated that project using both force and ideology. They sent foresters to Siberia and forbade citizens of the People's Republic of Poland from referring to ethnicity as a cause of suffering during World War II. The forgotten price paid in the present turn to ultraright nationalism is the erasure of how interwar ethnic politics and postwar (communist) politics denied plurality. An ecological interpretation would point to "multiplicities, disparate causalities, and unintentional creations of meaning" to make apparent the outbreaks of ultra-right-wing nationalism in relation to the forest, seizing Białowieża as one meaning (as a Polish forest created by Polish foresters or communism as a project without nationalist sentiments).

Ecologies of history can explain Polish nationalism in relation to communism. In a Polish nationalist narrative, communism is constructed as always alien. Where communism sought class consciousness, nationalism focuses a priori the anger felt in violation of the "natural" (roots, blood, soil) need for the nation. In the PiS narrative, there were no Polish communists, and Poles who belonged to the party were traitors, as enacted by the first PiS government's lustration of former Communist Party members between

2005 and 2007. The Białowieża Forest became center stage in this drama where the "communists" became "foreigners" when PiS won the election in 2015. Forest activists defending the forest were named "ecoterrorists" and "communists" as they came to the bark beetles' defense and sought EU support to terminate logging.

By bringing attention to the spruce bark beetle and its role in the physical ecology of the forest, here is price paid (to use Stengers's [2010] idea). When PiS "transform their inventions into norms," they have cut out not only the bark beetle but also a factual piece of history and memory, and it is leading to a diminished forest and a body politic that is rabidly nationalist. Polish nationalism, in its egotistical variant (the wrongs committed against our nation are more wrong than wrongs we might commit toward another nation), has to excise Russia, Germany, and communist internationalisms to remain Poland in some kind of pure ideal projection of the nation— a nation that was long without its own territory and that still retained a national consciousness (nationalism without a nation state).

The spruce bark beetle enters as an extraordinary agent of history and change in relation to the forester and his role as the figure of patriotic nationalism. Clearly distinct from humans and strategically employed by humans, the beetle has expanded its population at a specific historical moment (postsocialism), which is not the same as saying that the beetle knows what postsocialism is. The beetle, in ecological terms, cocreates an undeniable difference in the forest's composition and, in material terms, becomes the pretext for a logging intervention that is also, in political-economic terms, an intervention against those who do not live up to the ideal of the Polish nation under the PiS government or who betrayed the Polish nation in the postsocialist period.

Bark Beetle Ecology

I saw the bark beetle only once, and it was already dead. On one of our forays for mushrooms, Leszek (see chap. 4) poured contents of a plastic pheromone trap into my hand. I held about five tiny desiccated beetles in my palm. They seemed completely out of proportion to the exponentially larger images of the bark beetle I had seen silk screened onto the T-shirts of forest activists or printed on didactic posters meant to villainize the beetle. But I understood well that the beetles change the politics of survival in the forest. They are indeed big!

Ips typographus is a cylindrical insect, about a quarter of an inch long. It can hibernate for years in downed woody debris. Since the mid-1990s, foresters warned of bark beetle outbreaks and set up a trapping and monitoring program. There have been four outbreaks (1995, 2003, 2008, and 2012 to present), demonstrated by the volume of dead spruce. Commercial forests in Europe routinely conduct sanitary logging to control bark beetle numbers, but in a forest that is partly national park, partly protective reserves, and partly commercial forest, the question of control becomes all or nothing. If you cannot log in the national park or forest reserve, and these areas make up a large portion of your forest and provide habitat for the beetle, the cycle will continue (Jonasova and Prach 2008).

When conditions are hot and dry and there is a lot of forest litter, the beetles emerge, flying for miles in some cases until they find a host tree. They then bore their way into the phloem of both healthy and weak Norway spruce (*Picea abies*) (Michalski et al. 2004). Norway spruce flourished in the twentieth century under State Forests management and was valued for its long, straight timber harvestable in eighty years. Most deer avoid browsing on it unless deer populations are high. For these reasons, if you want a commercial forest, you need Norway spruce as one of the dominant species.

Climate change, which for Poland means hotter, drier weather, will increase the frequency of outbreaks, and a mosaic forest such as Białowieża provides an advantage for the bark beetle. Infestations are more severe in stands more than eighty years old. State Forests lands include planted mixed stands of oak, maple, and other hardwoods. Alder dominates swampy bogs. Lots of the monoculture stands in the forest have softwood spruce and pine, and many other stands are naturally reseeded with mixed tree species. Some of these stands are more than a hundred years old. In them, forest policy prevents the removal of dead wood.

Deadwood alone does not necessarily mean more outbreaks. The beetle nests only in spruce, and there are many other tree species. The moisture content of the forest can increase with more deadwood, and deadwood stores carbon into the soil, which is why old forests are so important in the fight against climate change (Fleituch 2010). The problem of climate change and forests arises as experts ask how much active management is preferable. How much commercial forestry can be done if one wants to keep forests as a carbon sink without letting them burn up or succumb to more severe insect and fungal outbreaks. Much hinges on the role of noncommercial forests for the future of Białowieża and all forests.

The science of how to approach bark beetle in an era of climate change is not at all settled (Fahse and Heurich 2011). Should active measures such as salvage logging be used to protect forest stands and biodiversity? If you are doing only sanitary logging in the unprotected areas of the commercial forest, and no logging in the strict reserve national park, will it restrain the outbreak?[1] There is a complex interplay among beetles, host trees, antagonists, mutualists, and forest management.

When and how the beetle will flourish exponentially is not entirely predictable, but as with any ecological relationship, the greater the food source and the less the predation, the more the beetle will reproduce. It can kill trees only when the beetle population is high. The beetles form elaborate larval chambers, spreading throughout the tree, and eventually kill off their spruce host. Who is eating the beetle when this happens?

The endangered three-toed woodpecker (*Picoides tridactylus*) eats bark beetle larvae deposited under bark. They are endangered precisely because of the lack of dead and dying wood in most European forests. A population of three-toed woodpeckers will flourish when the bark beetle population is high and may eventually control its numbers (Bütler and Schlaepfer 2002). The woodpecker, one of nine *Picus* species that live in the forest, nests in the cavities of dead trees. Białowieża is the only forest in Europe where one finds all nine species of European woodpecker.

Why should old trees with so much growth on them succumb to such a small insect, like the Lilliputians roping down the giant in *Gulliver's Travels*? The bark beetle is not acting alone; it has allies. The blue stain fungus *Ceratocystis polonica*, vectored by the spruce bark beetle, helps the beetle overcome the conifer's defenses. The spruce excretes unpalatable chemicals and seals up the ducts to its inner layers so nutrients can still flow within the bark; meanwhile, the blue stain fungus leaves its sticky spores on the beetle's body, and these spores weaken the tree's defenses. Parental beetles construct an initial egg gallery. The larvae they deposit form larval galleries. During these generational constructions, several different fungi can enter the nutrient-rich tree. The fungi provide nutrients that benefit the beetle.

The history of this encounter among bark beetle, Norway spruce, three-toed woodpecker, deadwood, blue stain fungi, industrial forestry, and nature protection is in the mix of current forest ecology. Ecology and politics are always part of forests. The question of what to do about the bark beetle is one that scientists are trying to address, but never outside of the sticky moral, legal, financial, cultural, and sovereignty issues. From all of this, a new value for the beetle is emerging; the beetle rewilds, but in large numbers because of the combined infrastructure of active management and nature protection.

Nature conservation measures secured in 2011 and agreed upon by State Forests developed a ten-year forestry management plan (2012–21). Many foresters felt that the Civic Platform (Platforma Obywatelska) government-negotiated process gave NGOs more concessions than they deserved. The plan mandated that dead and dying wood be left on the forest floor. It curbed logging (no more than 48,500 cubic meters per year) and stated clearly that logging was prohibited in "old growth" stands, defined as stands that contained more than 10 percent of trees over one hundred years old. This did not work well for profiting from the forest, which had been running a deficit when other protective measure were put in place. State Forests had enough income from its other forests to keep Białowieża as a Special Promotional Complex Forest, with a higher value placed on biodiversity than in its other forests, but foresters were resistant to adding further protections.

In 2014, UNESCO extended Białowieża's World Heritage designation to include the commercial forest, precisely because of the 2012–21 management plan. In 2016, it became impossible to ignore what this management meant for bark beetle outbreak and the productiveness of this forest. As soon as PiS came to power, it asserted authority and defied both Polish and EU law.

The PiS government's environmental minister, Jan Szyszko, annexed the forest management plan to allow salvage logging treatment for bark beetle prevention and damage. Logging was thus allowed in the old growth stands, a legality that the EU Commission challenged. Complying with the European Union's demands also meant admitting that PiS was breaking Polish rules. State Forests asserted that the beetle would have destroyed the forest had foresters not acted decisively against nature conservationists.

Biologists and entomologists in Poland and throughout Europe recognize the significant role that bark beetles play in the ecosystem (Bobiec and Bobiec 2012; Grodzki 2016; Lehnert et al. 2013; Müller et al. 2008; Müller, Bussler, and Brandl 2010). A number of prominent biologists agreed that the bark beetle could not be eliminated in the Białowieża Forest, nor could its damage be lessened through logging (Thorn et al. 2018; Gutowski and Krzysztofiak 2005). The beetle can fly, and when a tree is logged, the beetle simply flies to another tree; sometimes beetles are transported to another forest if they are still in their larval stage. The logging in

Białowieża took place after the trees were already dead. Unless 80 percent of the trees are removed before they are dead—which could not happen because Białowieża National Park does not control for the beetle—the bark beetle will presumably continue to flourish. Some spruce in the forest will die, but some can regenerate in the new openings created by the defoliation and toppling of dead spruce (Fahse and Heurich 2011; Gutowski and Krzystofiak 2005).

Foresters justified their actions within the Polish Forest Act (1991), which requires the district forest manager to control for any harmful organisms (Grodzki 2016, 328). National parks are excluded from this act. Foresters argued that bark beetles were attacking healthy spruce because the 2011–21 forest management plan curbed the harvest of old trees and left dead trees. If dead trees are left standing, foresters argue, they will threaten to topple over, giving way to a steppe ecosystem where a thick layer of grass prevents tree regrowth. By this logic, the forest will die without the forester, and the forest will not reestablish itself if the forester does not replant trees. In summer and fall 2017, foresters clear-cut more than 140,000 trees, 35 percent of them over one hundred years old, and removed dead and dying timber from the forest reserves. They reached their 2021 harvest quota by 2018, with plans to increase existing quotas by annexing forest law.

Enter the Forest Activist

Not all of the activists who came to Obóz dla Puszczy (Camp for the Forest) in 2017 shared the same political outlook, but they tried to stay on message: "Stop logging the Białowieża Forest." They also learned about, and some were experts in, rare and endangered species including insects, fungi, and larger animals that depend on deadwood.

Białowieża had a small, local group of activists in the postsocialist period who fought for the forest's protection against logging in the 1990s and early 2000s. We have met Adam Wajrak (chap. 4), Janusz Korbel (chap. 5), and a handful of biologists (chap. 3). Partly because of their agitations and foundational NGOs, such as Workshop for All Beings (Pracownia na rzecz Wszystkich Istot), larger national and international groups such as Greenpeace and the World Wildlife Foundation offered support. However, since massive logging began in 2017, hundreds of activists have set up camps in the villages. Some had no affiliation with any group, and others had visited the forest over the years and knew scientists or local activists.

The week I visited the Camp for the Forest was wet, which meant lots of mosquitos. I traveled with a Warsaw-based actress and a Gdańsk-based veterinarian and her newborn baby to a forest blockade, where activists tried to keep a harvester from cutting down trees. I stepped out of the car at a site with lots of people milling around. I approached a balding man in his midthirties sitting on a dirt driveway with his right arm inserted into a blue barrel with a hole drilled in one end. On the other side of the barrel, another activist was attached. He wore a cotton hoodie with a message silk-screened in Polish on the back: "Alarmuj! Las rośnie długo, znika szybko" (Alarm! Forests grow slowly and disappear quickly). Those who were not chained up secured a tarp to keep the rain off. Hand-painted signs warned in English, "World heritage is not for sale!" The activists blocked access to a shiny new harvester, which sat idle behind a fence at what seemed to be a forester's residence deep in the woods. There would be about sixty such blockades in 2017. Another protester set down a bowl of steaming vegan stew and warm tea, which the hooded protester tried to eat with his left hand, awkwardly, until someone offered to spoon-feed him.

After his meal, I approached. I introduced myself as a cultural anthropologist from the United States. Like me, the man spoke Polish with mistakes and an accent. He told me he was from the Czech Republic. There was something torturous about his appearance; mosquitos swarmed and landed on his forehead, and his back hunched from sitting in an awkward position for so long. I offered to spray him with mosquito repellant, which he accepted with relief. "Somebody has to defend the forest," he said. "It is a practice of direct democracy in undemocratic times." He told me that this was his return visit to the camp and that so far he had met two elderly American women, other Czechs, Hungarians, a handful of Italian anarchists, and a man who participated in the shipyard strikes with Lech Wałęsa in the 1970s. There were mostly Polish-speaking activists at the camp, although of many ages and occupations. I met a man who had heard about the camp from Silesia in southern Poland and drove to see the forest. He brought with him boxes of canned cooked meat. "That's what we ate in my army days," he told them, joyfully extending his arms with his contribution in plastic grocery bags. But the activists kindly declined, disappointing him with the news that the camp was entirely vegan.

Many activists stayed closer to the camp, cooking for those at the blockade, painting signs, and running meetings with the media. Others patrolled and monitored the forest, performing a type of citizen science.

Using handheld GPS devices, they documented, photographed, and inventoried trees slated for destruction or those already cut. They also recorded standing vegetation of herbivorous species and logged wildlife encounters.

The protesters managed to block access to this harvester for several days. It was the first time in State Forests' history that trees were removed with industrial harvesters instead of chain saws. With chain saws, foresters removed trees one at time with less damage to ground cover; harvesters chewed up the soil and undergrowth to get the same tree. After two days, foresters freed their equipment. They cut a hole in another part of the fence, avoiding the protest. This was one of the less confrontational blockades of that summer.

Activists lived largely at one site in Pogorzelce village, a former barn that still contained bales of hay but no animals. They used the barn as an auditorium for their nightly meetings of a few dozen to a hundred people, where they democratically set out strategies by consensus. Many activists prided themselves on being part of an international movement that also eschewed nationalism, patriarchy, and global capitalism. They based their camp on DIY (do-it-yourself) anarchist organizing principles similar to those used by the Occupy movement—no leaders and no followers, only spokespersons (like the spokes of a bicycle wheel) elected by councils of those present. Some tried to offer lectures on the connection between capitalism and logging the forest or between feminism and patriarchy, whereas others argued that such lectures took momentum away from the movement's main purpose of stopping logging.

Foresters saw the group as a swarm of unruly people. They called the protesters *szkodniki* (pests), charges I heard repeated often by people I knew in the villages, especially those who had family working for State Forests.

To deal with the growing movement, the director of State Forests, Konrad Tomaszewski, called in a special paramilitary unit of foresters with the right to carry guns. Foresters began using rough-arm and militaristic techniques—highly unusual for foresters. They wore the militarized gear of the police state, protective body armor and leather gloves, despite the peaceful nature of the protests and blockades. They confiscated the media's cameras and footage. They raided the protesters' camp to search for drugs (and found none). They dragged protesters from equipment, applied body locks, threw activists face down on piles of logs, and arrested those at blockades—all of which was captured on social media. One forester wore a button on his uniform that said, "Death to the enemies of the fatherland."

Fig. 6.1. Camp for the Forest. Strategizing. Photo by Jakub Szafranski. Used with permission.

Another told activists that "ecologists were planning a new world order." Some residents in the village said protesters should be lined up and shot. Others told me foresters were acting like the Gestapo.

The protesters faced numerous lawsuits but felt vindicated in multiple ways. Courts in Hajnówka passed judgment in their favor in 2018, citing European law, Polish law, and the right to demonstrate within Poland. The International Union for Conservation of Nature and UNESCO urged Poland to stop logging or risk having its World Heritage status revoked. The EU Court of Justice found that Poland had broken wildlife laws to which it was a signatory. And the entire parliamentary delegation from the opposition (Platforma Obywatelska) arrived at the camp without notice, wanting to officially collaborate and prosecute foresters who physically harmed activists (there were more than one hundred lawsuits against Lasy Państwowe) and vowing to better protect the forest through parliamentary action.

For activists and other nature conservationists, the bark beetle became a symbol of a new kind of ecological politics. The bark beetle was a rewilding agent that let conservationists tell a forest narrative to counter the circulation of nationalist narratives. They screen printed T-shirts and postcards with images of the beetle, which became as iconic as images of the famous bison. The bark beetle catalyzed a democratic response in new ways, both through direct democracy and through legal actions in Poland at the European Union and in nonbinding international arenas. In the age of the Anthropocene, this meant that the beetle (combined with the less-discussed blue stain fungus, three-toed woodpecker, deadwood, activists, foresters, scientists, and dry weather) catalyzed the idea that the forest must be freed to become what it will. This move marked an attempt to rearrange the aesthetics of the forest and draw attention to ecological processes as democratic processes, meaning that total defeat was not an option. The bark beetle had a historical evolutionary role, but evolution cannot evolve backward.

Wanted Posters: Justice

If forest activists were open to protecting the forest for its own evolutionary devices, a parallel and overlapping political formation in Poland suggested that the body politic had to do something strategic and surgical to correct a course of history "that went the wrong way," into the hands of those who would prevent historical "truth" from emerging from the debris of communism.

One day in July 2002, as I was cycling through State Forests land on my way to Narewka in the north, I saw a "wanted" poster, similar to those used in the American West of old to catch criminals: "Wanted for killing 25,000 spruce in 2001." It was a didactic information board, meant to reach the occasional traveler like me and warn us not to touch the plastic pheromone traps hanging from spruce, but its use of this Western motif struck me as remarkable. This catch-the-outlaw type of justice message reminded me of the Solidarity campaign posters from a decade earlier. Those posters used the image of Gary Cooper in the 1952 American western *High Noon* (F. Zimmerman 1952). Cooper played the marshal of a New Mexico territory who recognized his moral duty to stay on and fight a vicious outlaw when he might otherwise retire. Like Cooper, depicted on the poster wearing a Solidarity badge and holding a Solidarity ballot, the voter was supposed to make the moral choice and vote for Solidarity against the vicious and illegitimate communists. Although the two images (the beetle poster and the Solidarity poster) share few stylistic details, they draw on storied Western references to the good fight in the name of protecting decency and having a clear moral conscience. There is also a bit of hyperbole to both.

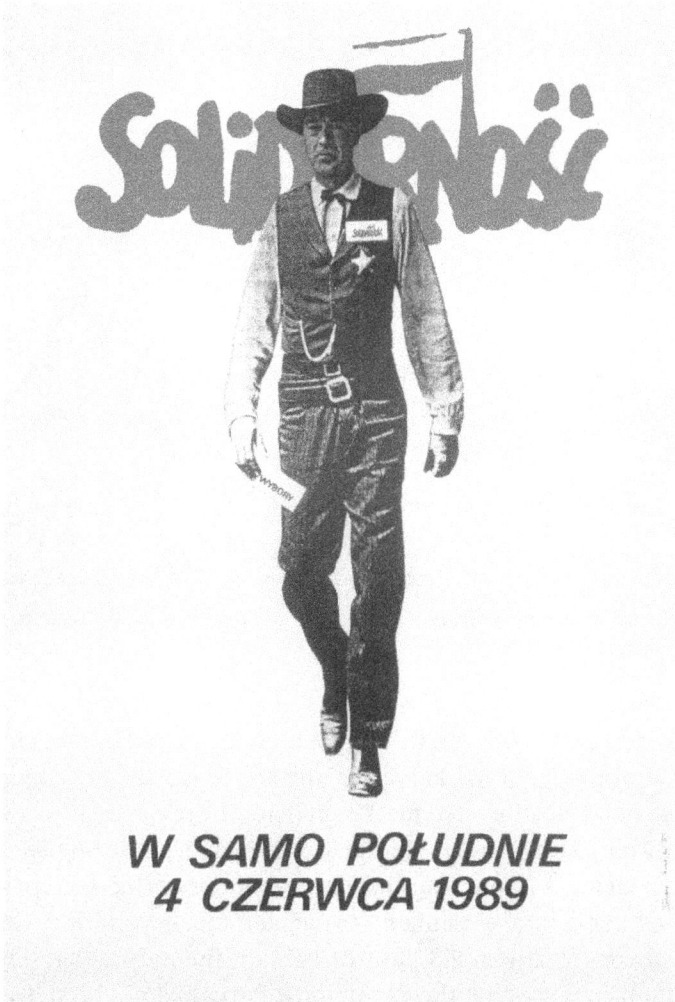

Fig. 6.2. At "high noon," June 4, 1989. Political poster featuring Gary Cooper to encourage votes for the Solidarity Party in the first semifree election in Poland. By artist Tomasz Sarnecki (1966–2018). Image courtesy of the Polish Poster Museum, Warsaw.

PiS built its entire political narrative on the accusation that Solidarity compromised itself in that historic period. In fact, the 1989 vote was not fair. Since PiS was founded in 2001 by Jarosław Kaczyński, twin brother of former President Lech Kaczyński (and who both were once members of Solidarity), the party has been dominated by social conservatism and the Catholic Church (some would argue it is the other way around). Starting as

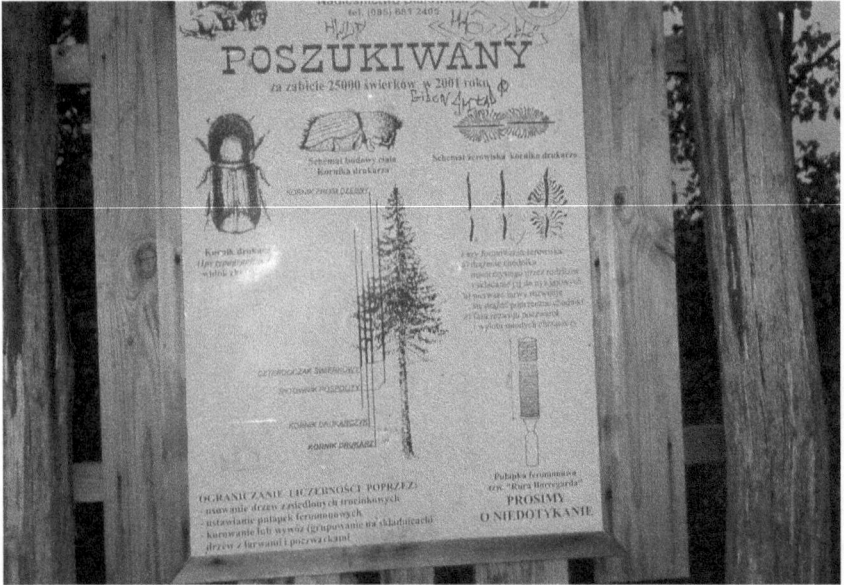

Fig. 6.3. "Wanted" poster for bark beetle located on forest road from Teremiski to Narewka. Photo by Eunice Blavascunas.

an opposition party, PiS won its first election in 2005; it lost to Civic Platform (Platforma Obywatelska), a socially conservative but economically liberal party advocating free market policies, in the 2007 elections; and then PiS won again in 2015. PiS's platform includes a strong social welfare component. As noted in chapter 3 about scientific legitimacy, the appeal of PiS's central organizing principle went beyond just Catholics and social conservatives. PiS built its base on the notion that Solidarity did not, in fact, win—that the Communist Party had not been overcome. Gary Cooper (that is to say, PiS) needed to stay in politics until everyone understood the brutality of the communist dictatorship. PiS would need to prevent communists from entering political life—and hold communists accountable.

According to PiS, Solidarity members including, and especially, Lech Wałęsa promised the Communist Party that it would not be excluded from politics in the new era; thus, Wałesa committed a crime against the nation. Where westerners like myself looked to Poland and eastern European revolutions in 1989 as mostly peaceful and heroic movements, PiS's founders considered Solidarity as a betrayer. Where I saw communists embracing democracy and renouncing their pasts, PiS saw an inauthentic narrative coming from the West. PiS wanted to create the Fourth Republic of Poland, delegitimizing the Third Republic and its communist corruption. According to PiS, democracy could not unfold until the nation was purged of its communists and its institutions reformed, and this platform extended to how they handled the bark beetle.

Although it did not appear in PiS's origin story, the bark beetle and its cyclical outbreak became a useful tool in PiS's platform to purge Poland of anyone who might thwart PiS's effort to unify the nation around the Catholic Church and social conservativism. The beetle fit within PiS's narrative about "threats" to the Polish nation, which were threats to Polish nature and Polish forests. The bark beetle made it easier to identify threats to national sovereignty and, more importantly, unity. This time, the old foes (communists, Bolsheviks, Soviets, Russians, German or British logging interests) appeared in the new guise of conservationists and ecological activists. "Green" activists became traitors of the Polish nation who served foreign interests and peddled rootless, cosmopolitan values.

Most forest activists and nature conservationists were not former Communist Party members, but what PiS saw in them was a reckless detachment from the past at the cost of unity. They saw *lewactwo*, a pejorative term for the new left ("pinkos"), as a group of countercultural radicals trying to break and corrupt not just the nation but human dignity. Those looking for general humanity, such as the claim that Białowieża is world heritage, denied people specific culture and history. PiS saw the activists wanting a new political order without God and Christianity that extended refugee status to Syrians and supported LGBTQ rights, veganism, and feminism.

Activists started gathering at the forest camp in May 2017. At the same time, under PiS-appointed director Konrad Tomaszewski, State Forests organized an official conference together with extreme-right Catholic clergy. The title, and a familiar anthem, was Jeszcze Polska nie zginęła— Wieś (Still Poland Has Not Perished—The Village). Eight thousand Polish foresters attended the conference in Toruń (central Poland). The conference program aimed to philosophically justify foresters' authority in relation to the ecological activists in the forest. Tomaszewski pronounced that Polish foresters were one of the four pillars of Polish society, along with hunters, the Catholic Church, and farmers. He rooted Poland in the idea that the country's true soul was in a kind of patriarchal village setting where the

Fig. 6.4. State Forests paramilitary unit guarding timber harvest against Camp for the Forest activists. 2017. Photo by Jacek Kusz. Used with permission.

highest authorities were priests, hunters, and foresters shepherding rural Catholic farmers who held onto traditional values over those of urban secularists. A theologian from the Catholic University of Lublin, Tadeusz Guz, gave a lecture titled, "The Philosophical Analysis of Human Animalization and the Humanization of Animals and Trees," in which he critiqued the deep ecology underpinnings of activists as more committed to nature than to human domination over nature. He called the ecological movement "atheist, materialist and nihilistic neo-communism," the aim of which is to "radically negate God as the creator of Poland, Poles and Polish women, animals and plants."

Attacking the activists and excising the beetle through the forester's authority became an excuse for capturing not only a definition of correct nature management but also for establishing the one and only proper history of (and for) the nation—a history that nature activists, in their tolerance for plurality, eschewed. PiS had to build its case that a forester's authority in Białowieża was central to rectifying the story of Poland, which was lost to the communist and postsocialist periods and could not be told properly when activists chose a forest or the earth above the nation.

The Forest Myth

By the logic of PiS and its nationalist agenda, the forest needed to be brought under the sole control and care of Polish foresters, as servants of the Polish nation-state. The story of Poland's forests and foresters, past and present, is the story of the Polish nation—a nation that has not always had its own state. As anthropologist Agata Konczal (2018) argued recently, this forest myth is based on an assumption that there is no Poland without forests and no forests without the "Polishness" of its foresters. Foresters set themselves up as the heroes of this myth. When Poles fought to self-govern—for example, during the 1831 and 1864 uprisings or in moments of occupation such as World Wars I and II—foresters saved the national soul, stretched between three different political territorial units, by saving its forests. The patriotism of previous generations of Polish foresters, especially those from the interwar period, is presented and interpreted by contemporary foresters as a sacrifice leading to the current political outcome: Poland as an independent republic with safe and healthy forests. Foresters' activities in logging and planting, administering, and acting as historical insurgents against occupiers explain today's legacy and, at the same time, are tested schemes of practice.

The myth needs to be performed for its historical continuity. History from the forest is not based on that what is within the forest (for that would need to include old growth and bark beetles) but rather on what is excavated from the forest through forester's management and labor. The superior knowledge of Polish foresters needs to be performed by fighting "ecoterrorists" who block harvesting equipment and seek extra-Polish legal means of nature protection. This performance takes place in response to and in concert with a version of national history. Nevertheless, the forest provides tools and materials for this performance: the bark beetle, the repeated foreign occupations, the martyrdoms vis-à-vis graves in the forest, Belarusian otherness that needs to be made Polish. Foresters do not build the national history in the forest according to their own will but based on historical fragments that need to be brought to life, such as reviving interwar stories about Polish foresters as partisans. PiS has been adept at calibrating local long-term opposition to nature conservationists to perpetuate its national forest myth.

This transition happened gradually in my purview. By about 2012, I began to hear fewer accusations that foresters were communists and more emphasis on Białowieża's foresters as patriots. Hard-line and controversial Catholic media founded by Father Tadeusz Rydzyk, known as "Father Director" (who coorganized the Toruń conference of foresters), took up the cause of logging Białowieża. Rydzyk's media criticized by the Vatican, broadcast nationalist religious messages that were rosary specific, antifeminist, and against the Islamization of Europe, Middle Eastern refugees, and gay rights. The radio station frequently referred to nature conservationists and environmentalists as "ecoterrorists." PiS environment minister Szyszko appeared many times as a guest on Rydzek's Radio Maryja and TV Trwam, where he often spoke about the need to assert the proper (forester) control over Białowieża.

A Hajnówka-based group called "SANTA: In Defense of the Białowieża Forest" organized an April 27, 2013, protest in which the first in situ signs of Polish nationalism appeared as the dominant driver of logging on the pretext of the bark beetle. The group's banners read, "Save the Polish forest from pseudoecologists and those who would sabotage it." The protest specifically railed against the 2011 forest management decision, with one of the speakers noting that "more than two million meters of cubic wood were rotting on the forest floor." An official "pastor of foresters," Tomasz Duszkiewicz also entered the political fray at that protest. He called nature activists "Satan's helpers" and told people in the forest region that rotting wood was "a sin." State Forests provided funds to SANTA for its work. Szyszko appeared as the protest's main speaker. Protesters in Polish folk costumes (central Polish costumes) milled about with Duszkiewicz and an Orthodox priest. SANTA's president, Walenty Wasiluk (notably, a Belarusian surname), owned several sawmills and spoke of nature conservation as a "Jewish" international plot to undermine Polish independence.

When Szyszko was nominated to the Ministry of Environment in December 2015, he made it his personal mission to radically transform the ecology of the forest through an attack on bark beetle and the message about the importance of Białowieża to the national identity. A few months later, Szyszko dismantled the National Council on Nature Protection, most members of which favored a national park expansion or backed the studies that native bark beetle could architecturally reconstruct a forest misdirected by forestry logic. Szyszko dismissed thirty-two of thirty-nine members and constituted a new council of twenty-nine members, among them mostly foresters, agricultural scientists, and directors of botanical gardens.

Fig. 6.5. SANTA organization says, "Don't depreciate the forester." From a 2014 calendar distributed to residents of the forest region to illustrate the dangers of a forest without a forester. Photo of calendar by Eunice Blavascunas.

In winter 2016, EU bodies watched Poland, first criticizing its moves to dismantle its Constitutional Court and then its breach of environmental law. In April 2018, the EU Court of Justice issued a finding that Poland would need to pay €100,000 per day (more than €4 million) for each day it had illegally logged. The European Union also gave Poland an ultimatum to drop judicial reforms that would have allowed PiS to put judges under its political control. If Poland did not comply, it might lose its voting rights in the European Union. But neither mandate could affect much change given the EU voting members, such as Hungary and Slovakia, that supported Poland.

PiS popular support enabled expressions, previously unseen in Poland, that mirrored far-right groups in Europe. Poland, like many European countries, witnessed extremists emboldened to hold prayer meetings for a "Muslim Holocaust" and white power marches with turnouts in the thousands where marchers carried the Celtic cross (a popular international symbol of white power). At the level of Białowieża, Belarusians increasingly became the target of local ultraright nationalists who took to celebrating a group of fighters known as "cursed soldiers" (*Żołnierze Wyklęci*).

For much of postsocialist Poland, memory politics focused on Poland's Home Army (Armia Krajowa), the dominant Polish resistance movement during World War II occupation. But the Home Army's legend focused mostly on resistance to German occupation and especially the Warsaw Uprising that tried to liberate the city. The anticommunist right needed heroes who fought Soviets. The newly invented term "cursed soldiers" refers to a variety of Polish anti-Soviet resistance movements that formed at the end of World War II. Many fought in Poland's Home Army but refused to put down their arms after Red Army "liberation" from German occupation. They chose to fight as partisans against "illegal occupants," meaning the new Soviet-imposed rulers and administrators. Some units operated until the early 1950s. Many soldiers died during fights with Soviets and Polish communists or were sentenced to execution by communist courts. These partisans were responsible in the larger Hajnówka region for revenge killings against Belarusian inhabitants who identified Polish foresters to Soviets during the Soviet occupation of eastern Poland (Kosel and Pirożnikow 2017). The Polish Communist Party strictly forbade any references to the memory of cursed soldiers. And cursed soldiers, if they lived, would have had to move to a new town and then invent a cover biography to avoid persecution and death.

Postsocialist ideological discourse revived the cursed soldiers' narrative, with a quarterly journal issuing its first volume in 2016. Poland's president, Andrzej Duda (PiS), called the cursed soldiers "a model for young people." On the first official state holiday of the cursed soldier, March 1, 2016, Duda claimed, "Those indomitable soldiers . . . were soldiers of the Polish state." After a long absence of this history, he mandated that the story of the cursed soldiers be included in the elementary school curriculum.

Organs not affiliated with PiS, yet supportive of Polish nationalism, seem to be adopting the extreme and literal interpretation of the government's nationalist position regarding the cursed soldiers. The popular election of PiS speaks to the uncoerced mobilization of part of the population. But since PiS's rise, the most influential organization strongly reviving the cursed soldiers is National Radical Camp (Obóz Narodowo-Radykalny [ONR]), a far-right nonpolitical movement that considers itself a descendant of interwar Poland's far right.

The first ONR was established in 1934, a period when non-Polish ethnic and religious groups constituted more than 30 percent of the population. It called for the elimination of national minorities from public life. An intellectual influence of ONR was the chief ideologue of the National Democracy political party (Endecja), Roman Dmowski (1864–1939). Dmowski was the main rival to the socialist leader of interwar Poland, Piłsudski, and wanted to overcome any notion that Poland would lead Europe to a brotherhood of nations—the romantic ideas of the nation embedded in Mickiewicz and Polish messianism. For Dmowski, the nation was not made up of those who inhabited the territory of Poland or those who wanted the restoration of the Polish nation; rather, it included those whose language was Polish and whose religion was Catholic. Outward conformity was not enough for anyone claiming to be Polish. And Dmowski was outwardly and brazenly antisemitic. Poland needed to direct its energies toward aggression, not just with German and Russian powers but specifically with political minorities within Poland. Dmowski believed that a true nation would become heartened in the struggle (Walicki 1982, 349–57). He referred to that process as "ingestion," directed specifically toward Ukrainians and Belarusians within Poland, who might be considered "tribes" (Groth 1969). For Dmowski, "pursuing its own interests is the primary duty of the nation," and the "only principle of international relations is that of strength or weakness, never that of being morally right or wrong" (Walicki 1982, 338).

In 2012, ONR legally registered as a common-interest association propagating many of Dmowski's views. It used violence against Middle Eastern and African minorities in Poland and against anti-PiS protesters. ONR organized several marches throughout Poland and coorganized an infamous 2017 Polish Independence Day march of more than sixty thousand people in Warsaw, where they carried banners reading "White Europe," "We want God," and "Clean blood, sober mind." A 2018 march was banned by the mayor of Warsaw.

The ONR branch based in the larger Hajnówka area revived Dmowski's ideas in relation to Belarusians and Ukrainians in the region. In 2017, local activists of ONR under the Narodowa Hajnówka (National Hajnówka) unit entered the Białowieża Forest conflict. The group's Facebook page, iconized as a slashed-through hammer and sickle (until ONR changed it to a saw cutting a tree and the Polish flag), called on members to form militias to track down "ecoterrorist" activities. Members exchanged multiple messages about Szyszko's correct ecology for the bark beetle and otherwise derided ecologists, suggesting, partly in jest, that harvesters kill and crush the activists. But their targeting of ethnic minorities was stark and painful, especially given that Polska B was designated as such because it contained the largest ethnic minority groups in Poland today.

I knew two of the main organizers of Narodowa Hajnówka: Alex and his sister, Monika. Although I did not know them well, I had frequent contact with their mother, Dorota, and their father, Piotr. I interviewed Piotr many years ago, when he was the *prezes*, or village tax collector. He did not identify himself as either Belarusian or Polish, Catholic or Orthodox. He wanted me to know that his family had been there from time immemorial, and they had owned land, served as forest guards for kings and czars, and were still there. Other people in the village saw him as Belarusian. He and his wife, who identified as Polish, owned a sawmill together. Twice they let me bring study tours for foreign groups who wanted educational tours of local sawmills. Piotr had more sympathies with nature conservationists than other small sawmill owners in the region and lamented the excesses of State Forests, who would not sell timber to him (or other small sawmills). He bought most of his raw oak from Belarus or Ukraine and turned it into wine casks for French buyers.

Alex and Monika (when they were teenagers) attended numerous events at the Teremiski school, where I taught English (Uniwersytet Powszechny). The school was infused with a multicultural curriculum. The school's rectors were Jacek Kuroń, known as the "Godfather" of the communist opposition movement in PRL Poland, and, after Kuroń's death in 2005, Zygmunt Bauman, one of the most highly esteemed social critics of Europe who was forced out of communist Poland in 1968 because of his Jewish background. Many school activities focused on how to both remember the past and search for new ways to move forward in postcommunist Poland by living with the wounds of the past. This approach involved theater performances about Jews in the region, concerts of traditional and contemporary Belarusian music, workshops on feminism and its ideas, and organized trips to visit local Catholic, Orthodox, Muslim, and Old Believer houses of worship. The school put up calendars themed, "I am Polish," with each month dedicated to a Polish citizen of Asian, African, Middle Eastern, Ukrainian, Belarusian, or other descent.

One of the intelligentsia in Teremiski told me about Alex, Dorota, and Monika's increasing extremism, which occurred after Dorota and Piotr divorced, after they had been invited to Christmas at Adam Wajrak's house, and after they wanted nothing to do with the Uniwersytet members in the Teremiski village. Alex and Monika began spending time with football clubs and martial arts groups in the regional city of Białystok. One night around a bonfire at their house with the "hooligans" from Białystok, the group set out, house to house, yelling "Kurwa!" (Whore!) in front of each house. This kind of emboldening experience made way for more organized public displays in broad daylight.

In February 2017, Narodowa Hajnówka organized its first march (there was a second in 2018 and a third in 2019) to commemorate the cursed soldiers, including one of its most controversial figures, Romualda Raisa Burego (code name Bury), who pacified whole villages in 1946, murdering more than seventy-nine Polish citizens of Belarusian descent. The marchers were mostly young men and women carrying Polish flags, portraits of the cursed soldiers, and ONR memorabilia and chanting, "A na drzewach zamiast liści, będą wisieć komuniści" (Instead of leaves hanging from trees, let's hang the communists).

In June 2017, Narodowa Hajnówka members joined a few hundred people to attend the opening ceremony for a highly controversial statue of another cursed soldier, Danuta Siedzikówna (code name Inka), in the forest. Monuments are built to initiate rituals around themselves and speak as collective memory at a site (Traba 2015, 26). Eighteen-year-old Inka worked for State Forests in Hajnówka and served in a morally pure context, given her age and gender. Her forester father was captured and sent to Siberia by the Soviets in 1940, and her mother was executed in the forest by the Gestapo for collaborating with the Polish Home Army. Her story is surely one of heroism against incredible odds as she smuggled all sorts of messages and goods through enemy lines. But the timing of the statue and its placement in the Białowieża forest outside the Browsk State Forest administration (with its majority Belarusian population) symbolized a renewed fight with anything that looked outside the Polish narrative of victimhood. This fight includes the bark beetle—that is, the pest inside the Polish forest and the enemy of Polish foresters—and whose ecology and science count. Szyszko; foresters in uniform; Narodowa Hajnówka members, including Alex, Monika and Dorota; and Siedzikówna's descendants all attended a highly regimented, two-hour commemoration as the statue was unveiled.

Fig. 6.6. Unveiling ceremony for cursed soldier "Inka," June 11, 2017. Photo by Agnieszka Sadowska. Used with permission.

In 2018, Alex was charged with a misdemeanor and forbidden from organizing further marches. Monika was charged with attacking a police officer and sentenced to four months in prison. Narodowa Hajnówka took to the streets to protest, carrying a banner comparing Monika with Inka. Both of their faces featured prominently on the banners with the message that Monika and Inka's fates were both sealed by "red Hajnówka," meaning communists of Belarusian descent. Members of one of the Orthodox churches in Hajnówka told me that the priest publicly announced the engagement of Alex with a woman from the congregation at a Sunday service. Two days before the wedding in fall 2018, Monika was taken to prison in Warsaw. On media channels and with the support of a right-wing professor, discourse spread quickly that Monika was a "political prisoner" who was given a sentence much harsher than her crime precisely because of her "patriotic" activities.

Simultaneously in the PiS and Narodowa Hajnówka narrative, forest activists were the worst version of a political operative who would deny national distinctiveness in the story of the cursed soldiers. Forest activists are political operatives against Polish foresters, who know which soil can best support pine, spruce, oak, and maple and who know the favored trees for lumber, and against commemorating the one true story of the fight for the forested region that needed to be known as Polish.

Teremiski village has one main street. No matter which direction you come from, the village starts with a wooden Orthodox cross and a wooden Catholic cross erected side by side, with an identical set of crosses as you leave the village. As long as I have been visiting Białowieża, the story of ethnic division was largely buried under polite pronouncements that "everyone got along" (meaning Poles and Belarusians) and that Białowieża was exceptional compared with other villages with stories of World War II pogroms. Long-term residents wanted me to understand that people intermarried and coexisted, even as they celebrated Christmas, New Year's, and Easter by both the Julian and Roman calendars. They worked together in their agricultural fields and for State Forests. The claim to being *tutejszy* (chap. 5) suggests that there are other forms of loyalty than radical nationalism. The type of "unity" propagated by Narodowa Hajnówka created a notion of community in which it is permissible for ethnic Poles to murder their Belarusian neighbors (or selves) for alleged communist collaboration, which sent good and respectable Poles to miserable fates in Siberia. That imagined community is more united in its youth culture, white power symbols, and cursed soldier symbol than unified by any common experience of living in the village with other Narodowa Hajnówka members. Yet they want to claim the forest region as "theirs," as "Polish" and "anticommunist," as "logged by Polish foresters," and free of "ecoterrorists."

The rupture for the village of Teremiski is not about the deterioration of face-to-face contact between long-term inhabitants of the village (or rather people who spent some part of their life working for State Forests) so much as whether modernity will advance along nationalist or cosmopolitan lines. Can the ideal of every person being a developed, nonpeasant, literate member of a national state exist together with modernity beyond the nation state?

Ecological activists were invited to use the school buildings in Teremiski by its legal owner, Adam Wajrak. The Jacek Kuroń Foundation continued to operate out of private buildings in Teremiski for purposes of concerts for the forest activists, plays about the Jewish history of the Białowieża region, and film screenings. Residents posted a prominent banner in Teremiski that read, "Pseudoekolodzy, brudne ręce precz od puszczy—Mieszkańcy"

(Pseudoecologists, your hands are dirty. Get out of the Forest!—[signed] The Residents).

Although Teremiski is the home of Wajrak, Poland's most famous environmental activist, most ecological activists are in the village temporarily. They represent a cosmopolitan world aligned with taking responsibility for environmental destruction, where one has to place the local in the larger context of diminishing global old growth forests and climate change. Ecological activists have used arguments about the forest as "the heritage of humanity." They have garnered the support of the international conservation community and have appealed to the European Union, its Court of Justices, and other international agendas—instead of the Polish government and environment ministry—as institutions having juridical and legal power over Poland. They scaled up, whereas Polish foresters became immersed in a nationalistic narrative scaled to the specific soil, with "their blood."

The stridency of Narodowa Hajnówka joined to State Forests suggests that the ethnic Polish forester, in militarized antiriot gear, would take care of the intruder—"the pest" and the "swarm" of these "pests"—in their midst. The swarm is both the nature activist and the bark beetle. PiS disarticulated any notion of foresters being attached to the communist past and mythologized the forester as Poland, as its historical embodiment of a martyred nation and the forest. The history of the Polish forester became the history of Poland. The fight for Białowieża became the struggle of Poland against Europe and against internationalism.

Ongoing Processes

A small unsightly insect can do ecological work that is drastic and historical. It can diversify monocultural forest stands and topple spruce unfit for a changing climate. It can also rearrange the icons of the forest; by recognizing the beetle as part of the forest's ecology, forest activists have directed attention away from Białowieża's stock icons to the processes of forest life. Białowieża is more than a static view of a beautiful forest with old trees. It contains more than just charismatic species as wolves and bison. Its story exceeds tales of its foresters. And its commercial forest includes outposts of old growth and places for complex self-willed biological processes. When one cares for the bark beetle and considers its role in Białowieża's ecology, one cares for the forest as a series of ongoing, dynamic processes that do not stop at the borders of either management zones or nation-states. These processes make people care about the forest for its ecology and its relationships of life and death, eating and being eaten. The forest has been evolving for ten thousand years, since the end of the last ice age, before national identities were formed. In this framing, forest activists thwart the nationalist story about the primacy of forester activities in Białowieża by attending to the beetle's long-term, creative, evolutionary role now and into the future.

The turn to nationalism in Poland is a study in what happens when a nation tries to rebuke the wrongs of a former regime or political system. Liberal, European-looking governments left Poland in a peripheral position economically and socially, as the European Union chided Poles for being "backward"—in either turning to nationalism or failing to forgo their communist habitus. PiS offered a program that redefined modernity and Polish interests: the paternalism of the village forester would set Poland on the correct modern course. Through State Forests, PiS excluded forest activists—and nature conservationists more broadly, who wanted a forest without commercial logging—from the community of "true Poles" and patriots. The forester must care for Polish trees and Poles and must mark the otherness of a beetle and win the sameness of the Polish people. Narodowa Hajnówka activated these same Polish people in their extremism, even as we learn of the ethnic "contamination" of some of its members. The ethnic mixing, though, suggests that Narodowa Hajnówka, like the forester in chapter 2, is more concerned with allegiance than blood. Belarusians can be "ingested" into the Polish narrative of the forest, especially if they accept that the cursed soldier Bury had to take revenge. He murdered Belarusians villagers after World War II because they betrayed Polish foresters to the Soviets.

This equation, however, does not take into account the larger ecological question set out at the beginning of this chapter: In the age of climate change and threats to European integration, what sorts of opportunities for theoretical and explanatory interventions are available to the anthropologist when the forest and the humans come together in an ecological assemblage?

Withdrawal into national belonging at a time of climate change seems regressive, a charge that furthers the nationalists' momentum. Acknowledging climate change means acknowledging the need for international cooperation. The type of modernity needed to reach political action on climate change is global; it demands that citizens detach from the nation and act on the prescriptions of a global regime of international experts. This detachment in the West has occurred precisely through globalized commerce, finance, culture, and consumerism, which fuel climate change in the first place. As Bruno Latour (2018, 7) noted, we have a "terrestrial question" (bigger than the nation) and a knot that is not easy to untie: "Matters of ecology cannot rely on the normal procedures of the [nation] state." Politics needs to be mobilized in a different way, and the anthropologist has a role in making visible what is happening on the ground beyond simply presenting two ideological positions at war or chronicling eras that have begun or ended in some kind of historical sense. The anthropologist can use the insights of postsocialist and posthumanist scholarship to think through the nationalist turn in postsocialist Poland and reorient how we think about the impact of the bark beetle three decades after the official end of communism.

Far-right activists in Białowieża are trying to connect to ancestors, soil, and blood. Like the ideologue and political leader Dmowski, they believe they need a homogeneous entity with spiritual and emotional bonds that give them both a common tradition and a future destiny in the region. This outlook is largely what the forest activists object to. For their refusal, PiS and Narodowa Hajnówka deride activists as "communists," "ecoterrorists," and "pests," with no attachments to any particular culture and certainly not to the Polish nation. Like the bark beetle, which flies around "disrespecting" borders of nations, national parks, and commercial forests, nature activists roam the forest, espousing socially liberal values as the values of nature. In the eyes of nationalists, this is their transgression.

When state socialism ended in Poland, this rupture redefined power relations between different ethnic and class groups. As nationalism reached "outbreak" proportions, it also served to redefine those relations. Whereas State Forests in communist Poland created more equal opportunities to address Białowieża's social inequalities by educating Belarusians as foresters, State Forests under PiS insists that the real inequalities are not between different ethnic or class groups but between those who benefited from their Communist Party involvement and those who could or did not.

Białowieża is a territory, which the nationalists covet (and want to convert), but also an ecological zone inhabited by people with wildly different political ideologies. As such, it presents the anthropologist with an opportunity to ask which fissures and faults might productively open when she illustrates "common sense" through her descriptions. A resurgence is not a repeat performance, which is why, as Anna Tsing (2015) insists, anthropologists need to cultivate the art of noticing. Narodowa Hajnówka might share one thing in common with the forest activists: a desire to inhabit the earth, albeit a particular piece of earth that can provide the group with cohesion. Although broad, this reconfiguration asks us to reexamine resurgences and outbreaks of particular ideologies and insects at particular points in time. The intensity of the bark beetle outbreak and of right-wing nationalism cannot be taken into account without also understanding the way in which the ecological crisis of climate change will inexorably create habitats and political possibilities.

There are processes through which places, ideas, and cultural groups appear threatening to the grand design of nationalist projects. Nativisms (e.g., bark beetle, ethnic or political otherness) challenge what is considered threatening or significant. The nationalist turn securitizes belonging through the protection of frontiers. An analysis of the postsocialist period using posthumanist and postsocialist scholarship teaches us about the resurgence of phenomena that look familiar but might take new turns, make new alliances, and require figuring out how to live together. The nationalist turn and the bark beetle outbreak also provide a temporal optic that allows us think about historical change and possibilities. In using the narrative and agency of the bark beetle, we radically rethink relations of belonging in a time of climate change and weakening European cohesion. Once we see the bark beetle as part of a plurality of radical difference—as posthumanism asks—and trace a history of that difference in social relations— as postsocialism asks—we open up to a way of becoming that might learn from all the ways the ultraright has tried to create difference as toxic or narrow Polish identity and forest diversity.

The key to metamorphosis is not to transcend the national question (as many of the forest activists are doing) nor to deny ethnic difference (as the communists did) but rather to see differentiated entities. In that sense, the terms "Poles" and "Belarusians" do not go away. Foresters can still be figures who all wear uniforms (chap. 2), and bark beetle have not surprised scientists by attacking oak instead of spruce trees. But Narodowa Hajnówka members can come out of a multicultural milieu and still espouse Dmowski's ideas. Forest activists include polyglot anarchists and, as one member told me, those who want an antirefugee policy for Poland. But only the nationalists are capable of solidifying and making "true groups" out of otherwise differentiated entities.

For now, the bark beetle has eaten thousands of spruce. And the forest has been heavily logged; after six thousand semitrucks hauled away more than 180,000 cubic meters of timber in 2017—bringing Lasy Państwowe more than US$10 million—PiS dismissed Szyszko and State Forests Director Tomaszewski (Bohdan et al. 2018, 7). PiS might have been Euroskeptic, but it was not anti-EU. PiS avoided paying the fine mandated by the European Court of Justice by terminating logging. But foresters continue to annex Polish law so they will be able to continue logging. And with PiS in power, controlling the judiciary, it seems increasingly likely that Polish law will try to distance itself from EU law. Foresters replanted self-regenerating areas with trees favorable to a timber harvest.

Note

1. The conference Managing Bark Beetle Outbreak in Białowieża Primeval Forest offers recent scientific debates on bark beetle in European forests (see Polska Akademia Nauk 2017).

7

TEMPORAL DIMENSIONS

The Past Is Not Safe at All

A RELATIONSHIP WITH TIME CAN BE MARKED BY erasures and replacements. Over my two decades of research, the most obvious markers of this phenomenon are Białowieża's old trees, removed on logging trucks and reseeded with those that the forester selects for their timber value. But logging is fungible, so removing old trees supports multiple diametrically opposed regimes, political parties, and interests across centuries and decades. And these regimes, political parties, and interests claim the forest through other markers that reference the pasts covered in this book. For example, the street name ul. Waszkiewicza (Aleksander, named for a Soviet military general of Polish descent) was changed in 2017 to ul. Stoczek (meaning "slight slope"), and another was changed from ul. Olga Gabiec (the local leader of the Western Belarusian Communist Party) to Pałacowa (Palace Street). The large granite marker in front of the Orthodox church was etched with a dedication to the "heroes of freedom and socialism"; in 2014, village officials melted the word "socialism" off the bronze plaque. Statues to the executed first director of State Forests, Adam Loret, went up near the Technical Forestry High School, and foresters erected their tribute to the cursed soldier Inka outside their offices in the Browsk Forestry District of Białowieża. In all these ways, the past was being made in the present and comprised not simply shared memories of all inhabitants but consequential visions driven by political interests. They mattered in how the forest would be used and managed.

In this book, unlike books on memory politics, I have tried to make the story of the forest not narrowly about memory but about the idea of a forest in relation to modernity over a period of time when the politics of the past occurred at the everyday level in the forest. The wide-reaching displays of Polish nationalism in the forest were clearly not the first time that the forest had been vexed by those who wished to control ideas about the forest as timeless or historical. The past 250 years have produced more chaos than order, as competing interests wrested the forest's meaning away from both previous rulers and local groups, as the Communist Party changed street names, as the occupying Germans in World War I erected full-scale industrial forestry operations, as Imperial Russia closed Roman Catholic churches in the village, and as the czars imported foreign game to supplement the bison in their hunts. The picture that begins to take shape from this book is that the human past in the present is not simply grafted to the forest; rather, what that forest *is* comes from the generative ecologies within the forest and the human infrastructures and ideologies that enable and cocreate different combinations of species and age classes, monuments, waterways, people, and meadows.

The people in this book show that they are flexible when recasting their identities across these eras in which the wrong interpretation of the past can be seen as treasonous. But that does not mean that people will align neatly with one camp or another. The past is actively constructed alongside official interpretations of history, and we see this in details from people's lives. Simona Kossak called for a Catholic priest on her deathbed and asked to be buried in the Kossak catacombs near Kraków. Her earlier patronage of guru Sai Baba and her disavowal of her upbringing in favor of her rugged life in the forest did not stop her from claiming her place in a dispossessed Polish aristocracy at the time of her death—a time when PiS would claim Poland as a Catholic nation seeking justice against lingering elements of communism. But near the end of her life, she facilitated the type of "illegitimate expertise" that she so railed against. She helps us see that individuals might act in opposition to their professed politics and social status in light of goals that were not just about getting rid of communism. Simona acted on her conviction of animal rights. Leszek Szumarski might have begun his life as a peasant, but he deftly crafted a social world to supersede options available to other men in his class background. As the capitalist path to development attempted to transform the peasant category and make it obsolete, Leszek would identify with the image of a free man of the forest. This identity folded in the idea that there were postpeasants who could defy communist and capitalist logic in their attachments to the land and kin. He would elevate himself to a new status, neither entrepreneur nor loser, in the transition. He was not just the *lumpenproletariat* who obeyed the foresters or conservationists. He exhibited tremendous agency in networking and bricolage to make himself as ambiguous as the forest itself. Foresters possessed a transhistorical staying power as figures in the local community, even as their professed ideologies bent to different regimes and politics. Foresters could be intelligentsia, gentry, working people, communists, and nationalists, depending on the political expression of the state. The institutional inertia of State Forests, with its ethos, uniforms, and bureaucracy, is a testament to contradictory processes. Similarly, in Janusz Korbel's story, the person who writes a multicultural narrative about what it means to be native to place finds his alter ego in the Belarusian quality of the forest region, where Belarusian is also symbolically referenced as authoritarian and passive, autochthonous, and the imposition of the Soviet Union. This image-based historical sensibility taps into the deep subconscious of Białowieża, which has had its fair share of authoritarian rule and multiculturalism, undergirded by both a *kresy* imaginary and a nostalgia for life during the communist period.

It is difficult to find a vocabulary that can capture and illuminate when individuals complied with political ideologies that would correct the past and when they were more committed to their respective social groups within their respective social hierarchies. Peasants, entrepreneurs, foresters, scientists, aristocrats, forest activists, nationalists, and communist sympathizers were categories with staying power but that clearly morphed depending on the individuals or social groups. Between these types of social actors, and always in the midst of the forest, there seemed to be an incubation of imaginaries about the past. When any one history was suppressed by the state or public demonstrations of compliance were expected, as under communism, people undid the order and pattern through intricate social practices over a decades of their involvement with the forest. I have shown these contradictions within social practices without restricting myself to anthropological debates about the study of power and resistance, as one might in a more Foucauldian analysis or in the field of political ecology. The social phenomena in this book come into dramatic focus when they take the form of long-term ethnographic commitments to people and forest over two decades.

The focus on people in the chapters has shown that structural ruptures such as the fall of state socialism did not overdetermine outcomes in relation to forest protection and use. Individual people and nature possessed a great deal of agency and creativity, even as social hierarchies were present and had not, in fact, disappeared during the communist period. This aspect matters in the kind of story I could tell, observing change up close but always at the risk of romanticizing this forest and its inhabitants. However, the chapters are not just ethnographic, descriptive sketches. Above all, the forest and its inhabitants offered too many problems to avoid, and this obliged me to listen deeply to people and to observe their concerns and life worlds. I would like to highlight how this book is, foremost, a self-conscious attempt not to become a pawn in the politics of memory while simultaneously not forgetting that nature is not outside of history and culture.

The nationalist insistence, or the communist insistence, or the liberal triumphalist insistence on one true story of the past turns the ethnographer's work into evidence gathering in the context of the vast historical and social science literature on these subjects. But first, the ethnographer must see what she brings to the story. The ethnographic puzzle over my two decades of research was how to interpret people's attachments to the past in the framework of a peripheral country and a peripheral place, in ancient forests that are themselves peripheral to the European continent— all in a country that has sought to be understood as central to European and civilizing projects of modernity, socialism, and political thought. Many people within Poland have done the discursive work to ensure that Poland is now identified as part of Central Europe, an area with imprecise borders, numerous criteria for definition as a region of a former multinational empire, socialist histories, and multiple religious identities. As I developed as an anthropologist with a commitment to scholarship on ecology and anthropological theory, these commitments to critical theory helped me identify strands of my unconscious in discourse about capitalist triumphalism at the end of the Cold War.

Anthropology initiated the critique of exoticism, but it was more challenging to excise myself from the paradigm that contrasts East and West. This was especially so as I began to hone in on people's heavy political and emotional investments in the unfairness of World War II; the number of Polish citizens who died at that time; how borders were drawn after the war; and why, how, and when individuals celebrated or excused their involvement in the communist project. All the while, I wrote this book over a period that added a new global understanding of periodization: the Anthropocene, an era defined by climate change and human excesses on a planetary scale.

As an environmentalist coming out of a US environmental education, the story of forest decline is one of mea culpa. With so few old growth forests left, it is imperative that a world of interconnected climate change consider the biological importance of such forest and how modernity has materially benefited from its loss, as the West controlled resource peripheries in the name of profit. I also understood what happens in the US context when the nation turns wilderness into a founding myth at the expense of seeing colonial conflict and Native American cultures within the land. The narrative sanctified Manifest Destiny on an emptied out continent (Cronon 1995). I kept this double consciousness with me over the course of my research.

For Poland, instead of asking how we can see history and culture in the wilderness without people, the question seemed to be how people in Białowieża can see beyond history to the larger context of this "last primeval forest" on the European continent as part of a story of global ecological degradation. I wanted Poland, at the political level, to recognize the global ecological crisis, but perhaps the failure of conservation is a failure of Western models as much as the failure of the nation-state. The failure of Western advisers, banks, institutions, and scholars was to believe that postsocialist Europe could simply modernize on Western terms by accepting free markets as the solution, which is not the whole story.

In that sense, postsocialist anthropology and anthropology invested in stories about world making and periphery in the face of an ecological crisis have been of central relevance for this book. This relevance was clearer in 2018 than in 1995, when I first visited the forest. When we see any of the people in this book eschewing their peripheral status, we see how resilient imaginaries of the past are shaped—by multiscalar representation; by the west projecting an image of "Europe proper," in which Poland is supposed to conserve this European relict and modernize; by Polish nationalists reacting to what the west does not see; by local Belarusian and *tutejszy* inhabitants who wanted more modernity and development over the course of the twentieth century but on their own terms, against the courtship and manipulation of authoritarian interests in Belarusians, as a people who had to serve violent goals of the Nazis and the Soviet empire.

The turn toward nationalism at the end of this book is the turn toward a way of being that the proverbial, liberal-democratic West did not want to see. The turn is against the internationalism of both communism and globalization (as represented by political parties that preceded the nationalists now in power) or, in the case of Białowieża, the national park ideal in which passive nature protection symbolizes a form of globalization.

It becomes clear within this book why certain people or interests rejected or embraced life in the communist era, but the flip side of the rejection of communism and internationalism is the question, "What's wrong with nationalism?" If communism disenfranchised people to the point of revolution and globalization failed provide justice or opportunity for most, then isn't nationalism a form of social solidarity that can protect and care for people and forests, as with the recent pro-logging slogans, "Protect Polish forests for the Polish nation"? Could there be a peaceful flowering of nations, each loving its own heritage without stepping on the sovereignty of others? What's wrong with taking ethnic identity and turning it into solidarity for the protection of nature or the nation, which is where many of the nature conservationists started heading when I began researching this topic?

Minorities and people who do not fit the national ideal always reside within territories. In times of economic or other stress, the nation needs to excise the "foreign" elements to create solidarity. Nationalists dig into "their" glorious pasts (victories of war, of territorial gain) and their "victimhood" (defeats in war, impositions of other or imperialistic powers) toward what they feel is the one and only solution to injustice: the nation (Neocleous 1997). The irony, as anthropologist Douglas Holmes (2000) has illustrated so well in ethnographic portraits of the far right, is that the very organization set up to hold postwar peace—namely, the European Community, which became the European Union—has so disenfranchised people through its bureaucracy that narrow nationalisms threaten peace and economic security in Europe once again.

In this estrangement, nationalists isolate themselves in the story of their nation and the support of their people, feeling that they are better than anything the supposedly liberal and seemingly secular West could offer. Nationalists use the past as an antidote to alienation. However, the turn to nationalism in Poland follows a period of relative prosperity, especially for Białowieża—one in which rising expectations could not be met, which has led to reactionary tendencies. Right-wing nationalism flourishes in Europe (west, east, north, and south), Israel, Brazil, Turkey, India, and the United States, among other places, at this writing. This rise suggests that it is not just the former communist world that feels its identities have long been suppressed by internationalist projects. A larger portion of the world's electorate apparently feels insecure about the future and looks to a narrowly defined national unity for stability in a world that seems increasingly threatened and threatening. This is especially important in the era of climate change, when nations must work together to achieve reductions in carbon emissions or face more catastrophic storms, droughts, fires, and war.

The challenge for the ethnographer who does long-term research at the Polish-Belarusian borderland in the forest is how to avoid reifying the "martyrdoms of the past" so as not to spread and reinforce nationalist projects for this era. Each ethnographer working within a national boundary makes difficult decisions about the national histories to present or leave out and how to describe formations that eclipse the nation. The invocation of the past and the idea that there are times and places to let the past escape oscillate throughout this book. The advantage of long-term ethnographic engagement, including both several year-long stays and then repeated shorter visits, is that the ethnographer cannot cement people in a presentist telling. In a big historical rupture, it takes time for people to sift through the wreckage, like the revolutions of 1989 in Central Europe. I imagine the same will be true for what appears to be the global nationalist turn at the time of crisis climate change. Critical voices in this ethnography show us that people like Leszek, Simona, Janusz, foresters, and others made surprising turns and alliances as they negotiated which pasts would be prominent in the story. Bark beetles and storks remind us that humans alone do not tell the stories. History, culture, and politics are deeply embedded within ecology. Nature plays into and constructs subjective senses of time and history.

Through intimate encounters with people in Białowieża, we can imagine what might be from what has been and is. This book frames and explores how space and time interact, how forest and history combine in anthropological analysis, always anchored to actual people living in the forest. In that sense, I would like to elaborate on a few more elements of the larger structural forces that inform this book.

Białowieża cannot easily escape its meaning as a borderlands ancient forest. Two major civilizations met in this forested borderlands: Orthodox and Catholic Christianity. In addition, Poland developed a national identity, over at least two centuries, as bordering Germany/Prussia/Austria-Hungary and Russia. Today Poland is in a different situation. As a member of NATO and a member of the European Union, with a populace that seems split on what kind of economic and cultural dependence they want, the forest has become a point of contention about Poland's relationship with the European Union.

The redrawn European border that folded Poland into the European Union and left Belarus out suggested the possibility of a unified Europe, which has clearly not played out. But a new world of multiple claims to center (between Russia and western Europe) the cultural border of Europe seems less clear than ever. The legitimacy of the border is no longer based on a democratic tradition in Poland and a dictatorial tradition in Belarus. There are still vast differences in democratic norms in these two countries; however, the increasingly illiberal democracy in Poland has drawn the condemnation of the European Union with regard to the way the Polish government logged the forest and to constitutional norms within Poland that have threatened judicial independence in the country. Perhaps Adam Wajrak's pronouncement that the Białowieża region was "little Belarus in a pill" was as much about the nondemocratic tradition in the region as it was about the meaning of the border not being fixed. Perhaps one might ingest this pill and become like Belarus—authoritarian and communist-like—but the option existed to take the pill when Adam said this. PiS changed the rules and the customs of democracy, which meant another round of historically heavy logging for the commercial forest with its remaining fragments of old growth.

The multicultural history of the region could have played out in the romantic tradition of Mickiewicz's Poland, where trees and humans become interchangeable in the struggle for the human, democratic spirit. Instead, the multicultural history has entailed mixed-ethnicity inhabitants not seeing Belarusian and Polish as inherently equal categories. Belarusians, or *tutejszy*, can claim Polish citizenship only when they disavow their past involvement with communism, a past that enabled many Belarusians to become literate citizens—foresters, teachers and doctors—when they were formerly peasants without any prospects of social advancement. However, this past felt alien for many Belarusians in its commitment to atheism over the Orthodox church and the murder of Polish neighbors.

Nature conservation is a temporal historical form and material-discursive construction. Nature conservation grew out of a heightened concern about modernity; too much modernity meant a self-consciousness about what was lost. Twentieth-century nature conservation in Białowieża, as a national park, sprouted from a quarreling marriage of scientists and foresters. Modernity is typically defined as being "outside" of nature and draws a protective border around the most pristine form of nature. National parks and nature preserves are wedded to unstable forms of nature, forms that move outside park boundaries and that cannot fully be protected in a Noah's Ark of correct species composition. Bark beetles lead us back to the premise that modernity is never outside of nature; people cannot just command the forest to do what they would like it to do. Forest activists want us to see the bark beetle's potential in this regard.

Conservation biologists question any steady state of nature that can be maintained within a national park. In the face of a global extinction crisis, biologists argue about the proper level of human intervention. These debates are far too complex to introduce in the conclusion of this book and are not the foci of my analysis. Nevertheless, I wish to enrich an understanding of forests and forest conservation through my long-term ethnographic lens, which is why I return to the emphasis at the beginning of this book—why a primeval forest can never just rest in its "primevalness." The deep time is always assembled and interwoven with historical subjectivity. Unstable nature is also human history.

By bringing the longue durée ethnography and history together with a unstable ecology embedded in historical contexts fleshed out in the chapters of this book, I have attempted to explain the "development of underdevelopment" in the postsocialist period. I mean the development of a feeling of disenfranchisement, even as people have more material wealth than ever before. People are led to nationalist populism because the present has not delivered on an expectation set long ago, during the communist era, about the abundance of material goods in the west. The forest has to do the work of modernizing both as a national park and as a commercially logged forest. But bark beetles show us that spruce-dominant forests—the forest type used to modernize—might disappear, despite foresters' best attempts to control dynamic insect populations and replant with profitable timber species.

The lands owned by State Forests hold the remnants of the primeval and of the hand of the foresters that will save people from underdevelopment. State Forests lands are at once labile, unpredictable, and contaminated by the strict reserve (the repository of the bark beetle and a type of forest not planted by foresters) of Białowieża National Park. With the national park established, conservationists and activists will always find justification for seeing the commercial forest as a remnant of the more pristine national park. The commercial forest becomes a place to grow the national park's wildness. In the face of climate change and hotter, drier years, the commercial forest threatens to become unmanageable, according to climate scientists' predictions; however, foresters hold onto the paradigm of active management rather than letting the forest evolve without interference in a new climate regime.

National parks have been criticized for kicking local people out of their boundaries (Dowie 2009), and we see how capitalism has shaped global imaginaries about nature (Igoe 2017). It is especially important for the anthropologist to highlight possibilities for emerging cultures and ecologies so that long-term ethnographic research does not merely serve to reify symbolic boundaries set up by people who would delimit our understanding of the past and of forests.

In the case of Białowieża, whether or not the whole forest is primeval or old growth is not the point. The point is how humans and nonhumans can create new combinations of culture and ecology that rely on subjective and national histories while also working synergistically and openly toward a forest that is an anchor in the midst of disturbances. As Leszek Szumarski disturbed our notion of a "wild man" for Białowieża, so too can a bark beetle alter our understanding and vision of Białowieża.

I hope that my book has also shown some of the ways that humans living in this area have invested their practices and imaginations into making the forest a historical production. I also hope that I have provided an ethnographic sensibility of change over time with attention to repurposing historical narratives. Contemporary life involves tremendous change. The forest is within time, both the deep time that sets ancient forests as a distinct and the historical time that enables us to see how the past constructs the present and the future.

BIBLIOGRAPHY

Abramsky, Chimen, Maciej Jachimczyk, and Antony Polonsky. 1989. *The Jews in Poland*. New York: Basil Blackwell.

Abu-Lughod, Lila. 1986. *Veiled Sentiments: Honor and Poetry in a Bedouin Society*. Berkeley: University of California Press.

Ahrens, Theodor. 1921. "The Present Status of the European Bison or Wisent." *Journal of Mammalogy* 2 (2): 58–62.

Allen, Paul. 1991. *Katyn: The Untold Story of Stalin's Polish Massacre*. London: Macmillan.

Anderson, Benedict. 1983. *Imagined Communities: Reflections on the Origin and Spread of Nationalism*. Rev. ed. London: Verso.

Bakic-Hayden, Milica. 1995. "Nesting Orientalisms: The Case of Former Yugoslavia." *Slavic Review* 54 (4): 917–31.

Bajko, Piotr. 2001. *Białowieża: Zarys Dziejów*. Białystok: Orthdruk.

———. 2017. "Rozstanie z Olga Gabiec." Czasopsis. Accessed February 2, 2019. https://czasopis.pl/rozstanie-z-olga-gabiec/.

Barad, Karen. 2003. "Posthumanist Performativity: Toward an Understanding of How Matter Comes to Matter." *Signs* 28, no. 3 (Spring): 801–31.

BBC News. 2006. "Belarus Jails Lukashenko's Foes." March 28, 2006. http://news.bbc.co.uk/2/hi/europe/4852130.stm.

Benjamin, Walter, and Rolf Tiedemann. 1999. *The Arcades Project*. Cambridge, MA: Belknap.

Benson, Etienne. 2010. *Wired Wilderness: Technologies of Tracking and the Making of Modern Wildlife*. Baltimore: John Hopkins University Press.

Berdahl, Daphne. 1999. *Where the World Ended: Re-unification and Identity in the German Borderland*. Berkeley: University of California Press.

Bhabha, Homi. 1994. *The Location of Culture*. London: Routledge.

Biehl, Joao, and Peter Locke. 2017. *Unfinished: The Anthropology of Becoming*. Durham, NC: Duke University Press.

Birks, John. 2005. "Mind the Gap: How Open Were European Primeval Forests?" *Trends in Ecology and Evolution* 20, no. 4: 154–56.

Blavascunas, Eunice, and Jodie Baltazar. 2014. *Black Stork, White Stork*. October 9, 2014. Rachel Carson Center, YouTube video, 42:32. https://www.youtube.com/watch?v=2bW8Qm3JvqY.

Blood, Phillip. 2010. "Securing Hitler's *Lebensraum*: The Luftwaffe and Białowieża Forest 1942–1944." *Holocaust and Genocide Studies* 24, no. 2 (October): 247–72. https://doi.org/10.1093/hgs/dcq024

Bobiec, Andrzej, and Małgorzata Bobiec. 2012. "Influence of Spruce Decline in Stands of the Białowieża National Park on Natural Oak Regeneration." *Sylvan* 156 (4): 243–51.

Bohdan, Adam, Marta Rachela Grundland, Michał Książek, Augustyn Miłosz, and Jakub Rok. 2018. *Puszcza Białowieska-Raport z Dewastacji*. https://oko.press/images/2018/04/RaportDewastacja2018.pdf.

Bohn, Thomas, Aliaksandr Dalhouski, and Markus Krzoska. 2017. *Wisent-Wildnis und Welterbe: Geschichte des polnisch wie weißrussischen Nationalparks von Białowieża.* Köln: Böhlau.

Boym, Svetlana. 2001. *The Future of Nostalgia.* New York: Basic.

Briggs, Jean L. 1970. *Never in Anger: Portrait of an Eskimo Family.* Cambridge, MA: Harvard University Press.

Brković, Carna. 2018. "The Same, yet Different: Ethnoanthropological Traditions in Europe." *American Anthropologist,* May 22, 2018. http://www.americananthropologist.org/2018 /05/22/the-same-yet-different-ethno-anthropological-traditions-in-europe/.

Broda, Józef. 2006. "Leśne dziedzictwo po okresie zaborów i powojenne uwarunkowania." In *Z Dziejów Lasów Państwowych i Leśnictwa Polskiego 1924–2004*, edited by Andrezej Szujecki Dyrekcji, 25–97. Warsaw: Generalnej Lasów Państwowych.

Brosius, J. Peter. 1999. "Green Dots, Pink Hearts: Displacing Politics from the Malaysian Rainforest." *American Anthropologist* 101 (1): 36–57.

Brosius, J. Peter, Anna Lowenhaupt Tsing, and Charles Zerner. 2005. *Communities and Conservation: Histories and Politics of Community-Based Natural Resource Management.* Globalization and the Environment. Walnut Creek, CA: AltaMira.

Buchowski, Michał. 2001. *Rethinking Transformation. An Anthropological Perspective on Postsocialism.* Poznań: Wydawnictwo Humaniora.

———. 2004. "Hierarchies of Knowledge in Central-Eastern European Anthropology." *Anthropology of East Europe Review* 22 (2): 5–14.

———. 2006. "The Specter of Orientalism in Europe: From Exotic Other to Stigmatized Brother." *Anthropological Quarterly* 79 (3): 463–82.

Bukowski, Paweł, and Filip Novokmet. 2017. "Inequality in Poland: Estimating the Whole Distribution by G-Percentiles, 1983–2015." WID.world Working Paper Series N°2017/21. World Wealth and Income Database. https://wid.world/document/bukowski -novokmet-poland-1983-2015-wid-world-working-paper-2017-21/.

Buscher, Bram. 2013. *Transforming the Frontier: Peace Parks and the Politics of Neoliberal Conservation in Southern Africa.* Durham, NC: Duke University Press.

Bütler, Rita, and R. Schlaepfer. 2002. "Three-Toed Woodpeckers as an Alternative to Bark Beetle Control by Traps?" In "International Woodpecker Symposium," edited by Peter Pechacek and Werner d'Oleire-Oltmanns. Special issue, *Forschungsbericht* 48:13–26.

Carr, Deborah S., and Kathleen Halvorsen. 2001. "An Evaluation of Three Democratic, Community-Based Approaches to Citizen Participation: Surveys, Conversations with Community Groups, and Community Dinners." *Society and Natural Resources* 14 (2): 107–26.

Chałupczak, H., and. Browarek, T. 2000. *Mniejszości narodowe w Polsce 1918–1995.* Lublin: Maria Curie-Skłodowska University.

Chayànov, Aleksandr V. 1966. *The Theory of Peasant Economy.* American Economic Association Translation Series. Homewood, IL: Published for the American Economic Association by R. D. Irwin.

Chvorostov, Alexander, Konrad Zieliński, Magdalena Cześniak-Zielińska, Ilona Matysiak, Anna Domaradzka, Lukasz Widla-Domaradzki, Hans-Georg Heinrich, and Olga Alekseeva. 2011. "The Belarusian Minority in Poland." *ENRI-East, European, National and Regional Identities.* 2008–2011. Research Report 10." Working Paper. http://doi.org /10.13140/RG.2.2.25455.23208.

Clifford, James, and George Marcus. 1986. *Writing Culture: The Poetics and Politics of Ethnography.* Berkeley: University of California Press.

Creed, Gerald. 1993. "Between Economy and Ideology: Local Level Perspectives on Political and Economic Reform in Bulgaria." *Socialism and Democracy* 13:45–65.

Cronon, William. 1995. "The Trouble with Wilderness, or Getting Back to the Wrong Nature." In *Uncommon Ground: Rethinking the Human Place in Nature,* edited by William Cronon, 69–90. New York: Norton.

Czykwin, Elżbieta. 2000. *Białoruska Mniejszość Narodowa Jako Grupa Stygmatyzowana.* Białystok: Trans Humana.

Daszkiewicz, Piotr, Tomasz Samojlik, and Bogumiła Jędrzejewska. 2012. *Puszcza Białowieska w Pracach Przyrodników I Podróżników 1831–1863.* Warsaw: Semper.

Davies, Norman. 1982. *God's Playground: A History of Poland.* New York: Columbia University Press.

Debord, Guy. (1967) 1983. *Society of the Spectacle.* Translation by Fredy Perlman. Detroit, MI: Black and Red.

Dunn, Elizabeth. 2004. *Privatizing Poland: Baby Food, Big Business, and the Remaking of Labor.* Ithaca, NY: Cornell University Press.

Dowie, Mark. 2009. *Conservation Refugees: The Hundred-Year Conflict between Global Conservation and Native People.* Cambridge, MA: MIT Press.

Eile, Stanislaw. 2000. *Literature and Nationalism in Partitioned Poland, 1795–1918.* New York: St. Martin's.

Escobar, Arturo. 2008. *Territories of Difference: Place, Movements, Life, Redes.* Durham, NC: Duke University Press.

Eurostat Statistics for Poland. 2012. Accessed January 13, 2020. https://ec.europa.eu/eurostat /web/lucas/data/primary-data/2012.

Fahse, Lorenz, and Marco Heurich. 2011. "Simulation and Analysis of Outbreaks of Bark Beetle Infestations and Their Management at the Stand Level." *Ecological Modeling* 222 (11): 1833–64.

Faliński, Janusz. 1968. *Park Narodowy w Puszczy Białowieskiej.* Warsaw: Państwowe Wydawnictwo Rolnicze I Leśne.

Fleituch, Tadeuz. 2010. "Breakdown of Particulate Organic Matter and Function of Stream Ecosystems under Anthropogenic Stress." *Studia Naturae* 57:1–154.

Fleming, Michael. 2010. *Communism, Nationalism and Ethnicity in Poland, 1944–50.* London: Routledge.

Franklin, Stewart. 2002. "Białowieża Forest, Poland: Representation, Myth, and the Politics of Dispossession." *Environment and Planning A* 34 (8): 1459–85.

Gal, Susan. 1991. "Bartok's Funeral: Representations of Europe in Hungarian Political Rhetoric." *American Ethnologist* 18 (3): 440–458.

Geertz, Clifford. 1973. *The Interpretation of Cultures: Selected Essays.* New York: Basic.

———. 1998. "Deep Hanging Out." *New York Review of Books,* October 22, 1998. Accessed via http://hypergeertz.jku.at/GeertzTexts/Deep_Hanging.htm.

Gellner, Ernest. 1983. *Nations and Nationalism.* Ithaca, NY: Cornell University Press.

———. 1998. *Language and Solitude: Wittgenstein, Malinowski and the Habsburg Dilemma.* Cambridge: Cambridge University Press.

Ghodsee, Kristen. 2005. *The Red Riviera: Gender, Tourism, and Postsocialism on the Black Sea.* Next Wave. Durham, NC: Duke University Press.

Graziosi, Andrea. 2014. *After the Holodomor: The Enduring Impact of the Great Famine on Ukraine*. Cambridge, MA: Harvard University Press.

Grewere, Bernd-Stefan, and Richard Hoelzl. 2018. "Forestry in Germany, c. 1550–2000." *Managing Northern Europe's Forests: Histories from the Age of Improvement to the Age of Ecology*, edited by K. Jan Oosthoek and Richard Hölzl, 15–65. New York: Berghan.

Grodzki, Wojciech. 2016. "Mass Outbreak of Spruce Bark Beetle *Ips typographus* in the Context of the Białowieża Primeval Forest." *Forest Research Papers* 77 (4): 324–31.

Groth, Alexander J. 1969. "Dmowski, Pilsudski and Ethnic Conflict in Pre-1939 Poland." *Canadian-American Slavic Studies* 3 (2): 69–91.

Grzywacz, Andrzej. 2014. "Adam Loret (1884–1940?): Pierwszy Dyrektor Naczelny Lasów Państwowych." *Studia i Materiały Ośrodka Kultury Leśnej* 13:93–120.

Guha, Ramachandra. 2000. *The Unquiet Woods: Ecological Change and Peasant Resistance in the Himalaya*. Berkeley: University of California Press.

Gutowski, Jerzy M. 2000. *Zasady funkcjonowania Białowieskiego Parku Narodowego: Powiększonego na Cały Obszar Polskiej Części Puszczy Białowieskiej*. Białowieża: Białowieża National Park.

Gutowski, Jerzy M., and L. Krzystofiak. 2005. "Directions and Intensity of Migration of the Spruce Bark Beetle and Accompanying Species at the Border between Strict Reserves and Managed Forests in North-Eastern Poland." *Ecological Questions* 6:81–92.

Halamska, Maria. 2016. "The Evolution of Family Farms in Poland: Present Time and the Weight of the Past." *East European Countryside* 22, no. 1 (December): 27–51.

Hale, Charles R. 2006. "Activist Research v. Cultural Critique: Indigenous Land Rights and the Contradictions of Politically Engaged Anthropology." *Cultural Anthropology* 21 (1): 96–120.

Handler, Richard, and Eric Gable. 1997. *The New History in an Old Museum: Creating the Past at Colonial Williamsburg*. Durham, NC: Duke University Press.

Hann, Chris. M. 1985. *A Village without Solidarity: Polish Peasants in Years of Crisis*. New Haven, CT: Yale University Press.

———. 2015. "Backwardness Revisited: Time, Space and Civilization in Rural Eastern Europe." *Comparative Studies in Society and History* 57 (4): 881–911.

———. 2017. "Multiscalar Narrative Identities: Individual and Nation, Europe and Eurasia." *Politeja* 49: 15–36.

Haraway, Donna. 1988. "Situated Knowledges: The Science Question in Feminism and the Privilege of Partial Perspective." *Feminist Studies* 14 (3): 575–99.

———. 2016. *Staying with the Trouble: Making Kin in the Chthulucene*. Durham, NC: Duke University Press.

Harvey, David. 2005. *A Brief History of Neoliberalism*. Oxford: Oxford University Press.

Hathaway, Michael J. 2013. *Environmental Winds: Making the Global in Southwest China*. Berkeley: University of California Press.

Heatherington, Tracey. 2010. *Wild Sardinia: Indigeneity and the Global Dreamtimes of Environmentalism*. Seattle: University of Washington Press.

Hecht, Susanna B., and Alexander Cockburn. 1990. *The Fate of the Forest: Developers, Destroyers and Defenders of the Amazon*. Chicago: University of Chicago Press.

Hedemann, Otto. 1939. *Dzieje Puszczy Białowieskiej w Polsce Przedrozbiorowej (w Okresie do 1779)*. Warsaw: Warsaw Księgarnia św. Wojciecha.

Herzfeld, Michael. 1997. *Cultural Intimacy: Social Poetics in the Nation-State*. New York: Routledge.

———. 2004. *The Body Impolitic: Artisans and Artifice in the Global Hierarchy of Value.* Chicago: University of Chicago Press.

Hirsch, Francine. 2005. *Empire of Nations: Ethnographic Knowledge and the Making of the Soviet Union.* Culture and Society after Socialism. Ithaca, NY: Cornell University Press.

Hobsbawm, Eric. 1962. *The Age of Revolution: Europe, 1789–1848.* London: Weidenfeld and Nicolson.

———. 1990. *Nations and Nationalism since 1780: Programme, Myth, Reality.* Cambridge: Cambridge University Press.

Holm-Hansen, Jørn. 1999. *Polish Policies in the European Borderlands: Ethnic Institutionalisation and Transborder Cooperation with Belarus and Lithuania.* Oslo: Norwegian Institute for Urban and Regional Research.

Holmes, Douglas R. 2000. *Integral Europe: Fast-Capitalism, Multiculturalism, Neofascism.* Princeton, NJ: Princeton University Press.

Hroch, Miroslav. 2000. *Social Preconditions of National Revival in Europe: A Comparative Analysis of the Social Composition of Patriotic Groups among the Smaller European Nations.* Cambridge: Cambridge University Press.

Humphrey, Caroline. 2002. *The Unmaking of Soviet Life: Everyday Economies after Socialism.* Ithaca, NY: Cornell University Press.

Hyży-Czołpińska, Beata. 2014. *Miejsce w Raju.* Polish Public Television/TVP SA.

Igoe, James. 2017. *The Nature of Spectacle: On Images, Money, and Conserving Capitalism.* Tucson: University of Arizona Press.

Ivakhiv, Adrian. 2006. "Stoking the Heart of (a Certain) Europe: Crafting Hybrid Identities in the Ukraine-EU Borderlands." *Spaces of Identity* 6 (1): 11–44.

Jedlicki, Jerzy. 2014. *The Vicious Circle, 1832–1864: A History of the Polish Intelligentsia—Part 2.* Frankfurt am Main: Lang.

Jonasova, Magda, and Karel Prach. 2008. "The Influence of Bark Beetles Outbreak vs. Salvage Logging on Ground Layer Vegetation in Central European Mountain Spruce Forests." *Biological Conservation* 141 (6): 1525–35.

Kamińska, Anna. 2015. *Simona: Opowieść o niezwyczajnym życiu Simony Kossak.* Warsaw: Wydawnictwo Literackie.

Kaneff, Deema. 2004. *Who Owns the Past? The Politics of Time in a "Model" Bulgarian Village.* New Directions in Anthropology, vol. 21. New York: Berghahn.

———. 2011. *Global Connections and Emerging Inequalities in Europe: Perspectives on Poverty and Transnational Migration.* London: Anthem.

Karpiński, Jan Jerzy. 1930. *Puszcza Białowieska i Park Narodowy w Białowieży: Forêt et Parc National de Białowieża.* Białowieża, Poland: Dyrekcja Lasów Państwowych w Białowieży.

———. 1932. "Sprawozdanie Kierownika Park Narodowego w Bialowiezy Za Rok 1932." *Ochrona Przyroda* 12:156–57.

Kideckel, David. 1993. *The Solitude of Collectivism: Romanian Villages to the Revolution and Beyond.* Ithaca, NY: Cornell University Press.

Kieniewicz, Stefan. 1969. *The Emancipation of the Polish Peasantry.* Chicago: University of Chicago Press.

Kirby, Keith, and Charles Watkins. 1998. *The Ecological History of European Forests.* International Conference on Advances in Forest and Woodland History. New York: Oxon.

Knudson, Ida, and Martin Frederiksen, eds. 2015. *Ethnographies of Grey Zones in Eastern Europe: Relations, Borders and Invisibilities.* London: Anthem.

Kohn, Eduardo. 2013. *How Forests Think: Toward an Anthropology beyond the Human.* Berkeley: University of California Press.

Konczal, Agata Agnieszka. 2018. *Anthropologia Lasu: Lesniczy a percepcja i kszaltowanie wizerunkow przyrody w Polsce.* Warsaw: Instytut Badawczy Literacki PAN.

Korys, Piotr. 2018. *Poland from Partitions to EU Accession: A Modern Economic History, 1772–2004.* London: Palgrave.

Kosel, Bogusław, and Ewa Pirożnikow. 2017. *Od Puszczy do Tajgi: Leśnicy wywiezieni z zachodniej części Puszczy Białowieskiej do ZSRS 10 II 1940 roku.* Hajnówka: Wydział Leśny Politechniki Białostockiej w Hajnówce.

Kossak, Simona. 2001. *The Białowieża Forest Saga.* Białystok: Muza.

Kowalczyk, Janusz R. 2015. "The Extraordinary Life of Simona Kossak." Culture.pl. July 22, 2015. https://culture.pl/en/article/the-extraordinary-life-of-simona-kossak.

Krasiński, Zbigniew. 1994. "Restitution of the European Bison in the Białowieża Reserve in the Years 1929–1952." *Parki Narodowy i Rezerwaty Przyrody* 4 (2): 2–23.

Krasiński, Zbigniew, Aleksei N. Bunevich, and Małgorzata Krasińska. 1994. "Characteristics of the European Bison Populations in the Polish and Belarusian Parts of the Białowieża Forest." *Parki Narodowe i Rezerwaty Przyrody* 13 (4): 25–67.

Kula, Witold. 1983. *Historia, zacofanie, rozwój.* Warsaw: Czytelnik.

Latałowa, M., M. Zimny, B. Jędrzejewska, and T. Samojlik. 2015. "Białowieża Primeval Forest: A 2000-Year Interplay of Environmental and Cultural Forces in Europe's Best Preserved Temperate Woodland." In *Europe's Changing Woods and Forests: From Wildwood to Managed Landscapes,* edited by Keith J. Kirby and Charles Watkins, 243–64. Wallingford, UK: CABI International.

Latour, Bruno. 1993. *We Have Never Been Modern,* translated by Catherine Porter. Cambridge, MA: Harvard University Press.

———. 2018. *Down to Earth: Politics in the New Climatic Regime.* Cambridge: Polity.

Łatyszonek, Oleg, and Eugeniusz Mironowicz. 2002. "Historia Białorusi, Związek Białoruski w RP." Report. Białystok, Poland: Białystok University.

Lehnert, Lukas W., Claus Bässler, Roland Brandle, Philip J. Burton, and Jörg Müller. 2013. "Highest Number of Indicator Species Is Found in the Early Successional Stages after Bark Beetle Attack." *Journal for Nature Conservation* 21:97–104.

Lehrer, Erica. 2013. *Jewish Poland Revisited: Heritage Tourism in Unquiet Places.* Bloomington: Indiana University Press.

Leonard, Pamela, and Deema Kaneff. 2002. *Post-socialist Peasant? Rural and Urban Constructions of Identity in Eastern Europe, East Asia and the Former Soviet Union.* Basingstoke: Palgrave.

Lowe, Celia. 2006. *Wild Profusion: Biodiversity Conservation in an Indonesian Archipelago.* Princeton, NJ: Princeton University Press.

Lowood, Henry. 1990. "The Calculating Forester: Quantification, Cameral Science, and the Emergence of Scientific Forestry Management in Germany." In *The Quantifying Spirit in the 18th Century,* edited by Tore Frangsmyr, J. L. Heilbron, and Robin E. Ride, 315–42. Berkeley: University of California Press.

Majchrowska, Anna. 2018. "The History of and Forestry in Poland." In *Managing Northern Europe's Forests: Histories from the Age of Improvement to the Age of Ecology,* edited by K. Jan Oosthoek and Richard Hoelzl. New York: Berghahn.

Malaby, Thomas. 2009. "Anthropology and Play: The Contours of Playful Experience." *New Literary History* 40 (1): 205–18.

Manser, Roger. 1993. *Failed Transitions: The Eastern European Economy and Environment since the Fall of Communism*. New York: New Press.

Mark, James. 2010. *The Unfinished Revolution: Making Sense of the Communist Past in Eastern-Central Europe*. New Haven, CT: Yale University Press.

Mathews, Andrew S. 2011. *Instituting Nature: Authority, Expertise, and Power in Mexican Forests*. Cambridge, MA: MIT Press.

Matteson, Kieko. 2015. *Forests in Revolutionary France: Conservation, Community, and Conflict, 1669–1848*. New York: Cambridge University Press.

Mauss, Marcel. 1925. *The Gift*. Chicago: HAU.

Menzies, Nicholas. 2007. *Our Forest, Your Ecosystem, Their Timber: Communities, Conservation, and the State in Community-Based Forest Management*. New York: Columbia University Press.

Michalski, Jacek, Jerzy R. Starzyk, Andrzej Kolk, and Wojciech Grodzki. 2004. "Zagrożenie świerka przez kornika drukarza Ips typographus (L.) w drzewostanach Leśnego Kompleksu Promocyjnego "Puszcza Białowieska" w latach 2000–2002." *Leśne Prace Badawcze* 3:5–30.

Michaluk, Dorota. 1997. *Dobra i Miasteczko Narewka na tle Dziejów Regionu: (Do Końca XIX Wieku)*. Narewce: Urząd Gminy.

Mickiewicz, Adam. (1834) 1992. *Pan Tadeusz*, translated by Kenneth R. MacKenzie. New York: Hippocrene.

Mikusińska, Anna, Bernadeta Zawadzka, Tomasz Samojlik, Bogumiła Jędrzejewska, and Grzegorz Mikunsiński. 2013. "Quantifying Landscape Change in the Last Two Centuries in Białowieża Primeval Forest." *Applied Vegetation Science* 16, no. 2 (April): 217–26. https://doi.org/10.1111/j.1654-109X.2012.01220.x.

Miłosz, Czesław. 1996. "Rozebrać Wawel Na Cegły?" *Tygodnik Powszechny: Katolickie Pismo Społeczno Kulturowe*, February 18.

Mironowicz, Eugeniusz. 1993. *Białorusini w Polsce: 1944–1949*. Wydawn. Naukowe PWN.

———. 1999. *Bialorus*. Warsaw: Wydawnictwo Trio.

Mucha, Stanislaw. 2005. *Reality Shock*. DVD. Bayerischer Rundfunk.

———. 2001. *Absolut Wharhola*. DVD. Hessicher Rundfunk.

Müller, Jörg, H. Bussler, M. Grossner, T. Rettelbach, and P. Duelli. 2008. "The European Spruce Bark Beetle *Ips typographus* in a National Park—From Pest to Keystone Species." *Biodiversity and Conservation* 17:2979–3001.

Müller, Jörg, H. Bussler, and R. Brandl. 2010. "Learning from a Benign Neglect Strategy in a National Park: Response of Saproxylic Beetles to Dead Wood Accumulation. *Biological Conservation* 143:2559–69.

Nagengast, Carole. 1991. *Reluctant Socialists, Rural Entrepreneurs: Class, Culture, and the Polish State*. Cambridge: Cambridge University Press.

Netting, Robert. 1993. *Smallholders, Householders: Farm Families and the Ecology of Intensive, Sustainable Agriculture*. Stanford, CA: Stanford University Press.

Niedziałkowski, Krzysztof. 2012. "Institutional Dynamics of Nature Conservation Policy in Poland." PhD diss., University of Leeds.

Niedziałkowski, Krzysztof, Małgorzata Blicharska, Grzegorz Mikusiński, and Bogumiła Jędrzejewska. 2014. "Why Is It Difficult to Enlarge a Protected Area? Ecosystem Services Perspective on the Conflict around the Extension of the Białowieża National Park in Poland." *Land Use Policy* 38:314–29.

Niedziałkowski, Krzysztof, Jouni Paavola, and Bogumiła Jędrzejewska. 2012. "Participation and Protected Areas Governance: The Impact of Changing Influence of Local

Authorities on the Conservation of the Białowieża Primeval Forest, Poland." *Ecology and Society* 17 (1): 2.

Nietzsche, Friedrich. 1995. "On the Utility and Liability of History for Life." In *Unfashionable Observations*, translated by Richard T. Gray, 83–168. Stanford, CA: Stanford University Press.

Nikitiuk, Borys. 1958. *Czerwona Hajnówka*. Hajnówka: Komitet Powiatowy PZPR.

———. 2003. *Z Dziejów Hajnowski i Jej Okolic*. Hajnówka: Starostwo Powiatowe w Hajnówce.

Neocleous, Mark. 1997. *Fascism*. Buckingham, UK: Open University Press.

Okołów, Czesław. 2009. "History of Protection." In *Białowieża National Park: Know It, Understand It, Protect It*. Białowieża: Białowieża National Park.

Oosthoek, Jan, and Richard Hoelzl. 2018. *Managing Northern Europe's Forests: Histories from the Age of Improvement to the Age of Ecology*. New York: Berghahn.

Opalski, Magdalena, and Israel Bartel. 1992. *Poles and Jews: A Failed Brotherhood*. Boston: Brandeis University Press.

Ortner, Sherry. 2016. "Dark Anthropology and Its Others: Theory since the Eighties." *HAU: Journal of Ethnographic Theory* 6, no. 1 (Summer): 47–73.

Parreñas, Rheana "Juno" Salazar. 2018. *Decolonizing Extinction: The Work of Care in Orangutan Habilitation*. Durham, NC: Duke University Press.

Pavlinek, Petr, and John Pickles. 2000. *Environmental Transitions: Transformation and Ecological Defense in Central and Eastern Europe*. London: Routledge.

Peluso, Nancy. 1992. *Rich Forests, Poor People, and Development: Forest Access Control and Resistance in Java*. Berkeley: University of California Press.

Pensky, Max. 2004. "Method and Time: Walter Benjamin's Dialectical Images." In *The Cambridge Companion to Walter Benjamin*, edited by David Ferris, 177–98. Cambridge: Cambridge University Press.

Petryna, Adriana. 2002. *Life Exposed: Biological Citizens after Chernobyl*. Princeton, NJ: Princeton University Press.

Pine, Frances. 1996. "Naming the House and Naming the Land: Kinship and Social Groups in the Polish Highlands." *Journal of the Royal Anthropological Institute* 2 (3): 443–59.

———. 2002. "Retreat to the Household? Gendered Domains in Postsocialist Poland." In *Postsocialism: Ideals, Ideologies and Practices in Eurasia*, edited by C. M. Hann, 95–113. London: Routledge.

Pogue Harrison, Robert. 1992. *Forests: The Shadow of Civilization*. Chicago: University of Chicago Press.

Pol, Wincenty. 1922. *Mohort*. Kraków: Krakowskiej Spólki Wydawniczej.

Rabinow, Paul. 1977. *Reflections on Fieldwork in Morocco*. Berkeley: University of California Press.

Radecki, Andrzej. 1996. *Agriculture in the Region of Białowieża Primeval Forest*. Warsaw: Fundacja Rozwój SGGW.

Rajan, S. Ravi. 2006. *Modernizing Nature: Forestry and Imperial Eco-Development, 1800–1910*. New York: Oxford University Press.

Rakowski, Tomasz. 2016. *Hunters, Gatherers, and Practitioners of Powerlessness: An Ethnography of the Degraded in Postsocialist Poland*. New York: Berghan.

Razsa, Maple. 2015. *Bastards of Utopia: Living Radical Politics after Socialism*. Bloomington: Indiana University Press.

Robbins, Paul. 2012. *Political Ecology: A Critical Introduction*. Maiden, MA: Wiley.

Rosaldo, Renato. 1989. *Culture and Truth: The Remaking of Social Analysis*. Boston MA: Beacon.

Rose, Carol. 1994. *Property and Persuasion: Essays on the History, Theory and Rhetoric of Ownership*. Boulder, CO: Westview.

Rudling, Per Anders. 2015. *The Rise and Fall of Belarusian Nationalism, 1906–1931*. Pittsburg, PA: University of Pittsburgh Press.

Sahlins, Marshall. 1985. *Islands of History*. Chicago: University of Chicago Press.

Said, Edward W. 1978. *Orientalism: Western Conceptions of the Orient*. New York: Pantheon.

Samojlik, Tomasz. 2005. "Stanisław August Poniatowski in the Białowieża Forest (30 August–2 September 1784)." *Kwartalnik Historii Kultury Materialnej* 53:35–52.

Samojlik, Tomasz, Anastasia Fedotova, and Dries P. J. Kuijper. 2016. "Transition from Traditional to Modern Forest Management Shaped the Spatial Extent of Cattle Pasturing in Białowieża Primeval Forest in the Nineteenth and Twentieth Centuries." *Ambio* 45, no. 8 (June): 904–18. http://doi.org/10.1007/s13280-016-0795-4

Sanderson, Fiona J., Marta Kucharz, Marek Jobda, and Paul F. Donald. 2013. "Impacts of Agricultural Intensification and Abandonment on Farmland Birds in Poland following EU Accession." *Agriculture, Ecosystems, and Environment* 168 (March 15): 16–24.

Schama, Simon. 1995. *Landscape and Memory*. New York: Knopf.

Schwartz, Katrina Z. S. 2006. *Nature and National Identity after Communism: Globalizing the Ethnoscape*. Pittsburgh, PA: University of Pittsburgh Press.

Scott, James C. 1985. *Weapons of the Weak: Everyday Forms of Peasant Resistance*. New Haven, CT: Yale University Press.

———. 1998. *Seeing Like a State*. New Haven, CT: Yale University Press.

———. 2010. *The Art of not Being Governed: An Anarchist History of Upland Southeast Asia*. New Haven, CT: Yale University Press.

Sharma, Ruchir. 2017. "The Next Economic Powerhouse? Poland." *New York Times*, July 5, 2017. https://www.nytimes.com/2017/07/05/opinion/poland-economy-trump-russia.html.

Sikor, Thomas, and Johannes Stahl. 2011. *Forests and People: Property, Governance, and Human Rights*. London: Earthscan.

Smart, Alan, and Josephine Smart. 2017. *Posthumanism: Anthropological Insights*. Toronto: University of Toronto Press.

Smith, Hugo. *Dancing with Wolves [Tańcząc z wilkami]*. Written by Ben Smith. Leeds, UK: Yorkshire Television, 1998.

Smoczyński, Rafał, and Tomasz Zarycki. 2017. *Totem Inteligencki: Arystokracja, szlachta I ziemiaństwo w Polskie Przestrezeni Społecznej*. Warsaw: Scholar.

Snajdr, Edward. 2008. *Nature Protests: The End of Ecology in Slovakia*. Culture, Place, and Nature. Seattle: University of Washington Press.

Snyder, Timothy. 2010. *Bloodlands: Europe between Hitler and Stalin*. NY: Basic Books.

Statistical Yearbook of Poland. 1921. Accessed January 13, 2020. https://www.wbc.poznan.pl/publication/54091.

Statistical Yearbook of the Republic of Poland. 2019. Accessed January 13, 2020. https://stat.gov.pl/en/topics/statistical-yearbooks/.

Stengers, Isabelle. 2010. *Cosmopolitics I*. Minneapolis,: University of Minnesota Press.

Sulimirski, Tadeusz. 1970. *Sarmatians*. Ancient Peoples and Places Series, edited by Glyn Daniel. London: Thames and Hudson.

Sunseri, Thaddeus. 2012. "Exploiting the Urwald: German Post-Colonial Forestry in Poland and Central Africa, 1900–1960." *Past and Present* 214 (1): 305–42.

Szafer, Władysław. 1920. "Plan Utworzenia Rezerwatu Leśnego w Puszczy Białowieskiej." *Chrońmy Przyrody Ojczysta* 6.

———. 1926. *On the Protection of Nature in Poland in the Last Five Years.* Nakładem Państwowej Komisji Ochrony Przyrody. Bulletin by the National Commission of Nature Protection.

Taussig, Michael. 1980. *Devil and Commodity Fetishism in South America.* Chapel Hill: University of North Carolina Press.

Thorn, Simon, Claus Bässler, Roland Brandl, Philip Burton, Rebecca Cahall, John Campell, Jorge Castro, et al. 2018. "Impacts of Salvage Logging on Biodiversity: A Meta-analysis." *Journal of Applied Ecology* 55 (1): 279–89.

Todorova, Maria. 2004. *Balkan Identities: Nation and Memory.* New York: New York University Press.

Traba, Robert. 2015. *The Past in the Present: The Construction of Polish History.* Frankfurt am Main: Lang.

Tsing, Anna. 2015. *The Mushroom at the End of the World: On the Possibility of Life in the Capitalist Ruins.* Princeton, NJ: Princeton University Press.

Vera, Frans. 1999. *Grazing Ecology and Forest History.* New York: CABI.

Verdery, Katherine. 1996. *What Was Socialism, and What Comes Next?* Princeton, NJ: Princeton University Press.

Walicki, Andrzej. 1982. *Philosophy and Romantic Nationalism: The Case of Poland.* Oxford: Oxford University Press.

Wanner, Catherine. 1998. *Burden of Dreams: History and Identity in Post Soviet Ukraine.* Pittsburgh: Pennsylvania State University.

Wedel, Janine. 1998. *Collision and Collusion: The Strange Case of Western Aid to Eastern Europe.* London: Palgrave.

Weiner, Douglas. 2002. *A Little Corner of Freedom: Russian Nature Protection from Stalin to Gorbachev.* Berkeley: University of California Press.

Więcko, Edward. 1984. *Puszcza Bialowieska: Problematyka Ochrony Puszczy Białowieskiej w ujęciu historycznym i społecznym.* Warsaw: PWN.

Wierzbicki, Marek. 2007. *Polacy i Białorusini w Zaborze Sowieckim. Stosunki Polsko-Białoruskie na Ziemiach Północno-Wschodnich II RP pod Okupacja Sowiecka 1939–1941.* Warsaw: Stowarzyszenie Kulturalne Fronda.

Wilczek, Lech. 2004. *Opowieść o borsukach.* Dom Wydawniczy "Benkowski."

———. 2011. *Spotkanie z Simoną Kossak.* Białystok, Poland: SMB-GM and Chyra.pl and Logo-art.

Witeska-Młynarczyk, Anna. 2014. *Evoking Polish Memory: State, Self and the Communist Past in Transition.* Frankfurt am Main: Lang.

Wolfe, Cary. 2003. *Zoontologies: The Question of the Animal.* Minneapolis: University of Minnesota Press.

Wolff, Larry. 1994. *Inventing Eastern Europe: The Map of Civilization on the Mind of the Enlightenment.* Stanford, CA: Stanford University Press.

Woolhiser, Curt. 2003. "Constructing National Identities in the Polish-Belarusian Borderlands." *Ab Imperio* 1:293–346. http://doi.org/10.1353/imp.2003.0022.

Wysocki, A. 2010. "Belarusians and Belarusianness in the Face of Soviet People and Sovietization in Western Belarus in the Years 1939–1941 in the Memoirs of Polish People." *Annus Albaruthenicus* 10: 137–52.

Yurchak, Alexei. 2005. *Everything Was Forever, until It Was No More: The Last Soviet Generation*. Princeton, NJ: Princeton University Press.

Zarycki, Tomasz. 2012. "In Search of a Usable Past: Who Were the Ancestors of the Polish Middle Class?" Eurozine, 26 September, 2012. https://www.eurozine.com/in-search-of -a-usable-past/.

———. 2014. *Ideologies of Eastness in Central and Eastern Europe*. London: Routledge.

Zarycki, Tomasz, Rafał Smoczyński, and Tomasz Warczok. 2017. "The Roots of Polish Culture-Centered Politics: Toward a Non–Purely Cultural Model of Cultural Domination in Central and Eastern Europe." *East European Politics and Societies and Cultures*. 20 (10): 1–22.

Zimmerman, Andrew. 2001. *Anthropology and Antihumanism in Imperial Germany*. Chicago: University of Chicago Press.

Zimmerman, Fred. 1952. *High Noon*. DVD. Stanley Kramer Productions.

Žižek, Slavoj. 2001. *Did Somebody Say Totalitarianism? Five Interventions in the (Mis)use of a Notion*. London: Verso.

Zubrzycki, Geneviève. 2006. *The Crosses of Auschwitz: Nationalism and Religion in Post-Communist Poland*. Chicago: University of Chicago Press.

INDEX

EUNICE BLAVASCUNAS is Assistant Professor of Anthropology and Environmental Studies at Whitman College in Walla Walla, Washington.

www.ingramcontent.com/pod-product-compliance
Lightning Source LLC
Chambersburg PA
CBHW020530270326
41927CB00006B/522